W9-AXQ-945

"This is a wonderful piece of gospel work. It is case-study rich, evidencing lots of wisdom in the ways of people who suffer. It is theology rich, exegeting in a very practical way the transforming power of the gospel and all the ways we are tempted to distort or minimize it. This needs to be published and distributed widely. I know of no other work that does what Wilkerson has done. It surely does advance the cause of applying the gospel to brokenness of this generation. Well done!"

Paul Tripp, President, Paul Tripp Ministries; author, *What Did You Expect?*

"I am weekly confronted by the harshness of life as a result of sin—abuse, neglect, consequences of sin. The list goes on and on. As a pastor of a church full of younger people, I have searched for a resource that I could with confidence recommend to those stuck in their sin. This book is that resource. It will help hurting people (which includes us!) come to grips with the reality of both our sin and the reality of being sinned against. Further, it will move people to Jesus, who is greater than our sin."

Darrin Patrick, Lead Pastor, The Journey, St. Louis, Missouri; author, *Church Planter*

"Backed by good scholarship yet accessible to all Christians, it brims with great stories of redemption and keen insights into the souls of broken sinners, challenging readers to follow the Christ who can set people free."

Eric Johnson, Lawrence and Charlotte Hoover Professor of Pastoral Care, Southern Baptist Theological Seminary; Director, Society for Christian Psychology

"Pastor Mike Wilkerson has penned a truly unique contribution both to small group literature and to the Christian "recovery" movement. His gospel-centered focus using the exodus theme of redemption provides an unparalleled biblical approach to facing our past face-to-face with Christ. The combination of gripping real-life vignettes, biblical narratives applied to sin and suffering, and the thought-provoking discussion-application guide makes *Redemption* the premier all-in-one book for small group recovery ministry."

Bob Kellemen, author, *God's Healing for Life's Losses*

"Praise God for *Redemption*, which is a gift to the body of Christ. God's story of redemption, which serves as both the source and framework of the book, is applied directly to the sin and suffering we all face both in and out of the church. It is, therefore, a great example of practical theology. This is a resource that enables reproducible training and ministry in any church and with all God's people. I wholeheartedly commend *Redemption* to anyone who is on the front lines of gospel ministry in the church and has a deep desire and vision to equip the saints for the work of ministry."

Robert Cheong, Pastor of Care and Counseling, Sojourn Community Church, Louisville, Kentucky

"Every genuine pastor and counselor prays to walk with the Savior freed 'from fleshly lusts which wage war against the soul' (1 Pet. 2:11), enjoying a fuller measure of abundant life in Christ each day. Every genuine pastor and counselor prays to see his precious flock walk the same road. *Redemption* provides a guide for the journey, bringing the richness of the exodus story to bear where we all live, feeding the gospel morsel by morsel to our souls, and helping us behold more of Christ along the way. I commend this resource to every pastor and counselor who prays for Spirit-wrought transformation in the hearts of people."

John Henderson, Counseling Pastor, Denton Bible Church, Denton, Texas; board member, Association of Biblical Counselors; author, *Equipped to Counsel*

"By God's grace, Pastor Mike Wilkerson gets it. He is a pastor who does not mind getting his hands dirty in the lives of people who are hurting and broken. But then he takes sufferers and sinners alike to the life-giving cross of Christ. Organized around the powerful story of the exodus, this book will point you to the marvelous Redeemer and his life-changing grace. Redemption—just think of it. In this book, Mike will help you think of it a lot. And you will be glad he did. I certainly was."

Steve Viars, Senior Pastor, Faith Baptist Church, Lafayette, Indiana; Administrator, Faith Biblical Counseling Ministries; author, *Putting Your Past in Its Place*

"So many tools for recovery groups deal only with wounds and desires, appealing to 'the god you envision,' and boil down to self-help programs. *Redemption* goes to core issues and shows how following the pattern of the exodus can redeem struggling people from their 'Egypts,' such as addictions and trauma. Because it takes us down biblical pathways in very applicable ways, it is an outstanding tool for ministry."

Gerry Breshears, Professor of Theology, Western Seminary

"This important book places the powder keg of gospel truth where it is most needed: on the frontline of pastoral ministry. A mixture of clear writing, real-life stories, and faithful Bible exposition makes this a powerful resource in the fight for redemption in the lives of those we are called to serve."

Joel Virgo, Church of Christ the King, Brighton, UK

"We have implemented the message and dynamics of this book with all the leaders in our church. It has led to a renewal on a massive scale. On each page of the book, Jesus is presented as the healer of every situation, helper of every circumstance, and advocate for every sinner. I recommend *Redemption* to every church pastor, leader, and sinner who wants to meet the healing of the gospel of Jesus on the other side of the Red Sea."

Ethan Burmeister, Core Community Church, Omaha, Nebraska

"The strength of *Redemption* is that it's rooted in the sufficient and transforming work of the gospel, using exercises and strategies to effect real change, and the process takes place in the context of authentic community. I have recommended, and even required, clients to go through the Redemption group process, and have seen life changing transformation in weeks that would take months to years in individual counseling. I have been waiting for something like this for a very long time!"

Elisa Hope, licensed mental health counselor

"As a leader involved in a Christian recovery ministry, *Redemption* has proven to be extremely powerful! Using it to lead meetings has given me a unique opportunity to share the 'good news' with believers and nonbelievers. I have seen tremendous breakthroughs in reaching and dealing with core issues, such as physical abuse, sexual abuse, and addiction, as participants identify with the book and hear of God's love for his children."

Mitch Thompson, Director, All The Way House Ministries, Delray Beach, Florida

"We need this book. In it God's grace is on full display. It begins and ends with the good news of God's story of redemption throughout all of Scripture, which culminates in the person and work of Jesus Christ. *Redemption* proclaims the faith, hope, and love we need and can offer to others. It is a gift to all who are suffering because of their sin and the sins done against them."

Justin Holcomb, Episcopal priest; Professor of Christian Thought, Gordon-Conwell Theological Seminary; co-author, *Rid of my Disgrace* and *Is It My Fault?*

"I had many fears about my future, living with the effects of the sin that was committed against me. As I read *Redemption*, I was blown away that the book put into words my unidentifiable worries and fears and addressed each issue with godly truths over and over."

Susan

"Alongside the Bible, *Redemption* was one of the most helpful and practical resources for applying the atonement of Christ to the darkest and most hidden parts of my life. Through reading it, overwhelming shame and fear that had led to my deep desire to end my own life was flushed out as the gospel was revealed more clearly—Christ died for me!"

Justin

"When I first picked up this book, I read and re-read chapter one over a hundred times. Coming from a childhood of traumatic sexual abuse, I related to the Israelites' slavery and desperate cries for help. Though God seemed absent (both to them and to me), he identifies with my pain. Realizing God's covenant love for me brought healing to my wounded heart. He is the God who sees and knows—and I can call him my Abba."

Stephanie

"After spending a decade in habitual sin and idol worship, including lust and homosexual prostitution, God showed up in my life. I was destroyed. I didn't know where to turn. Through the work of a church deacon and *Redemption*, God saved me from drowning in waves of torment and emotion. The eight weeks of the book followed me through the stages needed to put me back on solid ground. It helped me to realize my identity is in Christ alone, that he will never abandon me, and that God is love, true love that never lets go. *Redemption* was the map I needed to see that Jesus' death had paid for all my awful sin and I am now God's adopted son, bringing amazement I feel to this day. Should you need to help others broken and struggling with the intensity of sin, *Redemption* will be a great help in a time when people need it most."

Nate

REDEMPTION

FREED BY JESUS FROM THE IDOLS WE WORSHIP
AND THE WOUNDS WE CARRY.

MIKE WILKERSON

CROSSWAY

WHEATON, ILLINOIS

Redemption: Freed by Jesus from the Idols We Worship and the Wounds We Carry

Copyright © 2011 by Mike Wilkerson

Published by Crossway
        1300 Crescent Street
        Wheaton, Illinois 60187

All rights reserved. No part of this publication may be reproduced, stored in a retrieval system, or transmitted in any form by any means, electronic, mechanical, photocopy, recording, or otherwise, without the prior permission of the publisher, except as provided for by USA copyright law.

Cover design: Patrick Mahoney of The Mahoney Design Team

Printed in the United States of America

Unless otherwise indicated, Scripture quotations are from the ESV® Bible (*The Holy Bible, English Standard Version®*), copyright © 2001 by Crossway. Used by permission. All rights reserved.

Scripture quotations marked NASB are from *The New American Standard Bible®*. Copyright © The Lockman Foundation 1960, 1962, 1963, 1968, 1971, 1972, 1973, 1975, 1977, 1995. Used by permission.

Scripture quotations and works marked NET are from *The NET Bible®* copyright © 2003 by Biblical Studies Press, L.L.C. www.netbible.com. All rights reserved. Quoted by permission.

Scripture references marked NIV are taken from *The Holy Bible, New International Version®*. Copyright © 1973, 1978, 1984 Biblica. Used by permission of Zondervan. All rights reserved. The "NIV" and "New International Version" trademarks are registered in the United States Patent and Trademark Office by Biblica. Use of either trademark requires the permission of Biblica.

Scripture references marked NKJV are from *The New King James Version*. Copyright © 1982, Thomas Nelson, Inc. Used by permission.

All emphases in Scripture quotations have been added by the author.

Trade paperback ISBN: 978-1-4335-2077-8
PDF ISBN: 978-1-4335-2078-5
Mobipocket ISBN: 978-1-4335-2087-7
ePub ISBN: 978-1-4335-2088-4

Library of Congress Cataloging-in-Publication Data
Wilkerson, Mike, 1977–
   Redemption : freed by Jesus from the idols we worship and the
wounds we carry / Mike Wilkerson.
      p.   cm.
   Includes bibliographical references and index.
   ISBN 978-1-4335-2077-8 (tpb)
   1. Suffering—Religious aspects—Christianity—Textbooks.
2. Redemption—Christianity—Textbooks. 3. Exodus, The—Textbooks.
I. Title.
BV4909.W539   2011
248.8′6—dc22   2010031363

Crossway is a publishing ministry of Good News Publishers.

VP   25   24   23   22   21   20   19   18   17   16
20   19   18   17   16   15   14   13   12   11   10   9

To Trisha,
who—next to Jesus—is the most vivid daily reminder
of God's abounding steadfast love for me.

CONTENTS

PREFACE

This book was written to serve as a curriculum for Redemption Groups™, a ministry designed to help local churches provide care for many pastoral needs in their congregations.[1] A Redemption Group is an intense small group where participants experience the love of God shining into some of life's darkest areas of sin and suffering. It is a form of gospel-based biblical counseling, which is based on the belief that the ministry of the gospel of Jesus Christ is effective for helping people with how they think, behave, and feel in many areas of life.

A single Redemption Group may include participants with any number of life experiences and concerns. This book, therefore, lays out a general framework for the application of the biblical theme of redemption to one's life. While the book is not written to address a single concern like sexual abuse or drug addiction, the framework provided here is relevant and helpful to the lives of people with those concerns and others. Each chapter of the book includes personal stories that illustrate through real-life situations.

Early ideas for how Redemption Groups might work were conceived in collaboration with my team of pastoral colleagues in late 2007 and early 2008 at Mars Hill Church in Seattle. On that initial team were James Noriega, Brad House, and Phil Smidt. James, in particular, contributed from his pastoral experience of having pioneered a gospel-based groups ministry that helped participants with a range of life struggles. I have footnoted several of James's insights throughout the book. Bill Clem later joined the team, bringing his many years of experience teaching the Bible and writing curricula. Bill's guidance in the curriculum's early formation was essential. In fact, he drafted and taught *half* of the original curriculum modules.

My starting point for this book was the work we had done together as pastors, and especially the early drafts and recorded lectures from Bill Clem. Bill's influence is still strongly felt in the book's final form, most notably his work "God's Story" (woven throughout the Introduction) and "The Passover" (chapter 3), but also in many other places throughout the book. He also wrote early drafts of what have become chapters 3, 7, and 8. I have included footnotes at several points where I am particularly indebted to his initial work.

For information on how to develop Redemption Groups for your church, visit www.redemptiongroups.com.

KNOW YOUR REDEEMER'S LOVE

While writing this book, one key idea from my time saturated in Exodus grabbed me more than any other and planted a seed in my heart that would bear fruit in my own personal transformation over time. *God abounds in steadfast love* (Ex. 34:6). Such a simple idea, yet it changes everything.

Think of how God's committed, costly, one-way, covenantal love for his people, the Israelites, changed everything for them. Had God *not* abounded in steadfast love, keeping his promises to his people, I suppose they would never have been freed from slavery. He freed by this love.

Had God not *abounded* in steadfast love, then I suppose they might have come to the end of it in their unbelief and accusations. Yet, despite all the deprivations in the wilderness, his steadfast love abounded.

This was *steadfast* love: resilient and promise-keeping, covenant-bound, even when the people grumbled and were unlovely. The people could doubt, yet his love remained. They could forget, yet his love remained. They could defy him, yet his love remained. He was always faithful to love.

And it was *God* who abounded in this steadfast love. Not just a principle of love, but a *personal* love. In fact, a *person*. These were *his* people. God moved toward an oppressed people in slavery to identify himself with them and them with him: "I will take you to be my people, and I will be your God" (Ex. 6:7). The king of the universe would "come down" to them—to their level, in Egypt—so that he might "bring them up" and out of slavery (Ex. 3:8).

PATIENCE

There tend to be at least two different kinds of readers of a book like this: those who read it for their own edification, and those who read it again with others when ministering to them.

If you are reading this book hoping for help or change, hoping to experience Christ's work of redemption somehow specifically in your life, then I want to assure you that God abounds in steadfast love toward you, as he did toward the Israelites in the exodus. And yet the story of redemption in our own lives doesn't always match our expectations, just as it didn't match theirs.

As we see with their journey out of Egypt and through the wilderness, personal change is a process, and usually a slow one with a lot of ups, downs, and seemingly, detours. Keep in mind as you read that real stories of real people's lives—like yours and those told in this book—are always in progress. God does his work of progressive sanctification to change us into Christlikeness over the course of our whole lives. Neither this book nor a Redemption Group experience should be seen as a "quick fix." Rather, God uses these and many other experiences in our lives to help us know him and to transform us into his image little by little. I would encourage you to receive what help God brings to you through the experience you have with this book like the Israelites were to receive the manna in the wilderness— enough for the day—and thank God for what he provides.

If you are one of those friends or ministry leaders who may incorporate this book into your ministry to someone else, then I want to draw your attention to another idea: power. The idea of power is (or should be) closely related to the idea of love, the kind of love God showed in the exodus. Dr. Diane Langberg describes power as "the ability to make something happen...the capacity to have impact or influence".[2]

God's power is on display in the exodus for the whole world to behold (Ex. 15:14–16). What does he accomplish with his power? Freedom for those he loves. God loves powerfully. That's what you and I are called to as we follow him, to love others with God's powerful love. One of the effects of God's powerfully loving you and me is, eventually, the bearing of the fruit of the Spirit in our lives. The chief among these is love, and also gentleness and self-control (Gal. 5:22–23).

Gentleness that is the fruit of the Spirit should season our ministry to others. In my own experience of maturing as a minister and in equipping others for ministry, a common mistake for many of us seems to be untempered zeal: zeal for some truth or ministry method that lacks gentleness.

Sometimes when we try to help others, they make progress more slowly than we'd like. The Spirit's powerful work in us enables us to be patient and gentle in those times. Rather than being an occasion for us to "power up" and push harder for change in the other person, this is an opportunity to remember that the change we hope for in those whom we help is a work of the Holy Spirit, and he is powerful to accomplish it. As the Spirit works powerfully in us, he aims to make us a part of the work in another person's life while at the same time bearing in us the fruit of gentleness. He works on both of us at the same time. We would also do well in such times to be humbled by the reminder that he has been so gentle with us who are so often ignorant and wayward (Heb. 5:2).

Furthermore, if someone chooses to read a book like this with you, and in the process opens up his own life to talk about areas of deep sin or suffering, be mindful that this is a vulnerable thing for him to do. When someone is vulnerable with you, you have greater power for influence in her life in that moment—for better or for worse. It is a prime opportunity to respond in ways that will bring healing; and it is also a time when your response has greater potential to cause hurt.

How can you prepare for such a moment? We see this pattern in 2 Corinthians:

> Blessed be the God and Father of our Lord Jesus Christ, the Father of mercies and God of all comfort, who comforts us in all our affliction, so that we may be able to comfort those who are in any affliction, with the comfort with which we ourselves are comforted by God. (2 Cor. 1:3–4)

When we are in our own affliction and we make ourselves vulnerable—first to our merciful God, and also to trustworthy people who reflect God's mercy to us—it has a way of growing our hearts. Not only do we find help and healing, but also our capacity to be there for others amidst their sins and sufferings—in any affliction—expands. May each of us be changed by many moments of mercy before our Heavenly Father, and reflect his mercy to those around us.

A FINAL NOTE

While the statistics that appear in the Introduction are from the United States only, they represent the brokenness of the world we live in. There are similar trends around the world, along with many forms of human trafficking, racial discrimination, religious persecution, economic oppression and poverty elsewhere that may not be common among those who attend your church or mine. Yet the story of God's redemption is timeless and global; and one day, the redeemed from all the earth will be joined to sing of it together.

ACKNOWLEDGMENTS

Two key companions have been with me along the way, editing my drafts and helping me learn to write: Marsha Michaelis, and Matt Johnson. In the early days, it was Marsha who convinced me that I needed to rethink how to write a book! This triggered the *first* rewrite. Matt has taught me to hone my writing style through many, many substantial edits. His fingerprints are on every single chapter.

As much patience as I'm sure I've required of each of them, no one has been more patient and supportive than my wife, Trisha, and our four children. Through many months, several writing retreats, and countless bursts of inspiration at inconvenient moments, they have lovingly supported me. In fact, as I wrote about redemption, God used it to bring yet more redemption to my own life and marriage.

Many others have also contributed many hours reading and critiquing my drafts, including Katie Krombein; Adam Johnson; Steve Loosley; Justin Holcomb; Gerry Breshears; Lindsey Holcomb; Meredith Stinson; Greg Joines; Kerry Michaelis; Rick White; Lynne Wilson; Robert Cheong; Ryan Lister; Shannon Mead; Tami Hagglund; John O'Brien; my wife, Trisha; my parents; and many Redemption Group leaders.

Conversations with Mark Driscoll, Steve Loosley, Gerry Breshears, Justin Holcomb, Adam Johnson, Ryan Lister, and Robert Cheong have helped refine the book's theology. I am thankful to Adam, Steve, Robert, and Ryan for allowing me to read their dissertations and learn from their research—all of it has been very helpful. It was a conversation with Adam Johnson that sparked the idea for the "Red Sea" chapter (chapter 4). Ryan Lister's dissertation was helpful for chapter 8 (along with Adam Johnson's). Robert Cheong's work helped shaped the theology of forgiveness in chapter 3.

Without a doubt, the teaching of David Powlison of CCEF has most significantly influenced the biblical worldview and counseling philosophy backing this book. I'm grateful to Dr. Powlison not only for what I've learned through his books and lectures, but also for the time he has generously given to correspond with me face-to-face and by e-mail. Also, the Christian psychology of Eric Johnson in his book *Foundations for Soul Care* has strengthened my conviction that the Word of God, and especially the gospel of Jesus Christ, is central to understanding all of life and every aspect of human personhood.

Through many books, lectures, and personal interactions with the faculty of CCEF—Ed Welch, Mike Emlet, Winston Smith, Tim Lane, David Powlison—and Paul Tripp, I have been personally challenged and taught how to think biblically about people and how to help them practically and pastorally. More than anyone, they have provided the vision and guidance to put gospel counseling into practice in the local church.

Thanks to James and Heather Armstrong, Warren and Melissa Myers, Michael and Mary Van Skaik, Hank and Sharon Matthews, Cedar Springs, and Warm Beach for providing comfortable places for me to write.

I've often heard it said, "Without so-and-so this would never have been possible," and I've wondered if these are mere pleasantries. But now, having required so much help from so many people in writing this book, I get it. Without the Holy Spirit moving this work along toward completion through the hands of many helpers, it truly would not have been possible.

INTRODUCTION

Redemption. The word is so familiar its meaning is often taken for granted. In everyday use it suggests recovery, repayment, rescue, or vindication. But what does that look like in real life with real people who are broken, wounded, or addicted? Here's a true story of one man's need for redemption.

In a prison filled with thieves and murderers serving life sentences or awaiting execution, there is one innocent man. He is a slave, imprisoned on false rape charges alleged by his former master's wife. When she tried to seduce him, he ran; so she sentenced him with a lie. But this was not the first betrayal that had cost him his freedom.

He had grown up in a household where he was favored by a doting father and hated by jealous older brothers. Occasionally, he dreamed that he would one day rule over his brothers. Infuriated by his delusions of grandeur and their father's favoritism, his brothers plotted a terrible betrayal. They beat him up, threw him into a hole in the ground, and eventually sold him into slavery to the man whose adulterous wife would betray him again.

His name was Joseph and his story is told in the book of Genesis.[1] Your story has different details, but you probably know something about unjust suffering, betrayal, abuse, abandonment, or despair. You may even know the experience of being trapped in an abusive situation, a sort of prison, against your will. Or you've experienced the slavery and imprisonment of addiction. Whatever the case, you know that something has gone terribly wrong in the world, and this confronts you every day. You strain to make sense of it all; you search for answers.

LIVING STORIES

Life demands explanation, and the more intense the experience, the stronger the demand. "Why me?" has probably been on the lips of every victim and "What's wrong with me?" on the lips of every desperate addict.

We are *meaning-makers*, hard-wired to interpret life.[2] As Paul Tripp says, "We do not live our lives based on the bare facts of our existence; we live our lives according to our *interpretation* of those facts."[3] In other words, it's not our raw experiences that determine our lives but the meaning we make of them—the stories we tell and the stories we believe. Out of those stories, we live our lives.

Abuse and addiction are two particularly intense experiences we tend to build stories around. A third broader category of experiences is what I'll call *assorted trouble*—any combination of intense experiences of sinning or suffering that may not fit under the headings of *abuse* or *addiction* per se but nonetheless have exerted powerful influences on our story forming. Let's have a closer look at each of these.

Stories of Abuse

There are an estimated thirty-nine million survivors of childhood sexual abuse in America today.[4] Sixteen percent of boys and 25 percent of girls are sexually abused by age eighteen.[5] About 28 percent of children have been physically abused, up to 30 percent of boys in general.[6] Of these, only 10 precent are abused by strangers. The rest are abused by family members or trusted friends of the family. It is this betrayal of trust inherent in child abuse that does the most damage, such as when the parent who should be a trustworthy protector becomes the perpetrator.[7] The pain of child abuse extends far beyond physical or sexual damage; *betrayal of trust* sends shockwaves of anguish, fear, anger, rage, and temptations to react throughout the victim's life.[8]

Some are abused as adults—one day living life in a seemingly normal world, and the next, jarred by evil. On college campuses as many as one in five women are raped.[9] The violation of dignity and the stripping of any sense of safety in the world can linger and haunt for a lifetime. One woman I counseled was abused as an adult by a man whom she met at church. He befriended her, gained her trust, and then kidnapped her, violated her, and left her for dead. After being found by detectives, she fled her home country. The kidnapper had stolen and sabotaged her identity, using it to commit fraud. She now lives every day far from home with a lingering sense of danger all around.

My heart breaks when, in counseling and in groups, I hear story after story of abuse told by men and women whose lives have been so utterly devastated at the hands of evildoers. Yet what is even more devastating than the abuse itself is the way some have allowed it to define their lives: nursing bitterness; committing to revenge; desperately searching—even demanding!—affirmation against deep-seated, stubborn insecurities; believing that "I must have deserved this," carrying guilt that belongs to the abuser alone; believing that "*victim* is who I am at the core."

Even the word *abuse* is sometimes granted almost magical explanatory power, as if labeling something as abuse unlocks the deep meaning to explain what's wrong in our lives. Some reach for this word to label virtually any kind of suffering at the hands of another. Yet, as one biblical counselor cautions, "if *everything* is abuse, then nothing is abuse."[10] Using the term too broadly can trivialize the tragic reality of real abuse. But that doesn't mean we shouldn't find the right words to describe the suffering we *have* endured. We need to be able to talk about it, grieve it, and find grace and mercy in our time of need.

David Powlison suggests that we identify *abuse* as one particular evil among many. He asks: "Were you used? misused? abused? mistreated? betrayed? sinned against? done evil?"[11] Abuse, when seen in this context, is not an "all-determining, all-damning, all-condemning, all-controlling force."[12] It is, rather, one particularly terrible evil among many other evils that befall us in a broken world.

Stories of Addiction

Addiction is rampant:

- More than 70 percent of men ages eighteen to thirty-four visit a pornographic Web site in a typical month.[13]
- Forty-seven percent of families have said pornography is a problem in their home.[14]
- Twenty-eight percent of those admitting to sexual addiction are women.[15]
- Nearly eighteen million Americans (8.5 % of adults) meet the diagnostic criteria for alcohol abuse or alcoholism.[16]
- Nearly one out of five workers (19%) age eighteen to twenty-five used illicit drugs during the past month.[17]

Sex, alcohol, and drugs are only the most familiar addictions; we can get addicted to anything. One addiction-awareness Web site lists no fewer than twenty-eight varieties: alongside the usual—drugs, alcohol, and porn—are shopping, sugar, and video games.[18]

At one level, addictions defy all explanation; what could ever explain such foolish self-destruction? Yet, at the same time, they demand explanation; we want to know *why* because we believe that knowing will help us to break free or help others break free. So stories to explain addiction abound.

Some see addiction as a disease, a function of biology, chemistry, or genetics. This is the story told by some medical treatment programs. Shick Shadel Hospital, for example, makes the bold claim: "Give us 10 days; we'll give you back your life."[19] Driving their treatment program is their definition of addiction: "A compulsive physiological need for a habit forming substance . . . a neurological disease, not a mental or moral problem."[20]

Some see addiction as the consequence of low self-esteem and unmet needs. Patrick Carnes proposes that all sex addicts hold the following core beliefs:

- I am basically a bad, unworthy person.
- No one would love me as I am.
- My needs are never going to be met if I have to depend on others.
- Sex is my most important need.[21]

Some believe their addiction is an irreversible fact of life and can be managed only by healthy habits. I talked with one man who through AA (Alcoholics Anonymous) had stopped abusing alcohol. Unfortunately, in the process, he gained a new addiction: his preoccupation with sobriety. I heard the same story from another man who'd spent years in SA (Sexaholics Anonymous); it was a misguided attempt to replace sex with sobriety. Whether each of these men ran to the addiction, strained to break free, or managed to keep a sober distance, the addiction was always at the center, defining life.[22]

Assorted Trouble

Trouble is a catchall category for any kind of sin or suffering that you might experience.[23] While abuse is a particularly acute form of suffering, suffering comes in many serious forms. Even if abuse isn't the best label for what has happened to you, you may still have been sinned against in ways that have left lasting wounds. In addition to such personal suffering as abuse, there are ways we suffer that don't involve another person's sin against us: physical illness, natural disaster, or the loss of a job in a down economy.

There may be a habitual sin pattern in your life that you wouldn't call an addiction per se. Yet, much like an addiction, you find yourself foolishly falling into the same pattern of sin over and over again. So while your problem may be different in *degree* from abuse or addiction, it may not be so different in *kind*. It's all trouble; all trouble has much in common (see 1 Cor. 10:13), and each of us experiences it.

Just consider the following statistics. Even if you don't find yourself in these numbers, by the time you consider your close family—parents, spouse, children—chances increase that you are or will be affected by the trouble of someone close to you.

- *Alcohol:* More than one-half of American adults have a close family member who has or has had alcoholism. Approximately one in four children in the U.S. under eighteen years old is exposed to alcohol abuse or alcohol dependence in the family. Children of alcoholics are significantly more likely to initiate drinking during adolescence and to develop alcohol use disorders.[24]
- *Eating Disorders.* An estimated 0.5 to 3.7 percent of women engage in disorderly eating that could be labeled anexoria nervosa in their lifetime, and for 1.1 to 4.2 percent as bulimia nervosa.[25] The diagnoses of up to ten million females and one million males are considered life threatening.[26]
- *Anxiety.* More than forty million people exhibit the symptoms of anxiety disorders each year.[27]
- *Cutting.* Fifteen to 20 percent of adolescents have engaged in self-injury.[28]
- *Depression and Suicide.* At an average college with 18,000 undergraduate students, some 1,080 of them will seriously consider committing suicide at least once within a single year.[29] Nearly one in ten adults could be diagnosed with clinical depression each year.[30]
- *Mental Illness.* Almost 20 percent of children grow up with a mental illness in their home.[31]
- *Adultery and Divorce.* Half the children born to married parents in 2000 are expected before they turn eighteen to see their parents divorce.

> Children of divorced parents show higher rates of crime, drug abuse, suicide, school dropout, and becoming victims of abuse.[32] Twenty-five percent of all marriages are affected by adultery.[33]

Fill in the blank with your own trouble. You are surrounded by it. It is impossible to live life on the earth and not be stung by sin and suffering. Even more sobering is the fact that you are certainly the cause of some of that trouble to others around you.

Abuse, addiction, and assorted trouble send us searching for answers, explanations, and stories to make meaning of it all. We need to know the story that makes sense of life, the story about a personal Redeemer who offers hope for real redemption. This is the story of God as told in the Bible.

GOD'S STORY IS ABOUT GOD

Here's what's surprising about making sense of *your* life in *God's* story: the story is not about you—it's about him.[34] He is both the author and the main character, and he has written you into his story to say something about him. Yet, if we are honest, we tend to script our lives with ourselves as the protagonists and God in some supporting (or possibly antagonistic) role.

Often, God is cast as a mere extra. At best, he adds to the background action; at worst, he's overlooked. Some have written God into the story as an absent father who pays no attention to the damage being done to his child. Some have made him out to be a therapist whose job it is to prop up their self-esteem. Some treat God as debtor, holding him responsible for their pain and believing they are owed a free pass for sins of pleasure and escape in trade for their undeserved suffering. Others live a life of despair in a world they believe is controlled by a heartless mastermind, pulling the strings of the universe with no compassion for people afflicted by evil. Some treat God as though he were the source of a better high or a better escape than their drug of choice.

For others, he is known as "the God of our understanding," and they call upon him for help to walk away from an addiction.[35] Of course, coming to God with our broken lives is good—there's no better place to go—but we must be careful not to come to the right place with the wrong idea. Even more urgent, we must be careful not to come to the wrong God altogether, guided as we are by our distorted understanding of who he is.

26

Rather than trying to write God into our stories, we would be wiser to sit patiently with our Father and let him tell us his. We would surely find ourselves in his story and learn that we are not defined by our hurts or our sins, as we may have believed. As he tells us his story, we must be willing to let go of the stories we've told to make sense of our lives. We must let his story rewrite ours and sweep us up into something much greater than ourselves.

Joseph's life was shattered and fragmented, betrayed by his brothers and falsely accused by Potiphar's wife. We can assume he carried a lot of pain and asked a lot of questions. Yet when he later faced his brothers, he said to them, "You meant evil against me, but God meant it for good" (Gen. 50:20).

Despite his terrible suffering, Joseph had come to know God as the main character of his life's story and that God's purposes toward him were good. In retrospect, Joseph glimpsed God's redemptive plan, and this helped him make sense of his relationship with his brothers. Yet God didn't grant Joseph this insight until later on. While in prison, Joseph didn't have a clue; he could only trust God.

You may feel like you are still sitting in prison, crying out to be released. Take comfort in knowing that you are a character in the same story as Joseph, authored by the same Redeemer. Your hope need not rest in making sense of it all; rather, you are invited to set your hope of redemption in the Redeemer.

GOD'S STORY ANSWERS LIFE'S QUESTIONS

While God's story is ultimately about him, it is also about you and me and the world we inhabit. It gives us a worldview, a way of understanding life and all reality, including human nature—its important features, problems and causes, solutions, and the overarching goal for which we are meant to aspire.[36]

God's story moves "from creation to new creation by way of *redemption*, which is, in effect, the renewing of creation."[37] This pattern—creation, fall, redemption—will guide the following brief survey of God's story as we seek answers to our questions.[38] In a later section, "Redemption as Renewal," we'll see how God's story culminates in new creation.

Creation: What Does It Mean to Be Human?

Fixing a broken thing requires some knowledge of its design. Likewise, any attempt to address human brokenness requires some understanding of what it means to be human. So we will begin where humanity was designed, at creation, recorded in the book of Genesis.

First, to be human is to be created.[39] "In the beginning, God created the heavens and the earth" (Gen. 1:1). Even before creation, there is God ("In the beginning, God"). Therefore, Creation isn't even the beginning of God's story; all of creation—including humanity—begins somewhere in the midst of God's story. He was already there with a story before there was anything else at all. So once again, we creatures do not add the Creator to our stories; he has created us and added us to his.

Second, to be human is to live always before the face of God. Relationship to God is essential to what it means to be human, not just in the Christian sense (your *personal* relationship with God) but as creation relates to Creator. He made you a fundamentally related-to-God being, whether you know it or not.

Human life plays out on God's stage, before his eyes. Even our thoughts, motives, desires, and emotions are before his eyes, "for the LORD searches all hearts and understands every plan and thought" (1 Chron. 28:9). Every movement of your outward *and* inward life—every movement of your physical body—somehow moves in relationship to him.

I am on a plane as I write this. Suppose we were to hit some turbulence and I were gripped with fear. If you were to talk with me about it later—and you wanted to address the full reality and humanity of my experience—we couldn't simply talk about survival instincts, past experiences, or statistics about plane flight. The most significant aspect of that experience would be what my fear says in relation to God. Not to talk about that would be *subhuman*.[40] Do I believe God is near or far from me in that moment? Do I believe he cares about my trouble? Or do I believe he is indifferent? Do I believe that he controls what will happen or that he is as uncertain and helpless as me? You never have fears all to yourself; you have fears only in relationship to God. Theologians call this *coram Deo*, living all of life before the face of God.[41]

Third, to be human is to bear the image of God. "Then God said,

28

'Let us make man in our own image, after our likeness'" (Gen. 1:26). To be made in the image and likeness of God means you are designed to represent God, to make him known, to reflect his glory like a mirror, to look like him. God has made every human being in such a way that simply *being human* could make his presence known.

For this reason, you have great dignity as a human being, not primarily because of your own goodness but because you are made of the kind of stuff that is capable of making God's much greater goodness visible to others. This is the bedrock upon which the enduring dignity of every person is established—no matter how sinful, abused, impaired, or oppressed. Male and female from the womb, every race—we are all created in his image and likeness.

Fourth, to be human is to worship. We reflect God's glory by our worship of him, which means to hold him as the object of our deepest desires and as worthy of our imitation. Worship is not just singing songs in church; it's how we live our lives every moment of every day—every thought, word, deed, feeling, and desire. You worship what you live for, whatever is most worthy of your attention and devotion.[42] It is what drives you at the core, and it flows from the essence of who you are.

You can't turn off worship. It's your basic human wiring. To not worship is to not live. It's like a garden hose stuck on full blast. You can aim it at the grass, the car, or the shrubs, but you cannot stop its flow.

Or you might imagine yourself as a sort of human billboard, always advertising what you find to be important, valuable, worthy. What you pay attention to, how you spend your time, the way you work, how you relate to others in your life—all these things broadcast your heart's worship, making visible and advertising what is most important to you. God created you to broadcast him.

Fifth, to be human is to long for shalom. The universal peace, harmony, and wholeness of God's original design of humankind and the whole earth are conveyed by the Hebrew word *shalom* in the Bible (e.g., Isa. 32:14–20).[43] Cornelius Plantinga describes shalom as "the webbing together of God, humans, and all creation in justice, fulfillment, and delight . . . a rich state of affairs in which natural needs are satisfied and natural gifts fruitfully employed, a state of affairs that inspires joyful wonder as its Creator and

Savior opens doors and welcomes the creatures in whom he delights."[44] We have an inborn sense of shalom. It is home, and we long to return.

THE FALL: WHERE EVERYTHING WENT WRONG

It is perhaps *because* of this inborn sense of shalom that we are so grieved by the world in which we now live. You feel it in your gut and you see the evidence all around you and in you: the world is not the way it's supposed to be.[45]

It all began with the appearance of the Serpent in the garden, telling a different story.[46] The Serpent—Satan, the rebel-deceiver—moved in to spread his lies and rebellion to the fledgling human race. He invited Adam and Eve into his own way of understanding. He suggested that God is not as good as God had made himself out to be. He flatly denied the consequences of disobeying God (Gen. 3:1, 4). He even suggested an advantage to disobeying God: "You will be like God" (v. 5). In the first and greatest tragedy in the history of humankind, Adam and Eve believed the Serpent's story, and in their sin they rose up against God in attempt to become gods, just as the Serpent had done before (v. 6).

But it was a lie.

God's words had been true. So the consequences of their sin followed God's story, not the Serpent's.

Immediately, their eyes were opened and they realized they were naked (v. 7). They hid themselves from God's presence and were afraid because of their nakedness (vv. 8, 10). God cursed the Serpent (vv. 14–15). The woman would know greater pain in childbearing and frustration in her relationship to her husband (v. 16). The man's work would be frustrated by God's cursing of the ground, and God's people were driven out of the garden (vv. 17, 23).

What happened here? How could Adam and Eve go from the sheer bliss of living in the good garden under God's blessing to all-out rebellion? Surely, before the Serpent's lies entered the garden Adam and Eve were content to enjoy God and steward shalom as his image bearers. But the Serpent's story cast a shadow on their experience and offered to interpret their (already perfect) lives by lies: "Something is missing. God withholds his best. Why should you be satisfied living *under* God, when you could live *as* God?"

Behold the power of a story to define—and distort—life.

Sin Unravels God's Creation

Sin is not just the breaking of some Sunday school do's and don'ts. It is not the violation of some impersonal cosmic code of morality. Sin is a personal offense against the Creator. It unravels and corrupts God's creation. Consider how sin corrupts each aspect of creation introduced above.

First, sin distorts the distinction between Creator and created. We put ourselves at the center of the universe and the center of the story. We attempt to be god, defining good and evil for ourselves. We deify creation, trying to turn created things into gods (see Rom. 1:25).

Second, sin erodes our awareness of life lived always before the face of God (*coram Deo*). When this, the very platform for all life, is eroded, the results are pervasive, both at the individual level and at the broader, cultural level. At the individual level, we can become self-sufficient and autonomous, as if there is no one on whom we must depend and to whom we must give account for our lives. Culturally, worldviews emerge to explain reality in ways that are disconnected from a personal creator and sustainer. They explain human composition, motivation, and goals purely in terms of biology, social dynamics, or psychological needs. In turn, individuals who need help with their broken lives end up embracing ways of seeing their problems and solutions that are not shaped by the knowledge of God. This happens even within the church where agnostic theories are sometimes merely "baptized" in Christian lingo and then lived out.[47]

Third, sin corrupts the image of God in mankind and treats it with contempt. The image of God in man was not lost in the fall but marred and distorted (Gen. 9:6; James 3:9). In a sense, it would be less tragic if it had been utterly lost. Instead, with the very capacities God gave us to image him and steward his creation, we defame his name, vandalize his world, and violate his image in others, which amounts to treason. In so doing, we, in fact, image that arch rebel, Satan. Abuse, abortion, racism, and genocide are so heinous precisely because they violate the very image of God.

Fourth, sin corrupts worship. The result? Not a ceasing of worship but a distortion of it. We never stop worshiping. Rather, in sin, we worship anything and everything other than God. We tend to exalt a substance, an experience, a person, or a dream to the level of a god. We define life by its attainment, and we feel like dying when it eludes us. It becomes bigger in our eyes than God himself and takes his place in our lives. The Bible calls this "idolatry." So addictions, for example, aren't just drug, alcohol, food, or pornography problems. They are worship disorders.[48] They flow from hearts bent on worshiping created things rather than the Creator.

Fifth, sin spoils shalom.[49] Eden was the epicenter of a sin pandemic that has since enveloped the whole world. What began with Adam has spread to all people (Rom. 5:12). There is no one and nowhere left untouched. Shalom is spoiled not just by the sin I commit but also by the sins committed against me: the abuse, mistreatment, betrayal, lies, and abandonment.[50] It is important that we see both sides of this, because, as David Powlison warns, reducing the problem of sin to just one of these aspects has a blinding effect: either we become blind to God's compassion and mercy for our suffering, or we become blind to our responsibility for sin we commit.[51]

Some of the victims of abuse I've counseled have the clearest grasp on this. They have been terribly wounded by the sins of another. Yet they have also sinned in response—in bitterness, revenge, or promiscuity—at times even abusing others just as they had themselves been abused.

JESUS IS YOUR REDEMPTION

How can sin be overcome and shalom restored? To answer that question is to define redemption. And no Christian should be surprised by the biblical answer: Jesus himself is our redemption (1 Cor. 1:30; see also Rom. 3:23–24; Gal. 4:4–5; Eph. 1:7; Heb. 9:12).

Redemption is not a series of steps we practice or rules we follow. It is not the forced motions of religious practice. No human effort can accomplish redemption for oneself or anyone else. We need a Redeemer. Just as God's story is not ultimately about you but about God, so also redemption comes not from you but from God. God's story is about redemption. But more specifically it is about a Redeemer. Jesus is the main character of the story, and his life and work are the center of the plot.

For some, hearing the words "Jesus is your redemption" rings a bell and piques curiosity ("Tell me more!") For others, the same words seem hollow. They may have heard them a thousand times in sermons and Sunday school. But when real evil overwhelms, it just doesn't seem to work. At that point, they tend to move in one of two directions: they either pay lip service and pretend it's working to keep fitting in at church or grow cynical and leave. Either way, their hearts go in search of other solutions.[52] This is tragic, because it means they stray from their true hope at just the time when they most need it.

How is it that we can hear the words that *define* hope and yet not hear the hope they offer? I think it's partially due to a lack of context.[53] You can hear the climax of God's story—"Jesus is your redemption"—but a climax without context just doesn't pop.

Consider the movie *The Return of the King*, based on J. R. R. Tolkien's book by the same title. Imagine you knew nothing of the story and all you saw was a clip with some Hobbits clawing their way up a volcano to destroy a gold ring in its fire. A friend tells you that this is the part where they save the whole world, and you're thinking: "What does a gold ring have to do with the fate of the world?" Well, it's all in the back story. If you knew the story, you'd be on the edge of your seat. When it comes to understanding redemption, the key back story in the Bible is the exodus.[54]

THE EXODUS AS GOD'S MODEL OF REDEMPTION

When the New Testament authors wrote about Jesus as our redemption, the Old Testament story they had in mind was the exodus, the prototype of redemption.[55]

Christopher J. H. Wright says:

> If you had asked a devout Israelite in the Old Testament period "Are you redeemed?" the answer would have been a most definite yes. And if you had asked "How do you know?" you would be taken aside to sit down somewhere while your friend recounted a long and exciting story—the story of the exodus. For indeed it is the exodus that provided the primary model of God's idea of redemption, not just in the Old Testament but even in the New, where it is used as one of the keys to understanding the meaning of the cross of Christ.[56]

Exodus is more than one story of redemption; it also points to the larger story of redemption. Wright also says:

[The exodus] points beyond itself to a greater need for deliverance from the totality of evil and restoration to relationship with God than it achieved by itself. Such a deliverance was accomplished by Jesus Christ in his death and resurrection.[57]

So read Exodus expecting fresh insight into the truth that Jesus is your redemption. Immerse yourself in the drama as you would with any good story. Identify with the characters and the situations they faced. Encounter your Redeemer—not an abstract religious concept but a compassionate, powerful, steadfast, loving, and personal God who pursues and redeems his people.

Let's look at three related themes of redemption enacted by the exodus story: deliverance, ransom, and renewal. By considering each, we'll learn a bit more about what redemption involves and where it applies to our lives. We'll also get a survey of the exodus story and get a feel for how it points forward to Christ.

Redemption as Deliverance

Deliverance is about movement from slavery to freedom, from bondage in sin to life in God: "Redemption is synonymous with being liberated, freed, or rescued from bondage and slavery to a person or thing."[58]

Merriam-Webster defines *slave* as "one that is completely subservient to a dominating influence."[59] "Whatever overcomes a person, to that he is enslaved," wrote the apostle Peter (2 Pet. 2:19). And John wrote, "The whole world lies in the power of the evil one" (1 John 5:19). Our enemy seeks to overwhelm us with evil and take us captive.

If you've been abused, you may relate to the metaphor of slavery: being overcome by evil, taken captive against your will, and plunged into a world of pain, confusion, and fear. The wounds of abuse can be dominating influences, complicating relationships with people, sometimes resulting in difficulty trusting others, preoccupation with others' approval, or feeling alone in the world. It can also result in a seemingly irresistible urge to grow bitter or seek revenge.

If you've been addicted, you may also relate to the slavery metaphor. Your life has been out of control, dominated by the influence of the addiction. Perhaps, despite your desire to be free, you've gone back again and again to the addiction. It has cost you dearly—money, pain, and relation-ships—and has left you in misery beneath a load of guilt and shame. This is slavery; yet it's slavery you've chosen. It is voluntary slavery.[60]

In the opening chapters of Exodus, we find God's people in slavery. We are given no indication that they bear any blame for their condition. They have been overcome by evil, and his name is Pharaoh. God hears the cries of his people, and remembers them. He then stretches out his mighty hand to crush Pharaoh and deliver his people.

In the New Testament, we see that Jesus crushes our enemy (Col. 2:15), delivers us from slavery to sin (Rom. 6:6), and ultimately overcomes the power of the evil one (Rev. 12:9).

Redemption as Ransom

Ransom is the high price God paid to purchase our freedom: his own Son on the cross. According to theologian John Murray, "The language of redemption is the language of purchase and more specifically of ransom . . . [which] presupposes some kind of bondage or captivity."[61] The slaves in Egypt were bound by a ruthless enemy due to no fault of their own. Yet when God came to crush Pharaoh, the slaves were equally deserving of God's judgment because of their own sin (cf. Josh. 24:14). As an act of pure grace, God provided for them a Passover lamb whose blood would stand in their place as their ransom. By this blood, and this blood alone, God spared the lives of their firstborn even as he killed the firstborn of every Egyptian household.

However, notice what *isn't* happening here. God doesn't pay the ran-som price to Pharaoh, as if God owed Pharaoh anything. The ransom does not pay off the enemy; rather, it shows the great cost of redemption—a price paid by God as a gift of his grace.

There are some who hear that God forgives sinners and yet somehow find their own sin beyond forgiveness. The debt, they think, is just too great. Many exhaust themselves attempting to pay off the debt by good behavior, religious activity, or even by wallowing in their shame as a sort of self-punishment. But this ends only in misery and greater debt. We simply cannot repay what we owe. But Jesus, the spotless Passover Lamb, has paid it all (1 Cor. 5:7; 1 Pet. 1:18–19).

Redemption as Renewal

Redemption is "in effect, the renewing of creation."[62] In other words, it is *re*-creation. Terrence Fretheim, in agreement with many Exodus commentators, stresses the deep weaving of creation theology into the fabric of Exodus. He goes so far as to say, "While the liberation of Israel is the focus of God's activity, it is not the ultimate purpose. . . . Redemption is for the purpose of creation, a new life within the larger creation, a return to the world as God intended it to be."[63] So redemption restores God's original design in creation.

Meredith Kline elaborates on the significance of redemptive recreation for the individual Christian: "Redemption is a recovering and restoring of the original. The person who experiences redemption in Christ remains the same person, even though the transformation from the sinner dead-in-sins to the saint alive-forevermore-in-Christ is so radical as to be called a new creation."[64] Redemption restores you to your original purpose, to image God by your worship. God does this by remaking you in the image of Jesus, who is the perfect image of God (Col. 1:15; Heb. 1:3). That means when we look at Jesus, we see a perfect picture of what God intended for humankind.

And one day, when redemption is complete, God's original purpose for all creation will be completely restored. As in Eden, where God was present with his people, so also in the new creation "the dwelling place of God is with man"; where there was no death, "death shall be no more" (Rev. 21:3–4); where humankind ruled the earth on God's behalf, God's people will "reign forever and ever" (Rev. 22:5). There will be complete peace and perfect joy. Pain, shame, violence, oppression, fear, temptation, illness, famine, natural disasters—all of these pass away.

It's hard to imagine such perfection, isn't it? And yet when the Bible says you are a new creation, it means that you have already been made part of that whole new order of things. Jesus is the first of the new creation, and in him you too are a new creation (see 2 Cor. 5:17; cf. 1 Cor. 15:23).[65] In Christ, we are transformed. Idolaters, thieves, liars, sexual perverts, addicts, abusers, and victims—all of us already get new names, new identities, and new hearts with new desires (see 1 Cor. 6:9–11). Already, he is healing our wounds, covering our shame, and freeing us from the bondage to sin and temptation.

Already-and-not-yet

We sense, however, that we are not totally new: we still face temptation, and at times we give in; we still ache from past wounds. And there's no question that the world around us still lies in the power of the evil one. Misery—not peace—still dominates most of life on the earth. So how can we say the new has already begun, when so much corruption remains?

Theologians have spilled much ink trying to address questions raised by some biblical evidence that much of this re-creation has already begun, especially in God's people, and other biblical evidence that much is yet to come—the perfection of God's people and renewal of all creation. The view that seems to make most sense of this tension is called *inaugurated eschatology:* Jesus inaugurated his kingdom, and in him, a new creation has begun; yet the future holds the consummation of his kingdom and the perfection of all creation, including you and me. In the meantime, we live in a state of "already-and-not-yet." We already enjoy some of the benefits of the new creation, but we do not yet know the full freedom of perfection. For that we must wait eagerly. Between now and then, there is a process of renewal.

Colossians 3:9–10 captures the already-and-not-yet experience in the life of the Christian: "You have put off the old self with its practices and have put on the new self, which is being renewed in knowledge after the image of its creator." The old self here has been put off (already) and the new self has been put on (already). But look what's happening with this new self: it is being renewed. Renewal is a process.[66]

Worship in the Wilderness

The wilderness is an already-and-not-yet kind of place: the Israelites were already free from slavery, but they were not yet home. As Graeme Goldsworthy says, "The exodus is the end of captivity, but it is only the beginning of freedom."[67] Their deliverance freed them to worship God, but it didn't make them perfect worshipers. And though an evil oppressor no longer threatened them, they weren't free from all pain. They still carried their old wounds on their backs, and the wilderness held its own new troubles.

What we learn from the Israelites in the wilderness is that being free to worship God doesn't necessarily mean that we will. After all of his miraculous work to deliver them from Egypt, they doubted God's provision for them in the wilderness and grumbled bitterly for food and water. After he pursued them time and again, reiterating, "I am the God who delivers you from Egypt," they became impatient and erected a golden calf to worship, saying, "These are your gods, O Israel, who brought you up out of the land of Egypt!" (Ex. 32:4). It could even be said that they resembled unruly young calves themselves, astray in the wilderness, rebelling against their master.[68]

As shocking as their idol worship was, it was the natural result of their hearts' desires. They had turned their hearts to Egypt (Acts 7:39). Though they were free to worship God, when it came right down to it, they still lived for Egypt.

And this brings us all the way back to the core of our problems and therefore to the brink of the solution. We love the wrong things, so our worship is distorted. We have exchanged the worship of God for golden calves. The solution: renewed worship.

The Puritan preacher Thomas Chalmers, in his sermon *The Expulsive Power of a New Affection*, said that desires for God and desires for sin cannot coexist in the human heart. They are two opposing "affections"—one will always push out the other. So, he said, "the only way to dispossess [the heart] of an old affection, is by the expulsive power of a new one" (see Gal. 5:16–17).[69] You can't just "stop it," because the *it* is always more than behavior. It is always rooted in your affections, in what you love—what you worship. Chalmers points the way forward: we worshiped our way into this mess, and by God's grace, we'll worship our way out.[70]

Here is the moment-by-moment of our redemption: when bitterness surfaces, anxiety swells, fear stabs, or temptation lures, because we have been delivered from the bondage of sin into the freedom of the Spirit we can turn our eyes to Jesus, worship him then and there, and be changed from one degree of glory to another (2 Cor. 3:18).

RECOMMENDED RESOURCES

Emlet, Michael R. *CrossTalk: Where Life and Scripture Meet.* Greensboro, NC: New Growth Press, 2009. Emlet provides practical tools to help us deeply connect the meaning of the Bible to everyday life.

Keller, Timothy. *Counterfeit Gods: The Empty Promises of Money, Sex, and Power, and the Only Hope That Matters.* New York: Dutton, 2009. In his highly accessible and succinct style, Keller masterfully weaves biblical exposition, storytelling, observations of popular culture, and penetrating insight into human nature, to help us see idols within and all around us—and marks out the path away from them.

Lane, Timothy S., and Paul David Tripp. *How People Change.* Greensboro, NC: New Growth Press, 2008. This book lays a basic foundation for gospel-based life change (progressive sanctification).

Roberts, Vaughan. *God's Big Picture: Tracing the Story-Line of the Bible.* Downers Grove, IL: InterVarsity, 2003. Roberts concisely surveys the story of God, from Genesis to Revelation.

Tripp, Paul David. *Instruments in the Redeemer's Hands: People in Need of Change Helping People in Need of Change.* Phillipsburg, NJ: P&R, 2002. Especially for leaders and counselors. The first five chapters lay a foundation for understanding who we are as people and what it means to live in God's story in the face of life's trials.

SCRIPTURE READING

• Luke 24:13–35

FOR REFLECTION AND DISCUSSION

1) Write down some of the "big details" that stand out in your life. Look for details that seem significant to you even if you don't understand their significance yet. Consider key relationships, memorable events (good or bad), illness and injuries, times where you may have been harmed, notable sins and patterns of sin, dreams and aspirations.

2) Are there any stories you've told to make sense of some of these details—or your whole life in general—that may need to be reconsidered in light of God's story?

3) Where in your life do you feel enslaved?

4) What do you expect to get out of this book? Or if you are going through this book with a group, what do you expect to get out of the group experience?

1

WHEN YOU SUFFER, GOD IS NEAR

Sarah was conceived in adultery. Two years later, her mother had another girl by her husband. This is when she confessed to the adultery and revealed that Sarah was not her husband's daughter. He exploded in rage, nearly drowned Sarah, and forced her out of the house. Sarah was two years old.

The few years Sarah lived with her grandmother were happy ones: playing, singing songs, and going to church. But Sarah was returned to her mother's home at the age of five when her grandmother died from cancer. While Sarah lived with her grandmother, she'd had no contact with her mother or stepfather, and in the interim they'd had another child and adopted two more. Sarah's siblings didn't even know she existed. Her return forced her mother to tell the truth about their older sibling from an adulterous relationship.

Sarah was an outcast in her own home, and her stepfather treated her like an animal. If she angered him, he might force her to eat her food on the floor from a dog dish or lock her out of the house. Once, when she was in first grade, he locked her out for a whole week without food, water, or a change of clothes. She slept outside in the grass and awoke each morning to walk alone to the school bus, her hair matted with dirt and leaves. At least at school she could escape to a place where she felt human. But she couldn't escape for long. There was always more pain waiting for her when she returned home.

And it got worse.

She remembers the burning hatred in her stepfather's eyes as he entered her bedroom that first night. He raped her, not just that night but nearly every night for the next five years. Even this was not the worst of it. Sarah's stepfather beat her, tortured her, and sold her to other men. Sarah lived in a constant state of torment.

Sarah didn't deserve this suffering, and she was overwhelmed by it, helpless at the hands of evildoers. For those unsure about the actual presence of evil in the world, hers is the kind of story that leaves us without a doubt.

After hearing Sarah's story, some of us might conclude: "Well if that's suffering, then I haven't suffered at all; so what does this have to do with me?" While we don't all have stories as horrific as Sarah's, we still suffer in many ways, sometimes at the hands of others, sometimes not. All suffering takes its toll. Here are a few more examples.

I talked to a friend just a few weeks ago whose doctor had expressed concerns about some possible early symptoms of multiple sclerosis. Before he could make it to the CT scan to confirm a diagnosis, he awoke with severe abdominal pain and required emergency surgery. He's been in bed for weeks recovering. And what awaits him when his body heals? More tests for MS.

In January of 2010, a massive earthquake struck the already impoverished nation of Haiti, burying many under piles of rubble and leaving many more wounded and homeless. It was the largest earthquake in the region for some two hundred years. Death tolls quickly climbed into the tens of thousands, with an estimated third of the nation's population affected; estimates on the final toll soared into the hundreds of thousands.[1]

Yesterday at church, I prayed with a woman who was in tears as she explained that she'd always dreamed of being a mommy but has been unable to conceive.

I recently spoke with a man who lives with a mental illness that runs in his family; it affects him every day as he struggles with depression.

Another friend was devastated when she found out about her husband's addiction to porn. He wasn't the man she thought he was, and he'd been lying to her for years.

We haven't all experienced extreme physical abuse at the hands of a father, like Sarah has. But I've counseled enough people to know that absent, neglectful, and impossible-to-please fathers leave lasting, emotional scars on many of us.

Jeff was about the most likeable kid you could meet. Friendly and outgoing, he was born with a natural gift for connecting with people. Incurably yet forgivably talkative in class, even the disciplinary teachers fell into conversation with him. Jeff's father did a lot of "guy things" with Jeff's older brother, like hunting and playing ball. Jeff figured he'd be included once he got older. But the years passed and the rejection continued. Jeff faced daily disappointment as his father pushed him away. More than once Jeff heard his father say, "Get away from me. I don't like you. You remind me of myself." He was six years old. What is a little boy supposed to do with that?

Betrayal, tragedy, illness, abuse, neglect—suffering comes in many forms. And when it comes to you, me, Jeff, and Sarah, we share something in common—pain.

A friend of mine recently lost his wife to cancer. I was sharing with him about some hardship of my own and then stopped myself, thinking, *My concern must sound so trivial to him when he's lost his wife!* Knowing why I hesitated, he drew me back into the conversation and said, "This is the pain club. Even if your pain is different from mine, it's all pain." He wasn't saying all pain is equal, but what he was saying is that pain makes us aware that we need mercy and long for compassion.

Please don't miss the point: This isn't a who-has-the-saddest-story competition with compassion as the prize. The point is this: whether our misery is big or small, we all find ourselves under the fountain of God's mercy. But finding ourselves in that fountain begins with being honest about our suffering. So as we dive into the story of the Israelites suffering in Egypt, I invite you to honestly face the suffering in your life—whatever it looks like—and find a way to put yourself in their shoes.

GOD'S PEOPLE PLUNGED INTO DARKNESS

In the opening chapter of Exodus, we find the Israelites in Egypt. Some four hundred years earlier, Jacob, Joseph's father, brought his family to Egypt in hopes of surviving a famine. They remained in Egypt for many generations, multiplied, and in fulfillment of God's promise to Jacob's grandfather Abraham, they became a great people (Gen. 15:1–5; Ex. 1:7).

Their abundance in the land was a sign of God's blessing, and Joseph was responsible for saving the land from famine (Genesis 41). If it hadn't been for his godly wisdom and administration of Egypt's food stores, Egypt itself would have been crippled. So not only had God saved his own people by bringing them to Egypt; he had saved Egypt by sending his people. Egypt knew this, and they remembered Joseph and honored his family.

But then a new king arose in Egypt, and he did not know Joseph (Ex. 1:8). This doesn't mean he'd never heard of Joseph, the national hero; it means he refused to acknowledge Egypt's debt of gratitude to Joseph, and, by extension, he refused to see the Israelites (Joseph's people) as a blessing to the land.[2] All loyalties were forgotten, and the Israelites were suddenly in danger in the only homeland they'd ever known. As the king of Egypt, Pharaoh should have been the one to provide peace, protection, and provision for the people in his land.[3] But this Pharaoh grew fearful of them, and angry. He turned on the Israelites and incited the Egyptians against them with his propaganda (vv. 9–10).

Pharaoh plunged the Israelites into darkness and beat them into ruthless slavery (vv. 11, 13–14). They were oppressed, abused, and enslaved. They did nothing to warrant such treatment—they were innocent.[4] And it wasn't just one act of harm but the systematic oppression of a whole people through slavery, racism, and genocide (v. 22). According to scholar Nahum Sarna, the Israelites were "organized in large work gangs; they became an anonymous mass, depersonalized, losing all individuality in the eyes of their oppressors."[5]

Some would have been forced to work the fields where the toil was exhausting and the results were small, despite high expectations and harsh punishments for low yields. Imagine this scene: a field worker's harvest is half taken by worms and half by a hippopotamus, and then thieves steal whatever scraps are left. The slave masters then come to collect, with palm rods in hand. One Egyptian writing aptly illustrates their plight:

> They say, "Give us corn"—there is none there. Then they beat him as he lies stretched out and bound on the ground, they throw him into the canal and he sinks down, head under water. His wife is bound before his eyes and his children are put in fetters.[6]

The very land of salvation became their death sentence.

Imagine what it must have been like for the Israelites who were alive at the time of the enslavement. They were used to living peacefully there and would have been shocked by the initial blast of Pharaoh's hateful racism as all the safety, comfort, and freedom they'd known were ripped from them and replaced with chains and back-breaking labor.

Now think about Sarah's story. She knew about displacement and betrayal when she returned to her mother's home and was met with her stepfather's hatred and violence. You may be able to relate to this too if you've been stung by betrayal or abuse.

Now imagine being born into slavery and never knowing freedom at all. For the Israelites, Egypt was a place of pain from the cradle to the grave. They plodded through an exhausting life that ended in an unnoticed death, just one more nameless body spent and discarded. Sarah can relate. She never knew the love of an earthly dad but only the violence of a hateful stepfather. You too may have been born into an unsafe or dysfunctional home, or trained to believe lies from an early age.

The Israelites were under a fog of unyielding oppression: daily suffering was as far as the eye could see for as far as the memory could recall and as far into the future as the mind could imagine. They groaned bitterly and cried out to God for rescue. How hard it must have been to see their experience fit within God's grander story. Or was there a grand story at all? We can imagine, from their vantage point on the ground level—under the fog—that they felt abandoned by God in Egypt.

The opening scenes of Exodus don't present the reader with a present, active God. This is probably a reflection of the Israelites' experience—God *seemed* absent.[7] The most active character in this part of the story appears to be the evil Pharaoh. Where was God? How long did the Israelites have to suffer before God would intervene?

It may be too easy for us to take comfort in their place in God's story. From a distance, we have the advantage of seeing the big picture. The Israelites were multiplying in Egypt—an evidence of God's promise (Gen. 46:3; 47:27; Ex. 1:7). God in his sovereignty thwarted Pharaoh's plan, and the more the Israelites were in threat of extermination, the more they grew (Ex. 1:12). Not only that, but God had told Abraham that his offspring would endure a season of sojourn and slavery in Egypt and that he would deliver them (Gen. 15:13). We know that though God *seemed* absent, he wasn't really. We know that though Pharaoh *seemed* to have the final say in determining the fate of Israel, he didn't.

But when you're in the thick of it yourself, as the Israelites were, those truths so easily grasped from a distance can be elusive. The questions we ask in the midst of suffering aren't mainly intellectual ones about God's relationship to evil and evildoers; they are emotional ones such as, "How can I trust a God who has the power to make it stop, but doesn't?"[8] Who is this indifferent God who makes such grand promises and then watches as his people are treated so unjustly? Does he feel anything at all when he hears their wailings? Or does he just stand back at a distance, letting random events, the plans of evil men, and the forces of nature take their course?

SARAH'S WRESTLE WITH GOD

By age fifteen, Sarah had endured more violence at the hands of more men than she could count—or remember. Intentionally hardening in her anger, she wore black makeup, dyed her hair blue, and hated everyone. One of her favorite hobbies was arguing against the existence of God. Being a smart girl, she usually won.

Then in high school, two boys who were friends—the only nice and "normal" people she knew—began talking to her about God. They weren't skilled in debate like she was, but they weren't phased by her anti-God tirades either, and they kept being kind and inviting her to come along to their youth group at church. (One of their peers there, they thought, would be much more capable in the debate.)

The first night at youth group, she showed up and, per usual, got right into the argument. But then something unexpected happened. During a time of singing worship songs, she felt the palpable, undeniable presence of God. Her next feeling was holy terror: she had been the enemy of this present and powerful God, persuading many that he didn't even exist. She now knew beyond doubt that he did.

That night, she went home and read her Bible. Gripped by the new-found truth of God's existence, her desire to know about him was insatiable. Yet while this truth answered some of her questions, it also opened new ones: he was there, but he didn't seem good—at least not to her. Why had he so messed up her life, she wondered? It was as if God knew full well what she was going through; yet, despite having the power to stop it, he didn't seem to care. It was as if her cries for help fell upon deaf ears.

THE GOD WHO SEES AND KNOWS

Why did God wait some 430 years before delivering Israel?[9] We don't know, but the fact that he did wait doesn't contradict his wisdom, goodness, and mercy. When he breaks onto the scene, we are left with no doubt about what he is like: he hears the cries of his people and is filled with compassion.

> The people of Israel groaned because of their slavery and cried out for help. Their cry for rescue from slavery came up to God. And God heard their groaning, and God remembered his covenant with Abraham, with Isaac, and with Jacob. God saw the people of Israel—and God knew. (Ex. 2:23–25)

God's *knowing* here deserves some unpacking, because the significance of this language would have spoken volumes to the original readers. It is more than mere awareness of their situation; it conveys deep, personal, intimate knowledge and pity for his people.[10] He was paying attention to his people. He grieved that they have been denied their basic dignity as his image bearers. Commenting on this passage, William Edgar says:

> To be known by God is to be loved, to be in the best place you could possibly be. This is because God now bears the burden, not the people. Knowledge here means full acknowledgement and commitment to intervene.[11]

This passage reveals God's character in his commitment to intervene. Just as *knowing* here isn't mere awareness, so also *remembering* his covenant isn't mere recall; it is movement into action. These were his covenant people; Pharaoh would not ultimately have his way.

God is not a silent, detached, distant, dispassionate deity. He hears his people's cries. He knows their suffering. He will keep his promise. He will rescue them.

He spoke to Moses from the burning bush and said: "I have surely seen the affliction of my people. . . . I know their sufferings, and *I have come down*

47

to deliver them out of the hand of the Egyptians and to *bring them up* out of that land to a good and broad land" (Ex. 3:7–8).[12]

In the exodus story, God rescued his people by sending a redeemer, Moses, who was one of them. Moses prefigures the ultimate Redeemer, God himself, becoming one of us, in the man Jesus Christ. He came down to bring us up. Jesus is the ultimate expression of God's compassion for his people and the ultimate guarantee that God really does understand your pain. Jesus lived the kind of pain you are experiencing right now.

Jesus was made like us in all the frailty of humanity (Heb. 2:10, 17–18). He endured the hostility of sinners (Heb. 12:3). He was despised and rejected, a man of sorrows who has borne our grief: he was wounded, crushed, spit upon, and oppressed (Isa. 53:3–6). He knows the agony of betrayal from those closest to him, his own disciples. He knows the chill of abandonment (Ps. 22:1; Matt. 27:46).

He even knows the loneliness of suffering. In the garden of Gethsemane, knowing he would soon fall into the hands of those who would crucify him, Jesus said to his disciples, "My soul is very sorrowful, even to death; remain here, and watch with me" (Matt. 26:38). He said this to his closest two disciples, the two people on earth who would surely stand by him if anyone would. Then he fell on his face and cried out to the Father. When he arose, he found those two men—his closest friends—sleeping. While he was in agony, anticipating further agony in crucifixion and separation from the Father to the point of sweating blood, they were taking a nap (Luke 22:44). Not even Jesus' closest friends proved compassionate that night.

Jesus also knows the struggle to accept the Father's wisdom in allowing such pain. He knows what it is to trust a God who could make it stop but doesn't. For what was he praying in agony as his best friends slept? "Father, if you are willing, remove this cup from me" (Luke 22:42). You can be sure that there was no stoic resignation in his voice; Jesus desperately wrestled with the Father's plan—and not just once but three times (Matt. 26:39, 42, 44).

How do you feel when earnest prayers seem to go unanswered or are answered in ways that still leave you in difficult circumstances? How does this affect your faith the next time your prayers are desperate? Joan, a non-Christian, told me her story of a threatening situation with a boyfriend who pressured her to give him her virginity. She had always wanted sex to be special, but the situation she found herself in was just the opposite. She excused herself to another room in the house just long enough to utter the plea, "God, please don't let this happen to me." And then it did. That was probably the last time she ever prayed.

That night in the garden was not Jesus' first night of intense prayer entrusting himself to the Father. He had also prayed all night before he chose his twelve disciples (Luke 6:12–16). Surely he prayed for discernment to select faithful men, men who would live and die for the cause, men who would stand by him at all costs. The next day, he chose. And among the twelve was Judas, the traitor, the one whom Jesus, on that night in the garden, knew would betray him.

If you had been the one praying in that garden, would you not find it nearly impossible to entrust yourself to the Father after a whole night of prayer—and now a second night!—that ended with Judas? Joan refused to trust God again after concluding God had failed her. I think we can all relate to the reluctance to trust again when we feel we've been let down. But Jesus knew better that night in the garden. However bad the circumstances, however little we may understand them, the Father is always trustworthy. Jesus' faith, his trust, his dependence in a most vulnerable moment is almost unfathomable.

Notice too what Jesus *didn't* do in the garden: ignore the pain of his situation. He didn't drown it out with some addiction. He didn't deny it. And he didn't mask it with a platitude about God's sovereignty, either. He faced it and ran to the Father in his distress. The garden alone would have been more suffering than most could handle. Yet for Jesus, much more was to come: Peter's betrayal, the false trials, mockery, flogging, and finally crucifixion.

Jesus can identify with the worst suffering, for he suffered not only an excruciating death but also separation from the Father (Matt. 27:46). The fact is that none of us knows the full magnitude of what Jesus suffered, and those who put their trust in him never will.

In Exodus, God didn't turn away from the Israelites' pain; he faced it. He heard, saw, and knew their suffering. He invites us to do the same. The problem isn't that God has abandoned us in our pain, but that sometimes we refuse to face it with him.

SARAH FACES THE PAIN OF THE PAST

As an adult, Sarah had become a woman of steel, a tough survivor; yet she was lonely hiding so many secrets. She just didn't want to face the past, not even with her husband (she ended up marrying one of those boys who had invited her to their youth group).

In the first few months of their marriage, there was conflict in the bedroom. She was emotionally absent. Sex, even with her husband, felt like rape. But she didn't tell him what was going on. All he knew was that she wasn't engaged, and his confusion, disappointment, and hurt escalated into angry outbursts. Some good Christian friends were aware of the situation and confronted Sarah's husband. This was fine by Sarah, because the way she saw it, as long as he was angry the attention was off of her and on him. She intended to hide as long as she could, so she kept pushing his buttons. But by God's grace, her husband changed. He started moving toward her with greater sensitivity and patience. She knew she couldn't hide anymore. She was ready to talk.

Sarah and her husband met with a pastor at their church, and began talking through everything. After months of counseling sessions, Sarah's heels were still dug in. In her mind, God was disqualified to be God because he had failed her so many times. How could he be good and allow so many abuses? So she presumed to have free pass to play God in his place: she controlled her life, her emotions, and her husband.

After many compassionate conversations, the pastor confronted Sarah's arrogance. At first, she was furious. But the pastor, wisely, didn't merely confront Sarah's arrogance; he also turned her attention to how truly good and trustworthy God is. As Sarah's fury subsided and she settled into some personal Bible study on God's goodness, she felt God's grace and mercy flood into her heart. In the light of his goodness, she was convicted of her arrogance—trying to be God, trying to control her life, holding him in contempt for failing her. And God *forgave* her. Somehow, when she believed that God was good enough to forgive her sin, the dam broke and she was overwhelmed with a sense of his love and compassion for her suffering as well. Finally, she knew that he cares, that he loves her, and that he is good.

THE FATHER'S COVENANT LOVE

Sarah awoke to a great love—not just a vague self-esteem boost from a smiling but distant deity. Far greater than any fragile and temperamental self-love, she found the secure embrace of a loving Father. In the exodus, we can see an outline of this very special covenant love God has for his chosen people.[13]

Certainly, as Creator, God grieved the violation of his most prized creation, people created in his own image and likeness. Yet, as Sarah came to see, we have also sinned and rebelled against him, making ourselves his enemies (no less true for the Israelites, as we will later see). Thus, we have placed a barrier between ourselves and the only one who can truly love us out of our misery. But God, in covenant love, overcomes every obstacle that may stand between us and him, whether an evil oppressor, our own fears and doubts, or our own sin and folly.

"God remembered his covenant with Abraham, with Isaac, and with Jacob" (Ex. 2:24). For God to remember his covenant is in effect for him to say, "These are *my* people, I am their God, and I love them enough to overcome any obstacles to get to them" (cf. Ex. 6:7). He loved Israel as a Father loves his own children, as his "firstborn son," as a "treasured possession" among all people (Ex. 4:22; cf. Ex. 19:5; Ps. 103:13). In Jesus, we see the full picture of God's covenant love toward his children, for Jesus is the son in whom the Father is well pleased (Matt. 3:17). He is the true firstborn son of God drawn up from Egypt (Matt. 2:15; cf. Hos. 11:1). And in him, the Father has adopted us and loves us as his own children (Eph. 1:5; 1 John 3:1).

Tragically, for many of us the Father-child relationship is fraught with fear, shame, dread, disappointment, or absence. For some of us, like Sarah, the word *father* has been darkened by the worst evils. Can you ever hope to know God as your Father if your view of *father* is so broken? If we were left to know God as Father only by comparison to the fathers who have harmed us, we'd surely despair.[14] In fact, even the best earthly fathers are an imperfect reflection of the heavenly Father. Yet we have hope because Jesus has come near to reveal the Father, who has poured his love into our hearts by the Holy Spirit and drawn us near to himself as children.[15] Now, with full assurance of your Father's love, acceptance, and compassion, you can run to him for grace and mercy in your time of need (Heb. 4:16).

Yet will we run to him with such vulnerability? The reason many of us have given up hope on seeking our Father's grace and mercy is that, at an emotional level, we sense that he is the very source of our pain; it just hurts too much to draw closer to the one who could stop evil but hasn't. So we keep a safe distance. We may hold onto orthodox ideas about him, but our hearts disconnect; our affection cools; we just don't trust him. Even here, Jesus knows how you feel. In the garden of Gethsemane he was "sorrowful even to death" (Matt. 26:38). Yet it was in this moment that Jesus addressed the Father in prayer, not with cool formality, but with the familial term of endearment, "Abba, Father" (Mark 14:36).

Abba was a word heard at home on the lips of a child addressing a father, but it was rarely heard on the lips of a worshiper addressing God in prayer.[16] When Jesus called the Father his *Abba*, he revealed the great depths of intimacy with God that could be known by a son.

When was such deep intimacy revealed? Amidst Jesus' anguish, he pressed in even closer to the Father. "The very experiences that threaten to drive you the farthest from God are the exact experiences that bring you into closest possible fellowship with your Savior."[17] As God's adopted children, we have this same amazing privilege as Jesus himself—to call God *Abba*—and it is often in our worst suffering that we most need to (Rom. 8:15; Gal. 4:6).

SARAH GRIEVES WITH HER HEAVENLY FATHER

Sarah finally believed that God is good and that Jesus can identify with her suffering. All by itself, this was like having the light switched on in a dark room where she'd sat alone for so long. Yet this was only the beginning of her healing. So much damage done to her over so many years would take time to heal—time with her heavenly Father. Yet Sarah's only impression of *father* had been left by a man who had treated her like an animal. So when Sarah's pastor invited her to grieve with God the losses and wounds of her childhood, she didn't feel that she deserved to grieve. She didn't feel *human*.

Her human dignity was restored when she realized that, as God's daughter, she is precious. The evils done to her had been done to *his* precious little girl. Knowing that God grieves for her freed her to grieve as well (Ps. 103:13). There were many sleepless nights; her heart hurt too much for sleep. One hour she felt desperately alone and would cry out with Jesus, "My God, my God, why have you forsaken me?" (Matt. 27:46; Ps. 22:1).[18] An hour later she felt so close to him that it was as if he were gently holding her as she rested her head on his chest and cried. Later, she would feel alone again and would continue crying out. She had never felt such deep grief or felt so close to her Father. As she plumbed the depths of her sorrow, she clung to this promise and looked forward to the renewal at the end of all her grief: "God is good; I am his precious daughter; and that is enough."

RECOMMENDED RESOURCES

Holcomb, Justin, and Lindsey Holcomb. *Rid of My Disgrace: Hope and Healing for Victims of Sexual Assault*. Wheaton, IL: Crossway, 2011. The Holcombs offer compassionate, biblical help for victims of assault.

Keller, Timothy. "How Could a Good God Allow Suffering?" In *The Reason for God*. New York: Dutton, 2008, 22–34. Especially helpful for the non-Christian, Keller is both lucid in his philosophical arguments and compassionate in his pastoral applications.

Morgan, Christopher W., and Robert A. Peterson, eds. *Suffering and the Goodness of God*. Wheaton, IL: Crossway, 2008. A helpful biblical theological treatment of suffering by a team of theologians who explore suffering in the Old and New Testaments and in light of God's grand story. Sufferers will find comfort and practical help in John Feinberg's chapter, "A Journey in Suffering," where he shares his own story about how after he published a theological treatise on the problem of evil, none of his intellectual answers changed the way he felt when a personal crisis hit.

Powlison, David. "Broken through Child Abuse." CCEF Annual Conference 2006: Hope for Broken Relationships. http://ccef.org/broken-through-child-abuse.

———. "Enduring Hardship with the Psalmist." WorshipGod08 conference. http://www.sovereigngracestore.com/ProductInfo.aspx?productid= A2345-04-51. Insightful and compassionate guidance for sufferers on how the Psalms can teach us to cry out to God in faith.

———. "Suffering and Psalm 119." In *Speaking the Truth in Love* (Greensboro, NC: New Growth Press, 2005). Powlison explores the psalmist's personal, relational dealing with suffering before God. I have heard him say this is his favorite piece from among all he has written. Well worth a read.

_____. "Why Me? Comfort from Psalm 10." In *Seeing with New Eyes: Counseling and the Human Condition Through the Lens of Scripture*. Phillipsburg, NJ: P&R, 2003. Powlison applies Psalm 10 to the story of a woman in an abusive relationship with her husband; helpful not only to abuse scenarios of all kinds but also helpful as a guide in personal application of Psalms.

SCRIPTURE READING

- Exodus 1–3
- Matthew 26:36–46; Luke 22:39–46
- Romans 8:15–17
- Hebrews 2:10–17; 4:14–16

FOR REFLECTION AND DISCUSSION

1) If you could walk up to a few of the Israelites and ask them where they think God is in the midst of their suffering in Egypt, what responses do you think you'd hear?
2) If you were in the Israelites' situation, what do you think you would say? What would you ask of God? How would you be feeling as you cried out?
3) When we suffer, we are tempted. We are tempted to respond sinfully, and we are tempted to believe lies. Review the following and note any of these lies you've heard or temptations you've faced:
   - God is nowhere to be found. He has abandoned me in my suffering.
   - God doesn't understand.
   - If God were present and watching, he would act now to save me, but he hasn't. So I will take matters into my own hands and bring justice on my terms.
   - My pain and suffering are pointless. There's no reason to talk about them.
   - *Victim* defines me.

54

2

BRICKS WITHOUT STRAW: HOW LONG, OH LORD?

Peter thought he knew what a picture of his life's redemption should look like, but he was wrong. He married his high school sweetheart, who was soon pregnant with their first child, a boy. What Peter had wanted most was to be a father; he held his boy and beamed with delight. But the day before he was to take his son home, the baby's lips turned blue—the sudden onset of a fatal condition. Only three days old, Peter's son died in his arms.

The marriage was rocky after that; neither Peter nor his wife dealt well with their loss. Peter buried the pain and tried to look strong for his wife. Years later, they conceived again and had another son, and then again and had a daughter. Peter had never really faced the loss of his first son, but life had moved on: career, home ownership, and a growing family. On the outside, things were holding together.

Then Peter learned about his wife's adultery. She said she didn't love him anymore and filed for divorce. Losing his wife was bad enough, but this loss also brought to the surface the pain over his lost son. It was all too much too fast. Peter cracked.

Looking to escape a downward spiral of depression, he turned to methamphetamine, a drug which let him live in the illusion that he still had his life together. Before his divorce, Peter had never touched drugs or committed a crime—he had had only one seatbelt violation. After the divorce, he fell hard and fast and lost everything else in his life: his home, his job, and custody of his children. Peter was homeless, penniless, and enslaved to his addiction.

INCREASING PAIN

Which is more painful? To live without hope or to catch a glimpse of hope only to have it disappear? Often, this is our experience on the eve of redemption. Certainly, God is not a fickle redeemer. He is faithful. But if we expect redemption to be mainly about comfort, we may be disappointed when—at least for a season—it brings more pain.

Or you may have come to God with a life that was a mess with sin and were relieved to find that he accepts you in Christ, just as you are. But in time, you probably were confronted with the reality that some of those sins from your former life still had a powerful hold on you. Some new Christians at this point are so discouraged they question whether they were ever saved at all.

Or you may have found that after years of harboring the pain of abuse in secret, it's time to talk about it. It's time to tell the truth to God and to others. You may have to revisit some painful memories or confront someone who has harmed you. The battle to decide to speak out is pain unto itself, intensifying the pain of the original abuse. Maybe you've made your secrets known, and your confidants, rather than comforting and protecting you, have hurt you further by suggesting that you keep quiet or have even blamed you for stirring up trouble by digging up the past.

You may have developed various means of dealing with what's been done to you—self-protection, hypersensitivity, catastrophizing to grab others' attention, never trusting anyone or depending too much on their affirmation, getting even, withholding yourself from others, becoming the aggressor, or self-medicating with any number of substances or pleasures. In short, you may have constructed a comprehensive *manner of life* for surviving apart from God (Eph. 4:22).

In delivering you, God wants to show you that this manner of life, which may be all you've ever known, is actually death. He wants you to walk away. But walking away from the only life you've known can feel like death. This is all very risky. It may feel like it's getting worse before it gets better.

Maybe the breaking of your addiction began with a painful intervention by friends, or being caught by a spouse in an affair or with pornography. Perhaps you busted yourself but had no idea how painful it would be to tell the truth and begin changing. This new pain compounds the pain you already had and brings with it more temptation. The grip of sin does not loosen easily. Chances are that your sin has been some form of refuge for you, some means of comfort. But that comfort was merely bait on a hook, and now you're being reeled in, you're enslaved.[1] In delivering us from sin, God breaks the chains of slavery and beckons us to freedom. But faithful obedience is very costly; he calls us to abandon everything we have clung to in our sin, and pulling out the hook of false comfort can be very painful.

We have been bound in darkness; in redemption, God calls us into his light. This can feel like coming out of a dark cave into a midday sun—our eyes may hurt at first as they adjust to the light. How can we be so sure we know what the picture of redemption should look like, when we've been so blind?

LET MY PEOPLE GO

The glory of Egypt's kings, the pharaohs, was displayed by the towering architecture of Egypt's cities. The sixty-foot walls that encircled these cities, as well as the homes and public buildings that filled them, were made of bricks.[2] One pharaoh's pyramids (a tomb) required some 24.5 million bricks.[3] A skilled brick maker working at top speed could make at most three thousand bricks in a single day, but he rarely met his quota.[4] And standing over him all the while was a taskmaster, threatening: "The rod is in my hand, do not be idle."[5] An Egyptian writing describes the brick maker:

> He is dirtier than vines or pigs from treading under his mud. His clothes are stiff with clay; his leather belt is going to ruin. Entering into the wind, he is miserable. . . . His sides ache, since he must be outside in a treacherous wind. . . . His arms are destroyed with technical work. . . . What he eats is the bread of his fingers, and he washes himself only once a season. He is simply wretched through and through.[6]

Egypt's cities rose to prop up the pharaohs' fame as its slaves sank into despair, day after endless day in the mud, making bricks.

At the burning bush, God declared that he would deliver his people, sending Moses with his message and signs. After much wrestling with God over the assignment, Moses went reluctantly with his brother Aaron to proclaim the message in Egypt and demonstrate God's miraculous signs

(Exodus 3–4). No doubt to Moses' surprise, the people believed and bowed their heads in worship (Ex. 4:29–31).

Put yourself in the Israelites' place and imagine, after all those years of ruthless slavery, hoping against hope that God would deliver you, and finally he announces that deliverance is at hand—all those years of crying out to God, and he has heard and finally responded. He really is the God of Abraham who promised to deliver his people, and he's finally come. It was the eve of the redemption they'd longed for their whole lives.

PETER BELIEVES

After being in and out of jail for six felonies in only two years, most of Peter's family disowned him. Only his sister showed him some mercy at last; she fed him a meal and gave him money to get to the city where he might find help. He arrived alone and found his way to a park bench where he sat, without a clue what to do next. There was a time back in Peter's hometown when he had heard that God saves even the most terrible sinners and rescues people from the worst trouble. He had nowhere else to turn. So there on that park bench, he cried out for Jesus to save him.

Driven by the cold winter wind, Peter moved on to find shelter for the night in a doorway and slept. He awoke to find a line of people standing at the door. It just so happened that he'd slept in the doorway of a Christian mission, and they were lined up for breakfast. He learned that the mission had a program to help people walk away from addictions, so he got in line. Peter entered the mission's program, and his life began to change.

PHARAOH STRIKES BACK

After proclaiming the good news of deliverance to God's people, Moses and Aaron took the message to Pharaoh, saying: "Thus says the LORD, the God of Israel, 'Let my people go, that they may hold a feast to me in the wilderness'" (Ex. 5:1).

Don't miss the gravity of this confrontation. Pharaoh thinks he is the god of Egypt, the master of the Hebrews. He decides when they work and when they rest. He decides when, what, and whether they eat. And here come Moses and Aaron making a demand of him in the name of these slave-people's God. Pharaoh replied, "Who is the LORD, that I should obey his voice and let Israel go? I do not know the LORD, and moreover, I will not let Israel go" (v. 2).

But he did not just refuse to release them; he squeezed them tighter. Outraged at Moses' demand, he wielded his power to inflict them with life-threatening labor.

> The same day Pharaoh commanded the taskmasters of the people and their foremen, "You shall no longer give the people straw to make bricks, as in the past; let them go and gather straw for themselves. But the number of bricks that they made in the past you shall impose on them, you shall by no means reduce it, for they are idle. Therefore they cry, 'Let us go and offer sacrifice to our God.' Let heavier work be laid on the men that they may labor at it and pay no regard to lying words." (Ex. 5:6–9)

Pharaoh fought back, and he struck hard. Hear his intent. It wasn't simply to get more productivity out of the Israelites—they weren't expected to make any more bricks than before—it was to strike fear in their hearts and keep them busy so they would have no time or energy to entertain ideas about deliverance. So Pharaoh increased their toil, forcing them to gather their own straw (necessary for bonding the mud bricks) instead of providing it for them, brainwashing them to believe that the truths Moses told them about their God were lies. His purpose was to own them and flaunt his power as the god of Egypt.

PETER'S BAPTISM

That Christmas, a group from a church in Peter's hometown visited the mission to sing carols. Moved by how God had already begun to change his life, Peter asked the group if he could return with them to his hometown to be baptized in their church. In that church, with a few brothers that came along from the mission, Peter stood to give his testimony. He told of how God had reached out to rescue him from a life of drug addiction and pain. It was a time of great celebration.

Sitting in the congregation was a policeman visiting the church that day who happened to be aware of an outstanding warrant for Peter's arrest. Peter had made the county's most-wanted list for drug trafficking and had unknowingly delivered drugs to an undercover cop some months before he committed his life to Jesus. As Peter told his testimony, he noticed a uniformed officer show up in the back of the room. Then two. Then ten. Peter concluded his testimony and was baptized. He emerged from the water confident of his new life in Christ, and at that moment his hands were cuffed and he was taken out of the church, dripping, and off to prison. Peter looked over his shoulder as the police car drove away to see his brothers from the mission weeping on the church lawn.

A TEST OF FAITH

Faith is about evidence. If our primary evidence that God is at work is based on our circumstances, then our faith is strained when we are blindsided by circumstances that fail to meet our expectations. God's picture of redemption is not always the one we've imagined.

So what do you do when your hopes are dashed, when your faith is challenged by a devastating turn of events? How do you feel? Do you cry out to God for rescue? Do you continue to trust his promise of redemption? Or do you make a deal with God, painting a picture of redemption you can tolerate, saying, "As long as it looks like this, I'll follow you?"[7] Do you wander from God in search of comfort and refuge elsewhere? Perhaps even back to the very things that have enslaved you? Hebrews 11:1 says, "Now faith is the assurance of things hoped for, the conviction of things not seen."

It's all about weighing the evidence. We weigh the evidence of God's character, promises, and track record against the present circumstances we face and our fears of what might happen. To hold our picture of redemption out to God and say "Save me like this" doesn't require nearly as much faith as saying, "I know you're good. Save me like you want to." So we stand at a crossroads, and here is our dilemma: God is unseen while present circumstances stare us in the face and our fears are palpable.

PLEDGING ALLEGIANCE

When Moses and Aaron confronted Pharaoh, what was really happening was a clash of gods. Pharaoh went toe-to-toe with the God of Israel, vying for the allegiance of the people. He held the power to make their experience as slaves unbearable, to inflict life-threatening conditions they would feel in every fiber of their being. Or he could have let up and made their slavery livable again. In a sense, he held God's people hostage in an attempt to win the duel.

We don't see the cosmic war waged in unseen realms, and we are often inattentive to the corresponding war that rages in our own hearts. Yet when we take one step forward from the crossroads of this dilemma, we act in faith that one of these gods will save us. That act of faith is our pledge of allegiance. We either place our faith in the god who threatens to make us miserable but offers temporarily livable slave conditions, or we place our faith in the true God who has promised freedom for life.

Would Peter still believe that God was redeeming him even on his way to prison? Maybe you can relate to Peter's story because your sin has resulted in difficult consequences even on the path of redemption.

Or maybe like Margie, you are being redeemed amidst the allure of addiction. But you wonder, as a Christian, why are destructive habits so hard to break? Margie grew up in an alcoholic home filled with tension and fear. At age eight, while her mother was distracted with managing her alcoholic husband, she left Margie with a babysitter who abused her sexually. Margie kept it a secret; she'd learned to keep secrets in a home where daddy was often "on vacation" (read: rehab after a string of drunk driving arrests).

When Margie was only twelve, she found a hardcore porn video on the kitchen counter. At home alone, she watched for hours. She was curious, confused, aroused, and hooked. When she came of age, she gained access to thousands of videos and dove headlong into a fantasy world.

Margie became depressed, isolated, and constantly preoccupied, the disturbing images imprinted on her mind—some of which recalled what the babysitter had done. But she also couldn't seem to resist the comfort that came with escaping into her fantasies from the war zone that was her life.

In high school, Margie chased a Christian boy who took her to a church youth group. Eventually she came to faith in Jesus. She was saved! But one thing that didn't change was her destructive obsession with porn. As a Christian, she thought chaos at home would subside and the flood of explicit images would go away. But in some ways her pain increased as she struggled to resist her urges. She knew what the Bible says about escaping temptation (1 Cor. 10:13); but the only way of escape she knew to relieve the pain of temptation was to give in to pornography.

THE ISRAELITES CRY OUT

When Pharaoh withheld straw for their bricks, what had already been ruthless labor for the Israelites became unbearable. This stretched their seedling faith to the point of snapping, and they were driven to despair. At first, they had believed. When they saw the signs of Moses and Aaron, a flicker of hope was rekindled. But Pharaoh had snuffed it out. All they could see now were the inevitable beatings meted out on their kinsmen for failure to fill their quota.

Pharaoh's plan was working. They weren't thinking at all about deliverance anymore. They were preoccupied with mere survival. Their foremen cried out to Pharaoh for mercy, and he refused to let up (Ex. 5:15). So they turned and cried out bitterly against Moses and Aaron, blaming them for worsened conditions.

> They met Moses and Aaron, who were waiting for them, as they came out from Pharaoh; and they said to them, "The LORD look on you and judge, because you have made us stink in the sight of Pharaoh and his servants, and have put a sword in their hand to kill us." (Ex. 5:20–21)

Behind their resentment of Moses and Aaron was their ultimate resentment of God for bringing them worse trouble. When faced with the dilemma of either trusting God for their freedom or seeking relief by appeasing Pharaoh, they chose Pharaoh. They hoped merely not to stink in the sight of the Egyptians, so that some of their suffering might be alleviated. Had they forgotten how this ruthless slavery had driven them to cry out for deliverance? What "normal slavery" was it that they hoped to settle back into?

The fact is that there was no peaceful coexistence available to them in Egypt. That was not ultimately because Moses had made matters worse but because Pharaoh's heart was evil and stubborn. He wanted evil for them and glory for himself. Yet in the minds of the Israelites, it was as if *God* had brought evil upon them and *Pharaoh* was the one who could—if appeased—return some good by way of relief. God had become the enemy and Pharaoh the ally.

Even Moses staggered. This was his worst nightmare. At the burning bush he feared that Pharaoh would not respond and that the people would not believe him (Ex. 4:1–17). So Moses cried out to God in his distress:

> "O Lord, why have you done evil to this people? Why did you ever send me? For since I came to Pharaoh to speak in your name, he has done evil to this people, and you have not delivered your people at all." (Ex. 5:22–23)

Commentators debate about whether Moses was turning to God in faith here or beginning to doubt along with the rest. He appears bewildered and shaken in his own faith, to say the least. But he directed his cry to God, calling him 'adonai, or "master," acknowledging that God alone ultimately controls everything that happens.[8] Shaken though he was, Moses directed his plea to the right master, the one and only God who can save his people.

Of course, God was not surprised by any of this. He had foreseen it and had even told Moses at the burning bush that Pharaoh would not let the people go unless compelled by his mighty hand (Ex. 3:19). Pharaoh's hardening heart had not thwarted God's plans in the least. Nor was he thrown off by his people's lack of faith. Despite their disbelief, he would not abandon them.

God answered Moses' cry by reminding the people who he is and what he had promised to do. He didn't propose a new and less painful plan or apologize for how much worse things had become. Rather, he reassured them with the same words he had spoken to them at first. His message had not changed. He is faithful to his word even when his people are faithless (2 Tim. 2:13). He *would* deliver them: "I am the LORD, and I will bring you out . . . I will redeem you. . . . I will take you to be my people, and I will be your God . . . I am the LORD" (Ex. 6:2–8). Moses carried these hopeful words back to the people, but the people, because of their broken spirit and harsh slavery, would not listen to Moses (Ex. 6:9). Their broken hearts resisted hope.

CRY OUT TO GOD IN FAITH

Crying out in faith means brutal honesty with God about your suffering while still trusting him. Moses gives us a hint of this in his prayer, but Jesus' cry from the cross was filled with far greater pain—*and* far more faith: "My

63

God, my God, why have you forsaken me?" (Matt. 27:46). Jesus' expression of anguish was raw, honest, and fitting with his fatal circumstances. Yet, at first glance, it may not sound like a faith-filled cry at all. Let's dig a little deeper. In his cry, Jesus quoted Psalm 22. Yet he wasn't merely quoting it; he was living it.

> My God, my God, why have you forsaken me?
>> Why are you so far from saving me, from the words of my groaning?
> O my God, I cry by day, but you do not answer,
>> and by night, but I find no rest.
> Yet you are holy,
>> enthroned on the praises of Israel.
> In you our fathers trusted;
>> they trusted, and you delivered them.
> To you they cried and were rescued;
>> in you they trusted and were not put to shame. (Ps. 22:1–5)

There are feelings of abandonment and groans, and day after day of restless crying out. But it doesn't stop with brutal honesty; it moves on to proclaim who God is, who the psalmist *needs* God to be in this moment. He is holy and enthroned. He is trustworthy, and those who trust him—even in dire circumstances—are rescued! To live this psalm as Jesus did is to cry out the heart's anguish to God *and* to cling to his promise of rescue.

Jesus cried in desolation as he endured the very cup of God's wrath that he'd prayed in the garden of Gethsemane might pass from him (Luke 22:42). The fact that he found himself in the very worst imaginable circumstance—one that he'd prayed to avoid!—still did not deter his faith. It's scandalous to think that Jesus continued trusting the God who had permitted such suffering despite Jesus' prayers.

In fact, the religious leaders who stood back from the cross were so scandalized by it that they mocked Jesus for his faith: "He trusts in God; let God deliver him now, if he desires him" (Matt. 27:43).[9] They sneered, because like you and me, they measured the trustworthiness of God by present circumstances. The reasoning goes something like this: If God is trustworthy, and Jesus trusts him, then he wouldn't be hanging on the cross so shamefully; so it must be either that God is *not* trustworthy or that Jesus lacks faith. And those tend to be the very conclusions we draw for ourselves.

We, like broken-spirited Israelites, find it nearly impossible to keep trusting God as circumstances worsen. ("This does not fit my picture of redemption!") We are tempted to believe that God has forsaken us and that all hope is lost. Or some naïve Christian tells us that if we merely had more faith—if we just learned whatever lesson we're supposed to be learning—the pain would stop.[10]

But Jesus experienced worse pain than you or I will ever know. We may *fear* the worst—abandonment by God—but he actually *faced* it. And he didn't stop believing.

Did Jesus' cry of faith fix his circumstances? No. He spoke these despairing words in the face of death—and then he died. How could he cling to the hope of rescue when his death was imminent? Jesus knew the rest of the psalms as well, including Psalm 16:10, which says, "For you will not abandon my soul to Sheol, or let your holy one see corruption,"[11] a promise of resurrection. Yes, he would die; but he would also be raised to new life.

Because Jesus faced the worst in faith, you and I will never have to. We can cling to these same promises. We can face seeming (or certain!) death: emotionally, spiritually, and even physically, knowing we will not be put to shame. One way or another, God *will* deliver.

Like Jesus, our hope in God must extend beyond the desire for relief from present suffering to a deeper, ultimate relief. While it is not wrong to ask God to change our circumstances, our hope must remain in him whether he changes them or not. As we cry out to him, he becomes a refuge to us, a hiding place for safety and comfort. On this side of heaven, we will not experience *ultimate* comfort and refuge; there will still be pain and danger. Yet while we continue to hope in his promises for *ultimate* refuge, we can know him as a *true* refuge now. Even if we should die suffering, clinging to this hope as Jesus did, we can be sure of the same resurrection (2 Tim. 2:11–13).

And what if your anguish stems from the slavery of addiction? Here too it may get worse before it gets better. But that doesn't mean God is absent; it means he is at war against the gods that have enslaved you. It means the bonds of slavery have been tied so tightly that they've cut into your skin and can't be removed without some bleeding. Your slave masters are not only outside you, in the temptations of the world; they are also within you, wherever you have allowed those temptations to bond with your own sinful desires.

You must still cry out to God in faith for deliverance. Yet, as you are brutally honest about your anguish, you must be equally honest about your sin. You must know that you are in the midst of a war. Expect death and pain in the process because you have to put sin to death by the Spirit (Rom. 8:13). But also expect new life, for those who die with Christ also rise with him (Rom. 6:8). What this means is that your redemption is as certain as his resurrection.

SCRIPTURE READING

- Exodus 4:29–6:9
- Psalm 22

FOR REFLECTION AND DISCUSSION

1) Put yourself in the place of the Israelites when they first heard that God was about to deliver them (Ex. 4:30). How do you think you might have felt in that moment? What thoughts or questions might have come to your mind?
2) What picture of redemption have you painted for God to follow?
3) What in your life have you become cynical about (pessimistic, deeply distrustful)?
4) Where in your life do you sometimes experience despair (utter loss of hope)?
5) When you feel like giving up, what specific behaviors do you tend toward?
6) God heard his people's cry for help (Ex. 2:23). When Pharaoh retaliated, they cried out to Pharaoh (5:15). In anger and desperation, they cried out against Moses and Aaron (5:21). Then Moses cried out to God (5:22–23). What do your cries sound like, and to whom do you cry out?

3

THE PASSOVER: AT YOUR WORST, GOD GIVES HIS BEST

Christine grew up lonely. Her brothers were much older and had moved out of the house before she was six. Her parents worked full-time and were often not home. About the time Christine connected with peers in school, her family moved away; she had lived in seven states by junior high. Christine struggled with missing her parents and often longed for her mother to come home to be with her. Yet even when her mother was present, she was unpredictable. She battled depression, and when she became overwhelmed she lashed out and said terrible things to Christine and her brothers. Once, Christine's brother Jack jammed a drawer in an antique dresser. Her mother snapped at Christine, "If you do that again . . . "

"But Mom!" said Christine, "it was Jack!"

"I don't care! If you do that again, I'll send you both to the orphanage!" her mother raged.

Even more confusing to Christine, moments after making such threats, her mom might gush: "Sweetie, I love you. You are my reason for living." Over the years, Christine's confusion grew into hatred, suspicion, and contempt for her mother. How could she believe her mother loved her?

When Christine was seven, her father and brothers started exposing her regularly to violent softcore porn videos. She started having nightmares—which turned into fantasies—of being raped. At the age of ten, Christine found her brother's stash of alcohol and marijuana. She discovered that with these drugs she could find some relief from her pain—the loneliness, rejection, and emotional and sexual confusion. By age twelve, she had a daily drug habit.

Also at age twelve, Christine found a new way to deal with her pain: cutting. She spent sleepless nights in her room, crying and cutting her arms and chest. She once carved "no love" into her arm. Sometimes, she would cry outside her parents' bedroom door, hoping they would hear and come to comfort her.

By age fifteen, Christine had lost all hope and slipped into a severe episode of clinical depression, bedridden for nearly six months, on medical leave from school, and receiving regular medical and psychiatric treatment. She would go a week without eating, brushing her teeth, showering, or dressing. In the midst of that depression, Christine left home to immerse herself in a drug lifestyle on the streets. At age sixteen, Christine was homeless.

TENSION MOUNTS AS PHARAOH REFUSES TO LET GO

Christine's despair was not unlike that of the Israelites: broken-spirited and deaf to hope (see Ex. 6:9). Whatever hope had kindled in the Israelites when Moses arrived in Egypt with God's message of deliverance was snuffed out by Pharaoh's retaliation; as a result, they were happier to simply accept oppression (5:21).

Thankfully, God's promise to deliver the people was never contingent on their strength, but on his. God rolled up his sleeves to go to work on Egypt. He reassured Moses of his plans and sent him back to Pharaoh to show the signs of his sovereignty (Ex. 7:1–5). By his mighty hand, God would crush Pharaoh's kingdom; and by the same hand, he would draw his people out (vv. 4–5; cf. 3:19–20; 32:11).

Pharaoh had set himself up as a god over the people; but through the plagues, the true and living God showed that he alone is God, wielding the forces of creation to unmake Pharaoh. Each plague represented God's judgment against one of the false gods of Egypt (Ex. 12:12; Num. 33:4). For example, the Egyptians worshiped the Nile River as a god named Hapi and believed it to be the source of all life in Egypt. God's turning the Nile to blood with the striking of Moses' staff was, in effect, a declaration of his intent to claim the life of Egypt and render it desolate (see Ex. 7:14–25).[1]

The plagues increased in intensity. The first sign of God's sovereignty may have been confined to the banks of the Nile, but in the second, the frogs came up out of the Nile and invaded every bedroom, kitchen, court-yard, and field in the whole land (Ex. 8:3, 6, 13). Why frogs? The Egyptians worshiped the frog as the giver of the breath of life.[2] God mocked Egypt's idols; the very gods they worshiped, he turned into plagues against them.

After the second plague, the message was already inescapable: God, not Pharaoh, was sovereign over his people and Egypt. But Pharaoh's heart only became harder and harder with each plague; he would not let the people go.[3] So plague after plague, it escalated: gnats, flies, death of livestock, boils, hailstorms, locusts, and darkness. Each time Pharaoh had opportunity to release God's people and see an end to the plagues. Yet, despite the immense suffering brought upon Egypt, he foolishly and stub-bornly refused.

Each successive plague built up to the final and most devastating one: God promised to kill every firstborn in Egypt.

> Thus says the LORD: About midnight I will go out in the midst of Egypt, and every firstborn in the land of Egypt shall die, from the firstborn of Pharaoh who sits on his throne, even to the firstborn of the slave girl who is behind the handmill, and all the firstborn of the cattle. There shall be a great cry throughout all the land of Egypt, such as there has never been, nor ever will be again. (Ex. 11:4–6)

This final plague, more than any other, struck at the heart of Pharaoh's idol worship. He saw himself as god, ruler of all other gods in Egypt; and he saw his firstborn son as the next incarnate god to succeed him.[4] It's as if, throughout the first nine plagues, Pharaoh was willing to suffer the losses that came with every other god being crushed because his most pre-cious god had not yet been touched. At the very least (he could reason), *his* Egypt would survive through his son. But God had promised to overcome Pharaoh's resistance by his mighty hand, and this final strike would be the deadliest (Ex. 3:19).

CHRISTINE, THE PRODIGAL

The streets were hard on Christine. But this was how she'd chosen to live, chasing after drugs and the affection of men. At first, she stole to get cash for her drug habit. It wasn't long, though, before she fell victim to a sexual predator who roamed the streets, looking to take advantage of vulnerable, homeless teenagers. After that first rape, Christine felt like damaged goods—"What difference does it make? I'm already spoiled"—so she started selling her body.

Sometimes, though, it wasn't about the money but about the men. If she thought there was a chance of love—however small—she required no fee. Eventually, Christine found her first real boyfriend. Here at last (she thought) was the man who would rescue her from her loneliness. Together on the streets for a year-and-a-half, they lived a lifestyle of crime, drugs, and prostitution. In time, Christine's boyfriend began abusing her physically, verbally, and emotionally, and he thought nothing of putting her in harm's way. But she tolerated it all—because he was also her savior.

Then Christine got pregnant. The streets were no place for a baby, and she was only seventeen, so she decided to abort. She needed a safe place to recover, and her parents were happy to welcome her home. They hoped she would stay, recover from the abortion, and get clean from the drugs. By now, Christine was ready to get clean. She had been in and out of addiction recovery groups before, but her participation had always been half-hearted and apathetic, like she was waiting to hit rock bottom before she would take it seriously. But now, *abortion*. "Surely, *this* is rock bottom," she thought. "Surely, I'll get clean out of this."

Christine had agreed to come home on one condition: that she could bring her boyfriend, her savior. So what might have been a season of safe haven became a season of domestic violence and continued drug use as her boyfriend brought both with him into the house. Like Pharaoh's refusal to relent, Christine's sin had cost her dearly and left her devastated. By her own doing, she, too, had lost her firstborn.

GOD MAKES A DISTINCTION

In some of the plagues, God targeted only the Egyptians, not the Israelites. For example, in the fifth plague only the Egyptian livestock died, while the livestock of Israel lived (Ex. 9:3–4). This was part of God's demonstration of sovereignty to Pharaoh and all Egypt. The plagues were not accidents or random natural disasters; they were selective and intentional judgments against Egypt by the true Creator God of the universe.

In the final plague, the death of Egypt's firstborn, it was different. The death sentence was against every household in Egypt—every household that worshiped the gods of Egypt—including the households of the Israelites. Yet somehow God would still make "a distinction between Egypt and Israel" (Ex. 11:7).

Our natural reaction is to say, "Of course he made a distinction: the Israelites were the good guys and the Egyptians were the bad guys; he loves his people and hates those who oppress them." We tend to identify with the Israelites while we point fingers at other people we consider pharaohs and taskmasters, the real evildoers.[5] But this is where we see that suffering (the focus of the last couple of chapters) is polluted by sin. The sufferer is also a sinner.

The Israelites suffered terrible slavery in Egypt, but they also served its gods. We know this because of the way the Bible looks back on their time in Egypt. Some forty years later, as Joshua prepared to lead the next generation of Israelites into the Promised Land, he urged them to "put away the gods that [their] fathers served beyond the River and in Egypt, and serve the LORD" (Josh 24:14). Much later in Israel's history, the prophet Ezekiel would look back on Israel's days in Egypt and rebuke them for their idol worship. Ezekiel employs some of the most sexually graphic imagery in all of Scripture to make his point: Israel was a whore, passionately indulging her lust for Egypt (Ezek. 20:4–10; 23:19–21).[6]

Nobody in Egypt stood guiltless before God, not even the Israelites.[7] Every household stood to lose its firstborn unless God somehow made a distinction between them. But how could God justly distinguish between the Egyptians and Israelites when every one of them was an idolater? As shocking as it may seem, the Israelites deserved the same fate as their oppressor, Pharaoh. The blood of the firstborn would be shed.

CHRISTINE'S MISERY

Christine was consumed by feelings of worthlessness after so much neglect and abuse. She had been dogged by depression since childhood, and her "savior" boyfriend had now betrayed her and joined in her abuse (under her father's roof, no less!). All of this pain was compounded by the guilt from her sin—drugs, prostitution, theft, manipulation—as well as from her bitterness, self-pity, and wallowing.[8] She was a confused mess of sufferer and sinner, and the pain of it all was simply more than she could absorb.

She tried to boost her self-esteem, to love herself more, to forgive herself. She sometimes blamed others for her misery. But the pressure continued to build. In fact, the self-absorption inherent in these attempts at self-rescue only made things worse. One more word of rejection from her mother or her abusive boyfriend would stretch her to the point of bursting.

Cutting was the only release she knew; so she cut herself deeper and deeper, trying to bleed out all that pain. Yet her sin-stained blood could never atone, could never soothe her guilty conscience, could never satisfy the wrath of a holy God, could never make a pure plea for God's rescue.

PURE BLOOD

Like Christine, the Israelites in Egypt were stained with the guilt of idol worship, the same idols their oppressors worshiped. But God, abounding in love for his people and ready to make good on his promise to deliver them, knew what it would take to break them out of slavery despite their sin. He provided for them a substitute, a spotless Passover lamb, whose blood would be shed in place of their own. He promised that if they would paint the blood of that lamb on their doorposts, when he struck down every firstborn of Egypt he would "pass over" their homes, and all within would be spared the wrath they deserved:

> For I will pass through the land of Egypt that night, and I will strike all the firstborn in the land of Egypt, both man and beast; and on all the gods of Egypt I will execute judgments: I am the LORD. The blood shall be a sign for you, on the houses where you are. And when I see the blood, I will pass over you, and no plague will befall you to destroy you, when I strike the land of Egypt. (Ex. 12:12–13)

The lamb's blood signified the death the Israelites deserved. Yet God in his mercy provided the unstained blood of a perfect lamb to stand in the place of their firstborn.

Imagine, if you will, that fateful midnight when the Lord's messenger of death passed through Egypt from house to house. Imagine him arriving at the first home, looking through its windows and seeing the idols of Egypt strewn about. Clearly an Egyptian home filled with idols and idolaters, he enters and claims the life of that family's firstborn. He moves on to a second home: more idols, and another firstborn soul is claimed. Then he moves on to a third, and looking through its windows he finds the same Egyptian idols. But then he looks up and finds the blood of a lamb on the door. And he passes over.[9]

From Pharaoh's home a great cry was heard that night, a cry that echoed through every Egyptian house. The sons of Egypt were dead. Egypt's power was broken. Pharaoh not only relented at last, but he urged the Israelites to hurry away from Egypt so that no more harm might come to him (Ex. 12:31–33). This was a night God's people would never forget; they would commemorate it every year with the Passover and the Feast of Unleavened Bread, telling their children and grandchildren how the Lord had passed over them and redeemed them out of Egypt (vv. 43–49; 13:3–16).

RANSOM: THE PRICE OF REDEMPTION

God didn't just pluck the Israelites out of Egypt. A price had to be paid for their freedom because they deserved his wrath as much as the Egyptians. It was a costly redemption.[10]

Peter Enns points out that the terrible cost of the Israelites' redemption can be seen in both the death of the Egyptian firstborn and the blood of the perfect Passover lamb.[11]

First, there was the costliness of the firstborn. The Israelites understood that the first of the livestock, the firstborn child, and the first fruits of the soil were special; they belonged to God as a token of gratitude for his generosity (see Ex. 13:2). The firstborn "enjoyed a special status of sanctity and preciousness."[12]

In our culture today, we tend to have very individualistic hopes and dreams: *my* achievements, *my* goals. But as Tim Keller points out, "in ancient times, all the hopes and dreams of a man and his family rested in the firstborn son."[13] This insight helps us appreciate the magnitude of God's love for Israel when he called them his own "firstborn son" (Ex. 4:22); Israel was precious to him—special, chosen, and beloved. It also increases our sense of tragedy over the loss of Israel's infant firstborn sons when an earlier Pharaoh exterminated them by ordering them cast into the Nile. The cost of losing the firstborn was incalculably great.

Second, there was the costliness of the Passover lamb. As shown above, the Israelites were under just as much condemnation as the Egyptians. But, by God's merciful provision, the blood of a perfect and precious lamb (the best they could afford) would spare them and save the lives of their sons.[14] The life of another would be paid as ransom for their own.

When Jesus served his disciples at the Last Supper (a Passover meal) he said, "Take, eat; this is my body. . . . Drink . . . for this is my blood of the covenant, which is poured out for many for the forgiveness of sins" (Matt. 26:26–28; cf. 1 Cor. 11:23–26). He was, in effect, saying, "*I* am your Passover Lamb." This was fulfilled on the cross, when his blood stained the wood and he gave his life to pay ransom for ours. John in his Gospel takes care to point out that none of Jesus' bones were broken (just as none of the Passover lamb's bones were to be broken), "that the Scripture might be fulfilled" (John 19:36; cf. Ex. 12:46; 1 Cor. 5:7). Peter recalls this Exodus imagery when he declares that only Jesus' precious blood could serve as our ransom:

> You were *ransomed* from the futile ways inherited from your forefathers, not with perishable things such as silver or gold, but with the precious blood of Christ, like that of a lamb without blemish or spot. (1 Pet. 1:18–19)

Let's make this personal: the cost of our redemption was terrible. Our forgiveness cost God the Father his only Son, who is of far greater value than the entire world's silver and gold. Far too easily we take such costly forgiveness for granted. We don't see our sin as being so great. We just don't feel its weight as we should.

FORGIVEN AT YOUR VERY WORST—AND BEST

How do we accept the gift of Jesus as our Passover Lamb? The same way the Israelites did: by faith. God promised if they would trust him and paint the blood of the Passover lamb on their doorposts, he would pass over. This faith was no mere feeling or formality; God called them to put their faith to work, to paint the blood on the door, to obey. By grace through obedient faith, they received his provision for their protection: "And the people bowed their heads and worshiped. Then the people of Israel went and did so; as the LORD had commanded Moses and Aaron, so they did" (Ex. 12:27–28; cf. Eph. 2:8–10).[15]

As it was for the Israelites, so it is for us: God passes over our sins when, by faith alone, we receive Jesus Christ as our redemption, "for all have sinned and fall short of the glory of God, and are justified by his grace as a gift, through the redemption that is in Christ Jesus, whom God put forward as a propitiation by his blood, to be *received by faith* (Rom. 3:23–25).[16] Sin makes us God's enemies (Rom. 5:10). Enemies! Not only do we owe a great debt, but we continue to assault God with our sin! And that is true for you not only on your worst day, but also on your best.

Imagine your worst moment of guilt and shame, the memory that, when you let it, haunts you and threatens to hound you to the grave. In light of that sin, we sometimes cannot imagine how God could possibly forgive. Yet it was for *that* moment that Christ died for you. At your worst, God gave you his best. While you were still a sinner—of the worst kind—Christ died for you (Rom. 5:8). The Passover teaches us that no debt of sin is too great to be forgiven because the precious sacrifice of Jesus pays it all.

Now imagine your best day. You're on your winning streak, behaving well, keeping up with your spiritual disciplines, forgiving those who wrong you, helping those in need and leading non-Christians to Jesus. In light of such stellar Christian performance, we sometimes assume forgiveness, telling ourselves, "Of course God forgives me; I'm on *his* team." But the Passover teaches us that we don't—and never could—deserve God's forgiveness. Our debt of sin to him is so great that we couldn't possibly pay God back, not with a thousand years of a perfect performance (as if that were even possible). On your best day, when you can most easily see yourself as God's friend, your sin still makes you his enemy and requires Christ's death so that you might truly become his friend despite yourself. God shows his love for us in that while we were *still* sinners, Christ died for us.

AT CHRISTINE'S WORST

One New Year's Eve, Christine's church-going aunt invited her to a special church service, and she reluctantly agreed to go. She pretended not to be strung out that night, but in truth, she'd made sure to load up on dope before meeting up with her aunt.

At the small church, the pastor asked the congregation if anyone new had come that evening. Christine's aunt stood to announce that she was thankful Christine had joined her. To Christine's surprise, the pastor asked her to stand as well. Then he asked her in front of everyone, "Do you believe that Jesus is your savior?"

Christine replied, "That would be nice, but no. I can't even conceive of it." The pastor challenged her once more, "You know, the mystery of what God has done for you in Jesus *is* inconceivable. Can you accept that you won't be able to wrap your mind around it?"

With those words, in that very moment—right in the midst of her drug high—something changed for Christine. For the first time she saw Jesus in a new light. She left that night still affected by the drugs but carrying a Bible in her hand. At home, she threw herself onto her bed and wept, clutching her Bible. She faced withdrawal from the drugs clinging only to God's Word. God forgave Christine at her worst.

CHRISTINE'S FREEDOM

That was only the beginning for Christine. She still suffered greatly as before. There were still dark nights when she longed to be loved and was lonely; there were still hurtful words that stabbed her heart where so many wounds had been inflicted by abuse and rejection. In the past, she would cut herself for relief during those times. But what about now, when she'd come to know the rescuing and all-forgiving love of God?

Knowing that Jesus had absorbed immense pain, including the pain of *her* sin, she could rely on him to carry her ongoing pain with her. It was not through hollow affirmations of self-love; she now knew the immeasurably rich love of God. And it was not by bleeding out her guilt and shame, for she had entrusted her heart to the Healer. She envisioned God's surgery on her heart, an abscess filled with the infection of sin: he cut clean through, removed the corruption, and remade it—deep red, enlivened, and vibrant—healing her from the inside out. Christine's healing began with forgiveness—real forgiveness, not just the throwaway words of a formulaic prayer.

You may wonder: in her broken state, how could forgiveness bring her such joy and relief? At first, Christine was surprised at this too; she had always expected her relief to come with finding the right guy. So what is forgiveness, and how can it bring such joy?

FORGIVEN BY GOD

The joy of forgiveness comes with receiving a priceless gift from a God who lavishes his love upon his children. As theologian Miroslav Volf says, the heart of forgiveness is "the generous release of a genuine debt."[17] This gift presupposes a desperate need in its ill-deserving recipient.

God would have been unjust and his grace cheapened if he had blown off Christine's grievous sin with, "Ah, that's okay, you did your best. Plus, you were in so much pain from depression, neglect, rejection, and violence. Let's just put this all behind us." No. He named Christine's sin; he reckoned the debt; he condemned her wrongdoing. But then, her Judge became her Savior, and God granted her a gift so generous that only he could give it: he allowed his own Son to suffer the death she deserves. Christine can't do anything to earn God's forgiveness—it is a free gift of God's grace. All she can do is receive the gift.

Receiving God's forgiveness means receiving each part: both its condemnation of sin *and* its release from debt.[18] To receive its just condemnation is to confess the sin it condemns—to agree with God about what we've done wrong—and then to repent, turning from the wrongdoing back to him by faith.[19] For Christine, that meant, among other things: stopping her drug usage, breaking up with her abusive nonbelieving boyfriend, and asking her father's forgiveness for manipulating him for money in the name of keeping her off the streets.[20]

Then—and this is essential—we *believe* God and rejoice.[21] We rejoice that our debt has been canceled (Psalm 32; Col. 2:14), that nothing can separate us from God's love, not even our own sin (Rom. 8:38). We believe that our sin is not only forgiven but removed, taken away, as far as the east is from the west (Ps. 103:12), that he remembers it no more. We rejoice that no one can condemn us any longer because he has set us free (Rom. 8:1, 34).

For Christine, relief and rejoicing came in stages. Initially, it was like a huge weight had lifted, the burden of her sin's guilt was gone. She couldn't help but rejoice. Later, though, after the first wave of relief passed, she came to see that being restored to God meant worshiping him instead of chasing the love she'd longed for from parents and boyfriends. The feelings weren't always automatic. At her loneliest moments, it was *difficult* to remain satisfied in God when she was used to chasing others' affection. But as her faith was tested in this and her delight in God grew, she found him to be a far greater reward.

TROUBLE RECEIVING GOD'S FORGIVENESS

Sometimes, along the path of receiving God's forgiveness, we get stuck. Burdened by the guilt of sin for which we can't seem to accept God's forgiveness, we may even sink into the depths of depression.

Do you believe your sin is so great God cannot forgive it? Do you believe God has forgiven you but that somehow you still owe him? Or that you must work hard to keep his forgiveness? Or that you need to be reminded often of your forgiven sin to keep you from doing it again? It may be the Enemy accusing you of forgiven sins (see Rev. 12:10). But cling to God's promise of forgiveness against all claims to the contrary. Hold fast, even if at times you pray, "I believe, Lord. Help my unbelief" (Mark 9:24). Keep living and acting as if God's promise is true: act on the truth, remind yourself of it (meditating on the cross, the Passover, or such psalms as Psalm 32 or 130), refuse self-pity, and continually approach the throne of grace with confidence in your times of need (Heb. 4:16).

Finally, do you ever say, "I know God has forgiven me, but I just can't forgive myself"? If so, your problem is not about forgiveness; it is about pride. Here are five ways a preoccupation with self-forgiveness can express pride.

First, a preoccupation with self-forgiveness is to consider yourself a greater judge than God, as if you, acting as Supreme Court justice, could overturn God's lower-court ruling on your sin. But if God, your Creator, condemns your sin and then forgives you, sparing you from that condemnation, who are you to judge otherwise? Are you a greater judge than God?

Second, a preoccupation with self-forgiveness exposes a heart that still looks to an idol for justification instead of trusting God. According to

Tim Keller, "When people say, 'I know God forgives me, but I can't forgive myself,' they mean that they have failed an idol, whose approval is more important to them than God's."[22] One woman prized her parents' approval above all else. They had always wanted her to be a world-class violinist, and she built her life around reaching this goal. She was excellent, but she never reached the top of her profession, and she could not forgive herself for the failure.[23] As David Powlison says, "So often when people feel remorse for what they've done wrong, it is a remorse against their idealized self-image, a remorse in their own eyes, and a remorse against what other people think about them," *not* remorse for what they've done in *God's* eyes.[24]

Third, a preoccupation with self-forgiveness is to believe that your sin is a bigger deal to you than it is to God. You think, "Of course God has forgiven me," as if it were a small thing to him. The fact is that God is *always* the most offended by your sin, even when you sin against someone else. No one knows more than God just how big a deal your sin truly is. It cost him his perfect Son.

David confesses, "Against you, *you only*, have I sinned" (Ps. 51:4). What was King David's sin? He neglected his army during wartime, got the wife of one of his soldiers pregnant, and then had the soldier murdered to hide it (2 Sam. 11:1–12:14). He sinned against *everybody*. Yet in this confession, he saw his debt to God as towering so high as to overshadow his debt to everyone else. It is the height of self-centeredness to think your sin somehow offends you (or anyone else, even) more than it offends God.

Fourth, you may feel unforgiven because you haven't honestly confessed your sin to God. In this case, you *feel* unforgiven because—in a sense—you *are* unforgiven. As Volf says:

> Without confession I will remain unforgiven—not because God doesn't forgive, but because a refusal to confess is a rejection of forgiveness. Refusing to confess, I refuse to make forgiveness my own through confession of wrongdoing and joyful gratitude over it not being counted against me.[25]

Instead of owning that sin and confessing before God, you have become preoccupied with trying to forgive yourself.

Fifth, you might enjoy the feeling that all debts against you are canceled except for the debt you hold against yourself. It can give you a sense of control to think you have the last word on your own forgiveness. You may even feel noble for not letting yourself off the hook; it's your respectable show of penance.[26] It is better to be broken and desperate for God's grace and mercy, better to humbly accept his gift by faith and paint the blood of the Lamb on your doorpost, and better to find your joy in the sweet release of every debt canceled.

PASSING ALONG GOD'S GENEROUS GIFT OF FORGIVENESS

Forgiveness is a gift that God means for you to receive and then pass along to others.[27] It may be the most costly gift you ever give; yet, precisely because it is so costly, it is also one of the clearest ways you can show God's love as his image bearer.

Robert Cheong, in his doctoral work on a biblical theology of forgiveness, shows that to forgive is to love despite being sinned against. According to Cheong, forgiveness is an outworking of God's twofold command that we first love him with all our heart, soul, mind, and strength, and then love our neighbors as ourselves (Lev. 19:18; Deut. 6:5; Matt. 22:37–40; Mark 12:30–31; Luke 10:27). He summarizes: "Love is a work of God in the human soul that compels one to give oneself for another, *regardless of the cost*, so that the other might love God more deeply."[28]

The language of *cost* reminds us of the theology of ransom, the cost of our freedom from sin and suffering, the cost God generously paid, when, even while we were still sinners—his enemies—he sent his Son to the cross as our ransom (Rom. 5:8; 1 Pet. 1:18). He has poured out his love for us at great cost to himself; our love for him and for others may also at times be very costly.

Loving your neighbor becomes particularly costly when that neighbor is also an enemy, for one who sins against you *acts* like an enemy, even if he claims to be your friend.[29] Jesus raised the stakes in loving our neighbors when he taught us to love even our enemies—to pray for those who sin against us, to do good to those who hate us, and to bless those who curse us (Luke 6:27). How you treat your enemies is the ultimate test of your love for God and neighbor. Is it possible to love your enemy and not forgive him? Not according to the cross. God's love is expressed not only through Christ's sacrificial and substitutionary death but also through his forgiveness of sin through Christ's blood. Gospel love and forgiveness cannot be separated.[30] Therefore, forgiveness must be understood as an expression of love, especially *enemy love*. So Cheong defines forgiveness as "a work of God's love in the human soul that compels one to give oneself for another, *despite being sinned against* [that's the cost], so that the other might love God more deeply."[31]

With these two definitions of gospel love and forgiveness in view, two significant points stand out: (1) forgiveness can be seen as loving another despite being sinned against and (2) both love and forgiveness have redemptive motivation and purpose.

A helpful way to think about forgiveness is *absorption*. Imagine you're in traffic, and another driver swerves into your lane, cutting you off and forcing you to hit the brakes to keep from crashing into his bumper. What do you do? If you flip him off and slam on your horn (not for safety, mind you, but for payback), you offend everyone else around you. They have to tolerate your road rage on top of the usual stresses of commuting. Furthermore, maybe the guy who cut you off didn't mean anything personal by it—he just needed to move over quickly to make his exit. But you, in your swearing, definitely meant something personal against him. You have refused to absorb the offense and in the process have compounded the sin.

Absorption, says Cheong, "is at the heart of forgiveness, since it involves the ability to deal with the pain in a way that it will not be passed on to anyone else."[32] Or, as Tolstoy put it, to forgive is to "swallow" evil and prevent it from going further.[33] On the cross, Jesus overcame evil with good: he didn't return evil for evil; he didn't pass on the evil by seeking revenge; he absorbed it (Rom. 12:21; 1 Pet. 2:23). The only way we can truly absorb evil—the only way we can forgive—is to "roll it over" to Jesus who deals with it for us in perfect love and justice. To do that is to show love for our enemy because our desire that he should know the love and forgiveness of Jesus is greater than our desire to see him punished.

For Christine, receiving God's gift of forgiveness was so joyful and liberating that she didn't hesitate to pass the gift along to many of the people who'd harmed her, including the abusive ex-boyfriend and many anonymous abusers from the streets whom she'd never see again. Yet when it came to forgiving her parents, the progress of forgiveness slowed. She was still their daughter and, naturally, she still longed to be treated by them with respect, love, and affection. Could she forgive them even if they didn't love her in return? Could she absorb the pain of that rejection and continue moving toward them in love? Knowing she might never be well-loved by them, Christine nonetheless began to cultivate a desire for their well-being, a hope that they might receive God's gift of grace and join her in his family. Yet there also remained a genuine debt to be named. Forgiveness prepared Christine to confront her parents in love.

Despite the remaining tension in these family relationships, by naming the sin Christine reflects God's justice more clearly than if she were to pretend that her parents hadn't wronged her, and she reflects his grace more clearly than if she harbored bitterness about it. She is telling God's story with her life, and doing so she enjoys his peace.

Remember Sarah from chapter 1? Her stepfather treated her worse than an animal for most her childhood. Long after finding her refuge in God, with a safe husband, in another part of the country, she still feels the effects of her stepfather's abuse, sometimes daily. Her stepfather has never acknowledged one bit of harm done against her.

Why should Sarah forgive him? And how? How could she ever forgive him? Even if it were possible, is it fair for God to expect her to give such a costly gift? To even ask such questions seems scandalous. Yet, when compared to the scandal of the cross, Jesus' greatest demonstration of love (for his enemies who put him there, no less), it is not outrageous.

WHY SHOULD WE FORGIVE?

There are many benefits of forgiveness, such as release from anger, bitterness, and resentment.[34] For some, forgiveness is motivated by nothing more than these personal benefits. Dr. Phil, for example, says: "Forgiveness is a choice you make to release yourself from anger, hatred and resentment. [It] is not about [your wrongdoers]. It is about you."[35] This so-called therapeutic forgiveness emphasizes the "benefits for the forgiver as she transforms negative emotions and motivations into positive emotions and motivations."[36] It is not biblical forgiveness at all; biblical forgiveness is a gift given to someone else, not a favor to oneself.

So why should we forgive? First and foremost, we should forgive because God forgives, because we are moved by gratitude and compelled by the love of Christ to love others the way God has loved us (see 2 Cor. 5:14). Second, we should forgive because we were created to reflect God's glory, to declare his greatness, to show how good he is. These gifts, flowing through us, ultimately point to the greater Giver of such gifts. To tell someone, "I forgive you because God has forgiven me," is to tell God's story with our lives. Finally, we should forgive because God tells us to: "As the Lord has forgiven you, so you also must forgive" (Col. 3:13; cf. Matt. 6:14–15; 18:21–35; Mark 11:25; Luke 6:37; 11:4; 17:3–4; Eph. 4:32).

HOW SHOULD WE FORGIVE?

We should forgive "as God in Christ forgave [us]" (Eph. 4:32).[37] Let's look at five implications of this command.

First, *we should forgive genuine debt.* God knows exactly what sins he forgives. There is no turning of a blind eye, no shrugging it off, no naïveté. He knew you were a sinner when he sent his Son to the cross for you. He knew exactly what sin to place on Jesus to pay your debt (see 2 Cor. 5:21). When we forgive, it is fitting that we name the sin and the sinner, and we condemn the sin as wrong.

Second, *we should expect forgiveness to be costly.* The fact that God has given forgiveness freely doesn't mean it was cheap. It cost him his Son, worth more than the whole world. And before it cost Jesus the pain and agony of crucifixion, it cost him a life of humility; he descended from perfect fellowship with the Father and Spirit to the earth, where he would endure every humiliation and pain you've ever known, including mockery, temptation, betrayal, slander, social rejection, physical harm, separation from his Father, and ultimately death (Phil. 2:6–8; Heb. 2:10, 14, 17–18; 4:15; Matt. 27:46).

Sometimes, as in cases like Sarah's, forgiveness is especially costly and painful. Any Christian brothers or sisters who speak with Sarah about forgiveness should be wary of personal presumption. The cost for her to forgive is very great; she would have to absorb much evil, far more than most of us absorb in a lifetime. Yet it is not impossible, because God has poured his love into her heart through the Holy Spirit, uniting her with Christ and his love (see Rom. 5:5). When she forgives, she forgives *in Christ*, whose capacity to absorb evil is greater than the sin of the whole world (see 1 John 2:2).[38]

Third, *we should forgive generously.* This should be obvious from the very nature of forgiveness as a gift; God gives gifts generously. We have seen in the Passover, a foreshadowing of Christ's work on the cross, that God is an exceedingly generous giver of forgiveness. He has spared no expense to reconcile the world to himself (2 Cor. 5:19). You might think, "I'll forgive the person who hurt me, but he doesn't deserve my friendship, so that's where I draw the line."[39] Or you might force the words "I forgive you" out of your mouth but resist actually granting them from the heart. But "to forgive is to give people more than their due";[40] it is a gift from the heart (see Matt. 18:35).

Fourth, *we should forgive even before the wrongdoer repents, and even if the wrongdoer never repents.* "While we were still sinners, Christ died for us" (Rom. 5:8). God did not wait for us to repent before expressing his love toward us. Likewise, we can and should grant forgiveness to others, regardless of their repentance. This will lead some to ask, "But if they never repent, isn't that like letting them get away with it?" Remember: when someone sins against you, he also sins against God. In *your* forgiveness, you turn him over to God, not primarily hoping that he will be punished by God but first with the hope that he will eventually repent and receive God's forgiveness. Every wrong will be made right in the end, one way or another (Rom. 12:19). Ultimately, nobody gets away with anything.

Fifth, *after forgiving, we should allow for appropriate consequences.* Sin causes damage that cannot always be undone and sets things in motion that cannot always be stopped. In God's world, human choices have natural consequences. We reap what we sow (Gal. 6:7–8). When we forgive someone, it is not always wise—if it is even possible—to spare them the consequences of their sin.

A year ago, my home was burglarized. To my surprise, the burglars were caught—a man and a woman—and I attended the woman's sentencing hearing. She'd burglarized several houses in the neighborhood for drug money. In court, I saw her face and her cuffed hands behind her back. In my heart, I forgave her. Yet there were still consequences: prison time and the obligation to make restitution.

In cases of abuse, the consequences of the abuser's sin may include limited or no access to the victim. There are evildoers whose presence is always threatening. In such cases, we should not be naïve but seek protection. Love calls us to forgive even while wisdom warns us to keep our distance.

SARAH FORGIVES

Sarah knew the joy of God's forgiveness. He had spared her, not only from a life of suffering but also from her sin. Her heart welled up with gratitude for his mercy and kindness. She also took great comfort and hope in knowing that God would serve justice on her stepfather's heinous sins against her, that if he does not also repent and receive God's forgiveness, God will pour out his wrath on him in the end.

It took years for Sarah to hope more for her stepfather to find forgiveness than to find destruction. She knows she'll never see him again in this life—she must keep her distance. But there is still hope that she may see him in the next life, a forgiven and changed man.

Where are you stuck? Are you having trouble confessing your sin honestly? Accepting God's pardon? Passing along God's gift of forgiveness to another? These are indeed costly steps to take, but we can take them in obedient faith because God has already absorbed the greatest cost for us in Jesus, our ransom, our Passover Lamb.

RECOMMENDED RESOURCES

Lane, Tim. "Practicing Forgiveness." CCEF Annual Conference 2005: Redeeming Anger in a World Gone Mad. http://ccef.org/practicing-forgiveness.

Volf, Miroslav. *Free of Charge: Giving and Forgiving in a Culture Stripped of Grace.* Grand Rapids, MI: Zondervan, 2005.

SCRIPTURE READING

- Exodus 11–13
- Matthew 18:21–35
- Romans 5:6–11
- 2 Corinthians 5:17–21

FOR REFLECTION AND DISCUSSION

1) What makes it hard for you to receive God's forgiveness?
2) Do you have bitterness and unforgiveness against someone?
    - What debt do you feel that person owes you?
    - What would it look like for you to forgive that debt?
3) What have you not confessed for fear you've "gone too far" in your sin? Have you believed the lie that God won't forgive you for it?

4) What sin in your life do you tolerate, excuse, or minimize? One way to know is to consider the times you find yourself using the following phrases:
   - Yeah, I have sin, but nobody's perfect (dismissing sin).
   - Sure, it's sin, but at least I didn't . . . (minimizing by comparison).

5) Where in your life do you find yourself "working off your debt" to God? Consider some of these and add your own:
   - Church-going
   - Bible study
   - Mere confession of sin, without true repentance
   - Punishing yourself with harsh words or actions

4

CROSSING THE RED SEA: INTO A NEW LIFE FREE FROM SHAME

Ben sat alone in his car outside a house for thirty minutes, terrified. Inside, a men's small group from his church was gathering; Ben was sure he did not belong there. "Am I even a man? They'll see right through me," he feared. Finally, he prayed for strength, took a deep breath and, imagining reaching for the hand of Jesus to lead him, he stepped out of the car.

Desperation drove Ben's feet through that front door. He'd spent years living in the bondage of a homosexual lifestyle. One day he was struggling to break free, another struggling to prove his innocence. He was left broken, bewildered, and weary. But a new day had dawned—these steps forward were the most recent in his exodus, but not the first.

He had recently turned to God in genuine repentance, turning away from every comfort and security that had ever made him feel at home in this world. The gay lifestyle was everything: where you shop, the clothes you wear, how you cut your hair, your support network—socially, emotionally, and spiritually. And for Ben, it also included his life with a long-term partner. Ben had walked away from everything, sure to follow God into a wilderness of uncertainty. He was caught in a flood of opposing emotions. He felt relieved and revived but daunted all at the same time. The burden of guilt had been lifted, and he was hopeful for the first time in his life. But while he was encouraged, he knew his life needed a complete overhaul.

Ben's pastor urged him to join a group. It wasn't a support group for overcoming homosexuality; just a regular group of guys doing community and discipleship. But Ben snapped back, "There is no way I'm going there. I will not be the 'big fag' in the room among those men." In the past, attending specialized support groups had backfired—once, a *group leader* had hit on Ben. He was vulnerable and feared being cornered again. He felt spoiled and feared being cast out. He longed to be accepted yet dreaded being seen.

Broken and wounded, Ben was overwhelmed by waves of shame; even as he strained against the tide, he feared being swept away. The shame from his own sin weighed heaviest on him: He'd been a youth pastor in the past and a married man had come to him for counsel about his own same-sex attraction. They ended up having sex.

And then there was the shame he carried from others' sins against him. In grade school a janitor repeatedly coerced Ben and his best friend into a room to watch them act out sexually. This went on for years. Even home wasn't safe. His brother abused him sexually and then would lie awake at night on the floor beside Ben's bed and chant over and over, "You're gay, you're gay."

We saw in the last chapter how Jesus deals with the guilt of our sin, pictured in the Passover. Yet too often the message of the gospel ends here. We fail to grasp the magnitude of the gospel and its power to bring healing to every aspect of our lives. One reason for this is that our view of sin and its effects is too small. So it's not uncommon to hear, "I know God has forgiven me, but I still feel ashamed." Or, "When I remember what shameful things were done to me, I just can't get over it; I want to hide."

How can someone like Ben deal with wounds inflicted by others and also experience freedom from shame when the damage was already done? Put another way, how does the gospel, foreshadowed in Exodus, address all the damage done to us by sin—both our own sin and the sin of others against us? And what about the shame we may feel as a result?

Dan Allender and Tremper Longman define shame as "the traumatic exposure of nakedness."[1] A common way to distinguish guilt from shame is to say that guilt is about what you've *done* and shame is about who you *are*.[2] If you have a less-than-biblical view of sin and its effects on you, it may be tempting to conclude that the shame can be remedied by merely affirming yourself. It goes something like this: you are sorry for what you've *done*, but you don't feel bad about who you *are*. But according to the Bible, real guilt results in real shame. And, yes, it's not just a matter of what you do; it has to do with who you *are*—who you are in relation to God.

We can see this from the first moment sin entered the world with Adam and Eve. The moment they became guilty of sin, they also felt shame. They felt their nakedness, and they hid. The resulting distance from God is a picture of shame, being separated from the presence of a holy God.

But this experience of separation can also come when we are damaged by the sin of another. Second Samuel 13:1–22 tells the story of David's daughter Tamar who was raped by her half-brother Amnon. She pleaded with Amnon: "No, my brother, do not violate me. . . . Where could I carry my shame?" (vv. 12–13). Here, it was Amnon's sin, not Tamar's, that resulted in shame for them both: Amnon became an outcast, and Tamar was to bear the disgrace, living unmarried as a "desolate woman" the rest of her life (v. 20).

Shame can result from sin's effects even when they aren't personal. The cleanliness laws of Leviticus, for example, represent how sin contaminates everything it touches. So for instance, the leper was sent outside the Israelite's wilderness camp. Inside the camp one enjoyed belonging, culture, and most importantly, the presence of God at the tabernacle. Outside the camp was death: the waste from animal sacrifices, the scavenger animals that fed on it, and lepers. The leper was required to appear disheveled and shout "Unclean! Unclean!" if anyone walked by. There was no hiding even in exile (Lev. 13:45). Leprosy and exile were occasionally God's judgment on a person's sin, such as Miriam's (Num. 12:10–15), but most of the time, people just woke up as a contagious leper.

While my problem with sin and shame certainly includes sinful behaviors, it also includes sin's effects: the damage done by others (as for Tamar), and the filth of a sin-contaminated world (as for the leper). The world is simply not the way it's supposed to be.[3] Old Testament writers used the word *shalom* to describe the world of universal peace, safety, justice, order, and wholeness that God intended (see Isa. 32:14–20).[4] But sin wrecks the order and goodness of God's world. Sin vandalizes *shalom*.[5]

Sin's effects are truly and utterly devastating. But know this: God's plan of redemption is much, much greater. The end of the story is already written, and it's *really* good news: God will wipe away every last trace of sin's vandalism and re-create *shalom*. Revelation 21 gives us a glimpse of that new creation where there is no more pain, tears, or death. No one in that new heaven and earth is broken or ashamed; no one will want to hide; no one will feel contaminated:

> Then I saw a *new heaven and a new earth*, for the first heaven and the first earth had passed away, and *the sea was no more*. And I saw the holy city, new Jerusalem, coming down out of heaven from God, prepared as a bride adorned for her husband. And I heard a loud voice from the throne saying, "Behold, the dwelling place of God is with man. He will dwell with them, and they will be his people, and God himself will be with them as their God. He will *wipe away every tear from their eyes*, and *death shall be no more*, neither shall there be mourning, nor crying, nor pain anymore, for the *former things have passed away*." And he who was seated on the throne said, "Behold, *I am making all things new*." (Rev. 21:1–5)

When we look more closely at this passage, we find an arrangement of parallel phrases which sheds even more light on the author's vision of the new heaven and new earth.[6] Beginning with the paired phrases at the beginning and end of the passage (and working toward the center), we find "I am making all things new" (v. 5) and "a new heaven and new earth" (v. 1a). The link between them is pretty clear, right? Things are being made new. Moving inward, the next pair is "the former things have passed away" (v. 4) and "the first heaven and the first earth had passed away" (v. 1). Again, the connection between these phrases is straightforward. But the next pair is unexpected: the wiping away of all tears and the end of sorrow, pain, and death (v. 4) are paired with "and the sea was no more" (v. 1).

What does wiping out the sea have to do with wiping away tears? Some images in the Bible play a special role in telling God's story: the sea is one of those images. Commentators will tell you that the sea is an ancient symbol for chaos, which stands opposed to the good order of God's creation.[7] Before creation, there was chaos in the waters of the deep (Gen. 1:2). God ordered the chaos by creating through his powerful Word (Genesis 1; John 1:1–3). From this, we learn that life under God's Word becomes good and orderly; but sin always drives God's created order back toward chaos.

In Noah's day, chaotic floodwaters consumed the earth, a judgment against a world already consumed by chaotic sin (Gen. 6:5–7). Taming the waters of chaos once again, as in creation, God made dry ground appear (Gen. 1:9; 8:5–7).[8]

See the pattern? The chaos of the sea is like sin's vandalism of *shalom*: both threaten to unmake God's creation. Yet God is greater, for wherever we find chaos and sin unmaking God's creation, we find a God who ultimately triumphs over them by making a new creation.

Knowing what role chaos plays in God's story gives us a clue as to the significance of the Red Sea. As we come to these waters of chaos, we find the same pattern: God rules over the chaos and re-creates. It is the wiping away of something old and the dawning of something new.

CROSSING THE RED SEA

From their first steps away from Egypt to every key turn in the path along the way, God intimately guided the Israelites like a shepherd with his flock (Ps. 78:52), not only by speaking to their leader Moses (Ex. 3:17) but also by leading them miraculously by pillars of cloud and fire that never departed from them (Ex. 13:21–22).[9] If there had ever been any question of God's presence as they cried out in Egypt, there was no longer; they had a constant visible reminder. Present though he was, the path he chose for them was nonetheless fraught with peril. God led them straight to the impassible Red Sea and told them to camp there, facing it.

Back in Egypt, Pharaoh was changing his mind, regretting that he'd let the Israelites go.[10] He mounted his chariot and pursued them with the rest of his army in tow. As he neared, the people looked up in dread. As they had done when Pharaoh took away the straw for their bricks (Ex. 5:7), the Israelites panicked: "Is not this what we said to you in Egypt, 'Leave us alone that we may serve the Egyptians'? For it would have been better for us to serve the Egyptians than to die in the wilderness" (Ex. 14:12). They were hemmed in by evil on all sides. Behind them, a known enemy, filled with more wrath than ever, was advancing. Ahead of them was an impassible sea. They felt trapped. But Moses patiently and confidently spoke to them: don't be afraid; the Lord will save you; he will fight for you; and after this battle, you will never see your enemy again; you are safe here and need only to be silent and wait for God (see Ps. 78:53).

Ben needed to hear the same reassuring words Moses had given to the

Israelites. Two months after he joined that men's group—which accepted him warmly—it was his turn to answer the question, What do you want God to do in your heart this year? As every other man in the group answered, he wrestled inside: would he give an honest answer or would he say something easy? He knew he couldn't answer honestly without divulging some of his shameful secrets. This would test their acceptance of him, and it would test his trust in God. He waited and wrestled until everyone else had spoken; he went last.

Ben read from two psalms. The first one expressed his cry for forgiveness (Ps. 39:7–13); he knew he'd been forgiven. At last, he felt free from the guilt of his sin. Then, as he broke down in tears, Ben shared his second psalm. It was a cry of hope—teetering on despair—to be drawn up from the pit of destruction, restored, and made whole again (Ps. 40:1–9), not only to be forgiven of guilt, but also to be remade a new man. He still struggled to feel like he belonged among men. He was still tempted with same-sex attraction and filled with shame, from the abuse in his childhood to his life of homosexuality.

Ben faced his own Red Sea with Egypt at his back. He felt the enemy nipping at his heels, threatening to drag him back to that old lifestyle, back into his bondage. But he knew God had delivered him, and he wasn't going back. Yet what he held in his heart, the hope of being made new, seemed as impossible as crossing that sea. For the first time in his life, and with reckless abandon, Ben put all his hope in God. With bitter weeping, Ben wailed—from his gut—the cry that echoes throughout the Psalms: "God, please don't let me be ashamed for trusting you" (Pss. 22:5; 25:2–3, 20; 31:17; 34:5; 37:19; 69:6; 71:1; 74:21; 119:6, 31, 46, 80, 116).

The Israelites did not hope in vain. God, by his angel and a pillar of cloud, moved behind the camp and hid them from their enemy. He was their refuge (Ps. 78:53). Then, at the Lord's command, Moses raised his staff and God drove back the sea, parting the waters and making a safe path for the people to walk through the sea on dry ground. As the new day dawned and the Israelites emerged safely on the far side of the sea, the Lord's gaze pierced through the pillars of cloud and fire and fell dreadfully upon the Egyptians, striking terror in their hearts. He bound up their chariot wheels, which threw the fleet into chaos and panic. And just as they turned back, realizing the Lord was fighting for Israel and they had no hope, God turned the waters back upon them and drowned every one. The Israelites looked on as their enemies washed up dead on the seashore. Surely then they remembered Moses' words: "The LORD will fight for you, and you have only to be silent" (Ex. 14:14).

The old life of slavery was gone and a new life with God had begun. God's people had gone through a sort of death and resurrection.[11] So the apostle Paul looks back on the Red Sea and sees an outline for Christian baptism: death to an old life and resurrection to a new one in Christ (1 Cor. 10:2; cf. Rom. 6:3–4).[12] In fact, one commentator notes that many Christians celebrate the resurrection of Jesus at Easter with the Song of the Sea in Exodus 15:1–18.[13] God had wielded the forces of creation—wind, waves, water, earth—to unmake the enemy and remake his people.[14]

A NEW CREATION BEGUN

In his sermon *Before the Beginning*, Tim Keller shows how the plagues on Egypt represent the unraveling of creation in Genesis 1 and 2.[15] The second to last plague was darkness over the land, recalling the darkness over the face of the deep before God spoke "light" (Ex. 10:21–23; Gen. 1:2). What is surprising about the plagues, Keller says, is that they are so natural: frogs, gnats, boils. What God means for us to see in this is that the natural result of sin is the breaking down of the very fabric of creation.

Keller goes on to show how Jesus bore the full force of the plagues on the cross: in Egypt, the Nile turned to blood; at the cross, Jesus' own blood and water flowed. In Egypt, the firstborn died; at the cross, God's firstborn died. In Egypt, there was darkness; at the cross, the darkness fell upon Jesus (Matt. 27:45). Keller concludes:

> Jesus Christ is the Creator who came here not to smite us, but to be un-created so we could be re-created . . . the maker who came to be un-made so we could be re-made . . . the judge who came not to bring judgment, but to bear judgment, to take what we deserve so the Holy Spirit could come into our lives, once our sins are forgiven, and begin to remake us.[16]

On the cross, Jesus made an end to everything old and began something new. "Therefore, if anyone is in Christ, he is a new creation. The old has passed away; behold the new has come" (2 Cor. 5:17). When we are made alive in Christ, the change is radical. We stand, as it were, on the far side of the Red Sea, with the old life completely wiped away and a new life begun. This new life is none other than *new creation*, the restoration of *shalom* we saw in Revelation 21.

In that new heaven and new earth, Ben will no longer be tempted with same-sex attraction. The wound left by his absent father will be healed in the eternal presence of his heavenly Father. He will no longer fear rejection; he will know who he is and whose he is. He will not be haunted by the lie "you're gay," because the Accuser will be silenced forever (Rev. 12:10). He will be totally healed—a new man.

The Israelites on the far side of the Red Sea had every reason to celebrate: they were free, never to return to Egypt. They *saw* their enemies wash up dead on the seashore. And this God who had delivered on his promise to rescue them had also promised to lead them to a new land (Ex. 6:8). Yet, despite the finality and hope in that victory, they still bore scars on their backs and fears in their hearts. Like Ben, they desperately needed healing. They were creatures in need of re-creation. And almost immediately, in the first wilderness scene after the Red Sea, God promised his people that if they would follow him in this new life he'd made possible for them, he would heal them, sparing them from the diseases that had afflicted Egypt, saying "I am the LORD, your healer" (Ex. 15:26).

While the exodus was a mere foreshadow of what would come—the Israelites did not always walk with God and they did fall under plagues when they disobeyed, eventually even returning to captivity (2 Kings 17:6–19; 25:11, 21)—in Christ, everything here foreshadowed has been unveiled as a glorious reality.

When Jesus came healing the sick and proclaiming that the kingdom of God was at hand, he was effectively ushering in the new creation of Revelation 21.[17] As if through a crack in a dungeon wall, light from the new heaven and new earth poured in through Jesus. The Gospels are filled with stories of his healing the sick, demonstrating his authority as Creator and God to overcome sin and its effects and to restore *shalom*—both spiritually and physically (e.g., Mark 1:40–45; 5:1–43; John 11:1–44).[18] The end of the old and the beginning of the new had begun. The Old Testament was filled with promises that the Messiah would come with such divine authority to heal and restore *shalom*.[19]

In one healing scene in particular, Jesus demonstrated not only his authority to heal but also to forgive sins. This is instructive for us, to connect what we've learned in the last chapter about God's forgiveness at the Passover with what we see in this chapter about his healing. A crowd had gathered and was pressing in close to Jesus while he preached. A paralytic's friends tried to bring him to Jesus for healing, but the dense crowd made it impossible to get through. So they removed the roof over Jesus' head and lowered the man down before Jesus. At this point, we might expect Jesus to touch the man and heal him, right? But what Jesus does instead comes as a surprise to us and to everyone there. He said, "Son, your sins are forgiven" (Mark 2:1–5).

If you're like me, you may be tempted at this point to think Jesus withheld his healing power by "merely" forgiving him. But this is probably because we underestimate the power of that forgiveness. Those who were present saw the situation more clearly. They knew that a claim to forgive sin was a claim to be God. (In fact, it was because of this that they accused Jesus of blasphemy; Mark 2:7) You see, far from withholding his power from the paralytic, Jesus demonstrated his greatest power *first*. The point is that if Jesus has the power to forgive, then he is God; and if he is God, then he also heals. Jesus explained all this and then said to the paralytic, "Rise, pick up your bed, and go home." And the man was also healed (Mark 2:11–12). Imagine how that man's life was changed. That day, he *walked* away from an old life of guilt and paralysis into a new life made possible by Jesus.

In another story, a woman who'd heard about Jesus' healings had been bleeding for twelve years. She'd gone to every doctor she could find and spent all the money she had looking for a cure. Not only did she fail to find the cure, but she grew worse. She was desperate, penniless, and weak—and she knew it. Finally, she thought, "If only I could press through the crowd and touch his clothing." So that's what she did, and she was healed (Mark 5:25–34).

A leper dropped to his knees before Jesus and implored him, "If you will, you can make me clean" (Mark 1:40–42). Recall from Leviticus the biblical significance of the leper's plight. Such a man was afflicted with a disease that made him unclean and forced him to live on the fringe of society in a paradoxical blend of hidden isolation and vulnerable exposure. The fact of his contagion would have been well known, so he would have been avoided and he would have avoided others because anyone who touched him would also have become unclean. The leper lived a life of shame. But Jesus loved this leper. He *touched* him, healed him, and made him clean. This one touch from Jesus ended the leper's old life of shame and isolation and began a new one. The leper would no longer live "outside the camp," outside the city, outside of society, and at a distance from God's presence represented by the temple. The leper's life of shame had ended; Jesus had healed him and made him belong once again.

There are two things for us to learn from those who were healed by Jesus: (1) they knew their desperate need, and (2) they put all their hope in Jesus.

They knew their desperate need. Too often, we masquerade as though we have everything under control. We'd like to think we aren't broken and in need of healing. To let on that we still ache from past wounds might seem weak or embarrassing. To admit that we still feel vulnerable after a long season of habitual sin might seem shameful. Sometimes, we are simply unwilling to soil the reputation we've built by admitting we're broken. So we pretend to be strong. We try to cover our wounds and Achilles' heels. The Israelites, facing the impassible Red Sea, rather than crying out their desperate need to God, cried out against Moses for leading them into such need, momentarily abandoning all hopes for healing and wishing they'd been left in Egypt to die (Ex. 14:10–12).

But Jesus said it's the poor in spirit who inherit the kingdom of heaven, those who know their desperate need and don't try to hide it (Matt. 5:3). The paralytic and his friends, the woman with the issue of blood, and the leper are each a physical portrait of what "poor in spirit" looks like. They are reminders that you don't have to feign composure in Jesus' presence, because he heals the broken. Like Ben's cry, their cries were simple: "I'm broken. Please heal me!"

They put all their hope in Jesus. They also knew they had one shot at healing and that it could only come from Jesus. The leper was doomed to a life of shame apart from some miraculous healing that he knew only Jesus could provide. The woman with the issue of blood had already spent everything she had seeking a cure. She had proven there was no other hope for her and had surely begun to despair. Like the paralytic, they believed, put all their hope in Jesus, threw caution to the wind, and pressed in as close as they could.

The same urgency was in Ben's voice as he cried, "Don't let me be ashamed for trusting you." It was the first time in his life that he had entrusted himself to God without reservation. He clung to no other hope. And he knew he was taking a big risk. This is how it is with hope: if the object of your hope fails you, you will feel shame.

This theme turns up time and again throughout the Psalms: "O my God, in you I trust; let me not be put to shame" (Ps. 25:2). So Allender and Longman conclude:

> Shame is rooted in our inherent preference to trust false gods rather than depend on God for each and every moment of our existence. . . . Shame is not primarily an experience of feeling bad or deficient as it is the exposure of foolish trust in a god who is not God. . . . Shame exposes what we worship.[20]

If you put your hope in your mere will power to stop your habitual sinning, or in your track record (e.g., days of sobriety) to keep distance between you and your shameful past, you'll be put to shame the moment you stumble and those false hopes fail you. If your hope lies in your ability to mask your wounds by acting strong, in the constant affirmation of another to make you feel worthy, or in your vigilance to avoid being harmed again, you'll inevitably be put to shame because you are not strong enough to save yourself; no one can ultimately secure your identity against your own deep doubts, and you'll never have a risk-free life as long as you live in a fallen world.

Your only true hope for lasting healing that shields you from shame is Jesus. "But," you may ask, "how can I be healed by him when he isn't here for me to reach out and touch the hem of his garment?" The answer is that he has *already* begun the healing. When you are in Christ, the old has *already* passed away, and the new has *already* begun (2 Cor. 5:17). You are *now* a new creation in Christ. He has already touched you with his forgiveness and his healing power. Like the leper, he has already taken away your shame, adopting you into his family where you now belong with no more shame. What's more, he has sent his Spirit to live in you to complete the restoration. The same Spirit that raised Jesus from the dead has been sent to give you new life and reverse sin's effects, remaking you from the inside out (Rom. 8:11; 1 Cor. 15:45; 2 Cor. 3:18; 5:17; Col. 3:9–10). The Holy Spirit will not stop until you are perfected. In the end, you will be fully redeemed, fully healed, body and soul—not merely returned to "normal" (whatever that is), but made glorious, fit for a new heaven and a new earth in God's kingdom (Rom. 8:23; Phil. 1:6; 1 John 3:2–3.).

Now, while the healing has begun, it usually doesn't happen all at once. There are days when it seems to be going so slowly, and you don't feel like a new creation; you are painfully aware of the lingering corruption in your soul, or haunted by memories of some past sin, or feel a pang from some old wound. Shame sneaks up and whispers, "This is the real you: guilty, corrupt, violated, damaged."[21] The Enemy seizes the moment of weakness to condemn and accuse you, pointing to the not-yet completeness of your healing as evidence that you aren't who you thought you were. He would have you believe that those past sins and wounds are what define you, instead of the new creation. He may even plant the seed of doubt in your mind about God himself: "How can you believe God heals? *You* aren't healed. Look at you!"

The experience may be somewhat like that of the Israelites when they approached the Red Sea, terrified of the threat ahead and harassed by the enemy gaining ground from behind. For a moment, they seemed to have forgotten who God was, the Redeemer who had freed them from slavery. At the same time, they forgot who they were to him. When he brought them out of Egypt, he called them "my firstborn son" (Ex. 4:22), showing how dear they were to his heart. As a Father, he had promised to defend and protect his children as he brought them home. Would he now abandon them?

What we find at the Red Sea is that God not only redeems his people from slavery and gives them a privileged status as his children but also acts to defend them against any evidence that they are not truly his children or that he is not truly their God.

VINDICATION: THE FATHER DEFENDS HIS CHILDREN

Vindication is being proven right in the face of evidence against you. In modern-day America this happens in a court of law when one is falsely charged but in the trial is proven innocent. In the Ancient Near East the most difficult judicial decisions were given to the gods to decide (false gods, of course—shudder to think of their decisions!). It was called *trial by ordeal*, and it usually involved either fire or water, and life or death. In one case, the accused was thrown into the river, which, in the religion of the day, was a river god who would judge the man's guilt or innocence. If the man survived the river, it showed he was innocent, and his false accuser was therefore put to death. But if the river drowned him, his accuser was given everything he owned.[22] It was winner take all; the last man standing was vindicated.

The Red Sea crossing, in which God's people emerged safely as the Egyptians drowned, was one such trial. In the words of theologian Meredith G. Kline, "God vindicated the cause of those who called upon his name and condemned their adversaries."[23] Despite the myths of ancient Near Eastern religions, at the Red Sea God showed that the fate of his people rested in his sovereign hands alone, and neither the sea nor Pharaoh—and no other enemy—could do a thing about it.[24] So God used the same trial elements, the waters of chaos, to both save his people and destroy the enemy.

At the cross, Jesus underwent the trial by ordeal of which the Red Sea crossing was a mere shadow. There at the cross, the Enemy did his worst to shame Jesus. The Romans designed crucifixion to be the most shameful death sentence imaginable, not only taking the life of its victim but also subjecting him to the scorn of every passerby. But Jesus overcame the Enemy by that same cross and threw its shame back in his face, making a public spectacle of him, just like God turned the waters of the Red Sea against Pharaoh's army and watched them drown (Col. 2:13–15 NIV, NKJV). In his resurrection, as though emerging victoriously from the Sea, Jesus was vindicated as the righteous Son of God whom death could not hold.

When Jesus rose from death, he was the first to be fully vindicated as the Son of God, but not the last. Romans 8:29 says he is the firstborn among many brothers. That means that in Christ, you and I are adopted children of God. That is our new identity—children of God, loved by the Father, healed by the Healer. At the cross, Jesus secured our new identity, and in his resurrection he defended it against all shameful accusations once and for all. So the cross has become a symbol for God's children—not the symbol of shame the Enemy intended, but a symbol of hope and healing because, as Hebrews 12:2 says, Jesus *despised* the shame of the cross.

To *despise* means more than we often mean by it in everyday language. We usually mean something like "extreme dislike," which is a legitimate meaning; but the context of this verse suggests that more is happening here.[25] *Despise* can also mean: "to regard as unworthy of one's interest or concern."[26] A biblical Greek dictionary captures the nuance of the original language: "to consider something not important enough to be an object of concern when evaluated against something else."[27] David deSilva explains that Jesus despised the shame of the cross by overlooking the shameful claims the world made against him by it and instead looked only to the Father for his identity. Who he was in the Father's eyes was all that mattered—not who the world said he was and not what his shameful circumstances might have implied.[28]

Imagine you were to fix a theatre spotlight on a stage actor and then point a toy flashlight at a blemish on the actor's face. What happens? Nothing. Why? Because the spotlight is so bright that the flashlight has no effect.[29] It's not that the flashlight isn't shining; it's just that it doesn't make any difference. The glory of God in the face of Jesus—his grace, mercy, forgiveness, cleansing, and healing—simply outshines any of the blemishes that haven't faded yet; but they are fading, and in the end they'll all be gone (2 Cor. 4:6).

The shame question really comes down to this: who are you in the Father's eyes? We come to this question from at least two places: (1) Who are we in light of our past sin? (2) Who are we in light of the damage that's been done to us?

In light of past sin. When Jesus stands before the Father in your place, your guilt is pardoned and your shame taken away: "If we confess our sins, he is faithful and just to forgive us our sins and to *cleanse* us from all unrighteousness" (1 John 1:9). Romans 8:1 declares, "There is therefore now no condemnation for those who are in Christ Jesus." So the shame of your own sin no longer defines you. You are cleansed and no longer condemned.

Ben used to feel overwhelmed by the shame of his past sin. It drove him further away from God; he became more self-absorbed, wallowing in shame as a sort of penance, as if God's forgiveness was insufficient.[30] Then he realized that the sin in the midst of his self-induced shame was believing the lie that somehow Christ's forgiveness wasn't enough. He wasn't seeing himself through his heavenly Father's eyes but through someone else's. When he finally put his full trust in the complete forgiveness and cleansing power of Jesus, the shame lost its grip on him. Does he still feel bad when he remembers his past sin? Sure, but where he once wallowed in shame, he now feels sorrow and grieves for his sin—and this sends him running to God for more mercy and grace (Heb. 4:16).

In light of the damage done. Jesus abounds in compassion for you in your hurt. More than that, he rescues you from your wounds, so they do not define you. It is his glory to make you a new creation, to adopt you as a child of God, and to heal you, and that glory outshines any shame that could possibly come from what's been done to you.

As I counseled one Christian woman, she recalled a memory of shameful childhood abuse. She could hardly tell her husband, it was so terrible. I reminded her that there was no more shame for her in that memory. "In your Father's eyes, you are chosen, precious, and protected." While that memory was new for her, it was not new for God; he has already loved her and redeemed her—all of her—even the parts she's forgotten. And in God's all-redeeming love, he can overcome the pain of one more shameful memory with one more healing touch—just as the cross and the confrontation at the Red Sea were meant by the enemy for evil but were redeemed by God for the good of those he loves (Gen. 50:20; Rom. 8:28).

When you feel broken and vulnerable, do you stand in the confidence that you are a new creation in Christ? Do you see your new identity in Christ through the Father's eyes? Or do you allow the memories, remnant flesh, hostile world, and the Enemy's lies to define you? Do you admit your need for healing and put your hope in Christ alone? Your answer to those questions, more than any past sin or lingering wound, determines your susceptibility to shame.

The old is gone and the new has come. In Christ, you are already new and being renewed. You already stand, as it were, on the far side of the Red Sea. Your enemy has been disarmed and drowned, along with the power of his condemning lies and shameful wounds. The burden of shame is not yours to bear any longer. It belongs with the rest of Egypt, buried in the sea. So cast your burden into the sea and walk free in your new life in Christ.

SCRIPTURE READING

- Exodus 14–15
- 2 Corinthians 5:16–21
- Hebrews 12:1–2

FOR REFLECTION AND DISCUSSION

1) When do you feel shame?

2) What sin do you hide in shame?

3) What abuse, damage, or beliefs do you keep as shameful secrets?

4) How do you act around others when you are ashamed?

5) How does shame affect your relationship with God?

6) When are you most likely to doubt that you are an adopted child of God?

7) When you imagine being completely renewed in the new heavens and new earth, what specific part of your life do you most look forward to being healed?

8) What evidence do you see in your life that the healing has already begun?

5

DEMANDING MANNA: THE SUBTLE SIGNIFICANCE OF EVERYDAY DESIRES

Lisa used to plan every day around food, but you'd never know it. At a glance, she just appeared to be a talented Christian girl. But behind the scenes, she was spinning lies and throwing people off her trail.

It began in high school, when, despite already having an average healthy body, Lisa decided to lose a little weight, hoping to gain the attention of her peers. She started exercising in place of meals. With many school and church activities, she was always on the go, so her meal skipping went unnoticed by others—until she lost some forty pounds in only two months. Her parents and teachers expressed concern, but she blew them off. She was happy with the trade, though, because for the first time in her life, the boys noticed her. She had attracted the attention she'd craved.

But this wasn't the beginning of her craving for attention. As a child, she had longed for the affection of her task-focused mother and seemed to gain it only in small portions after completing long lists of household duties and homework.

While it might be easy to condemn Lisa's vain wish for all the boys to notice her, it stems from the same root desire as that little girl in the kitchen proudly presenting a picture she had drawn, hoping to capture the attention of her preoccupied mother.

Who could not sympathize with the disappointment of such an innocent desire? Surely God created little girls to long for the affection of their mothers.

Lisa's story is a clear example of the subtlety of our troubles: often, the very desires that lead to our ruin start as healthy longings. Pure desires can be polluted; justice can become vengeful; lovely aspirations can be perverted; noble endeavors can become petty; and moderate desires can become inordinate by indulgence (cf. Phil. 4:8). Because of sin's blinding effect, we can look at our own motives and see only what is pure, just, lovely, noble, and moderate, when, in fact, pollution, revenge, perversion, petti-ness, and indulgence may be lurking in our blind spots.

Eventually, Lisa's body began breaking down from starvation. Her parents sent her to a treatment facility, hoping to spare her life. Nutritionists taught her healthy eating. Counselors taught her how to curb her behavior by addressing her irrational fears and depressive moods. It was all fine advice, but she didn't care. She was driven by a single desire, and she saw nothing wrong with it: "All I want is to be loved." So she drove on, from meal skipping to violent swings of binging and purging to fueling her daily food obsession by shoplifting. Before she realized it, she felt trapped in a cycle she couldn't break and was near death. What had begun as a desire to attract the attention of the boys at school had become life-threatening slavery.

INTO THE WILDERNESS

We pick up the Israelites' journey in Exodus 16, two months after their flight from Egypt.[1] On the far side of the Red Sea, the Israelites celebrated their freedom from Egypt and God's epic victory at the sea (Ex. 15:1–18). They were truly grateful for being delivered—weren't they? Yet no sooner had they finished singing a song of victory than they turned from the sea to face their next obstacle, the wilderness.

Imagine looking up with tired eyes to see what they saw: a barren wilderness as far as the eye could see. The rest of their journey—the rest of their lives—would be in that wilderness, under the desert sun. Food and water were scarce, and fears were fierce.

God had delivered them from the hand of Pharaoh, but could he also deliver them from the wilderness? He had promised a land flowing with milk and honey but had brought them to a barren wilderness (Ex. 3:8). How many times had their faith been tested? First, they were promised freedom, only to see their slavery worsen when Pharaoh withheld straw for their brick making. When freedom was finally in view, it was blocked by an impassable sea. Then God parted the waters, only to lead them into a wilderness. How much could a human heart take? Well, they couldn't take it anymore, and broke out in grumbling:

> And the whole congregation of the people of Israel grumbled against Moses and Aaron in the wilderness, and the people of Israel said to them, "Would that we had died by the hand of the LORD in the land of Egypt, when we sat by the meat pots and ate bread to the full, for you have brought us out into this wilderness to kill this whole assembly with hunger." (Ex. 16:2–3)

Despite their faithlessness and ingratitude, God showered them with blessing, promising a miraculous daily supply of bread they would come to call *manna* (vv. 4–18). It wasn't because they deserved it, especially after their grumbling, but because he is a generous Father and cares for the needs of his children—even when they whine.

While their minds were obsessed with food, God had something bigger on his mind—their hearts. Even as he provided graciously, he did so in a way that would test their hearts, "whether they will walk in my law or not" (v. 4).

Now the word *law* here needs some explaining because it can be misleading to a modern reader. In contemporary usage, it typically brings to mind a list of do's and don'ts. But here, it's better to see that God was making their grumbling an occasion to reveal something about the kind of relationship he wants to have with his people: he wants to bless them, and he wants them to respond with trust in his provision, receiving the blessing on his terms rather than on theirs. As commentator Douglas Stuart observes, "It was not just a test to see if they could follow instructions but a test to see if their hearts were inclined to be his covenant people."[2] In this case, to walk in his law would have meant to "trust him every day afresh" to meet their need for food.[3] This would have put him at the forefront of their daily desire for sustenance: *he* would provide their daily bread. Now the test: would they follow him, or would they only chase the bread?

The first test of manna came with God's promise to provide enough bread each day for every man, woman, and child to have all they could eat.

They were to gather a day's supply and save none of it till morning (vv. 16, 19). And sure enough, when they gathered and measured, it was enough (vv. 17–18). The fact that there was enough was no credit to their gathering abilities. As John Sailhamer comments, "[It] was another sign that God was *intimately* involved in providing for each of them."[4] After dinner each night, when all the day's manna was gone, they were to go to bed and sleep, trusting that when they awoke, there would be more waiting for them.

Could they trust that the same God who had kept his promise to deliver them from slavery could also provide food each day? Or would they hoard it to secure themselves against hunger?

They hoarded.

Everything kept until morning bred worms and stank (v. 20). Perhaps some of them, like their parents Adam and Eve, thought, "Did God really say that we couldn't just keep a *little* until morning? What harm could come of it? Just a little extra for good measure . . . " (see Gen. 3:1, 6).

The second test of manna came with God's instructions for how they were to observe the Sabbath, the weekly day of rest devoted to the Lord. The weekend manna gathering rules were a bit different: on the sixth day, they were to gather two days' worth, because there would be none to gather on the seventh (Ex. 16:23, 26, 29). Could they devote a day to the Lord, and trust him for a day's rest? Would they diligently gather two days' worth, trusting that the extra would keep for the Sabbath?

Nope. Instead of resting, they went out to gather more manna on the seventh day (vv. 27–28).

Lisa reached a point in her downward spiral where she was desperate to break free. She cried out to God for deliverance. Her cry, however, came not from any deep conviction over sin but out of fear for her life. By God's grace (though she wouldn't have thought so at the time), she remembered the tactics she'd learned in the treatment centers and finally began using them to control her destructive behavior. This was enough to restore her health. And once she could say that she no longer had an eating disorder, she thought she was healed. Yet still, all she wanted was for people to look at her, think she was beautiful, and love her. As her eating habits improved, she remained lonely and depressed. Lisa's problem of desperately seeking love is not unique, but the issue is subtle, and it can come out in different ways.

Meet Bill. The same pattern emerges in his life, transcending differences in gender and driven by different desires. As a boy, Bill grew up with two overpowering men in his home: his intellectual, outspoken father, who won every argument and left Bill feeling defeated every time, and his twelve-years-older brother, who was bigger, faster, stronger, and funnier. Bill lived in a house with two giants, and he burned with desire to be a powerful man himself. Looking for ways to act like a man before his time, Bill began collecting empty mini alcohol bottles, and, filling them with colored water, he built his own bar in his bedroom. He imagined his stuffed animals were women and acted out "adult" sexual fantasies with them. This was what the world had taught him a real man is. These were the small beginnings of a life Bill would later live out on the road in real bars every night, playing in a band, and seducing real women, still burning with the boyhood desire to be a powerful, charismatic man.

WHAT'S SO WRONG?

Lisa wanted love; Bill wanted to be a man; the Israelites wanted food. What could be more innocent, right? If we could interview one of those Israelites trying to gather a little too much manna, what do you suppose he'd say? I think he would say something like this: "What's so wrong with providing for my family, with protecting them against starvation?" It might have been hard to convince him there *was* a problem. And you know, on one level, he would have been right: God never condemned the Israelites for wanting bread. After all, he created people to want food when they get hungry—a perfectly natural desire—and then he led a bunch of them out into a wilderness.[5] There's nothing wrong with wanting to eat, and there wasn't anything wrong with asking God for food.

But here's the problem. The Israelites didn't have just a natural desire for food; they wanted food, *and* they wanted it on their terms, *and* they disbelieved that God would provide. So they tried to take matters into their own hands. Being helpless in the wilderness, their only recourse seemed to be grumbling. Something was deeply wrong in their hearts, and it was about far more than bread. As subtle as their grumbling and hoarding may seem, God's tests revealed their truly significant sinfulness. He was concerned not only to fill their stomachs but also to expose their hearts. I'll make two observations about what was revealed.

First, their desire wasn't simply for a daily fill of bread. That was merely a thin cover over a bottomless pit of desire to have life on *their* terms. They wanted bread, and they wanted it now. Gathering it a day at a time wasn't good enough; they wanted to stockpile. Taking a break from gathering to give thanks on the seventh day wouldn't do either; they wanted more and more at every opportunity.

The Bible has a word for such insatiable desire: *lust* (e.g., Rom. 13:14; James 1:14; 1 John 2:16 NASB).[6] Though *lust* usually connotes sexual desire, a lust can be any sinfully excessive desire. Like a poison ivy itch, when you scratch it, it itches even more. It's never satisfied, never grateful—it only grows. Ephesians 4:19 captures the greediness of lust with the phrase "a continual lust for more" (NIV).

This view of sinful desires as bottomless and insatiable corrects the common misunderstanding that such desires are basically good, though misguided, and must instead be met in healthy ways. This is true enough, but without a biblical understanding of how sin corrupts good desires, this reasoning leads to one of two traps: either fixating on desires that *must be* met, leading to attitudes that are demanding, entitled, and at worst, blame shifting, or else feeding desires that should rather be put to death in the first place.

Lisa's counselor told her that her food problems arose out of an unmet need for love that went all the way back to her failed attempts to gain her mother's affection as a child.[7] The solution, therefore, would be to go and get the love she always craved but never got enough of. The problem with that solution is that she was already living life under the rule of that desire, and no matter how much attention she gained with her body, no matter how much weight she lost, it was never enough.

But maybe you think her problem was that she was trying to get the wrong *kind* of attention, and if she sought the right kind instead, that would fix her. But let's look at what happened with Steve when he followed that same advice.

Steve grew up deeply dissatisfied with his emotionally distant father. He would see an older man and wish *that* one could be his father, take him under his wing, and teach him what it means to be a man. Without such an ideal relationship with a surrogate father, Steve was convinced he would never become a man. This desire ruled his life.

In puberty, Steve became aware of his feelings of sexual attraction—they weren't for girls his age but for men his father's age. This was very confusing to Steve. He kept it as a shameful secret for years, all the while indulging homosexual fantasies. When Steve became a Christian and admitted his desire to change, he was encouraged to pursue healthy relationships with older men as a means of fulfilling this so-called need that had gone unfulfilled in childhood. This encouragement reignited his obsession to find a surrogate father. So he pursued increasingly desperate relationships with older men until eventually one of those relationships turned blatantly sexual, and his sinful fantasies became sinful reality.

Steve's longing for a surrogate father was never questioned. His belief that he had to have an intimate relationship with a man to affirm his masculinity was never challenged. Gone unchecked, this desire ruled his life, subtly undermining every attempt to change his behavior and put his fantasy life to death.

If the root of your problem is a sinful desire masquerading as an innocent (or even noble) need, then feeding it will only make the problem worse. Even if you feed it with something basically good—like a healthy relationship—it may amount to nothing more than manna hoarding, greedily gobbling up some otherwise good gift from God with no thought of God at all.

In their greed, the Israelites in the wilderness put their own desires at the center of the universe and demanded that God, Moses, and the wilderness revolve around them. But such boundless desire can never be satisfied on human terms and was never meant to be. Only God gets life on his own terms.

That brings us to the second observation: God's terms. Was it just red tape, all that policy about gathering only a day's worth at a time and resting on the seventh day? No, it was God making the daily gathering of provisions a part of his personal relationship with his people. A personal God makes a promise to a people, saying: "I want you to remember me as often as you get hungry. I want you to know that I provide for you." Rather than just leaving a note on the counter that said, "Kids, there's a lifetime supply of frozen dinners in the fridge. Later," he invited them to dine with him any time they were hungry.

But the Israelites would have preferred a manna machine to guarantee their perpetual satisfaction, one not requiring them to acknowledge God or trust him. They acted as if he didn't even exist in the wilderness—it was Moses' and Aaron's fault they were out in the wilderness without food (Ex. 16:2–3)! If God did exist, he did so (in their minds) only for the purpose of meeting their need, the all-consuming center of their thoughts. But he certainly wasn't the God who had saved them from slavery, forgiven them at his own expense, made them his treasured people, called them to worship him, and swept them up into a story far bigger than the wilderness.

Moses had it right: "Your grumbling is not against [me] but against the LORD" (v. 8). Their grumbling accused God of being a bad God. We live moment by moment—thought, word, and deed—*coram Deo*, before the face of God. There are no idle thoughts or deeds. He searches every one (1 Chron. 28:9; Ps. 139; Eccl. 12:14; Heb. 4:12–13). There are certainly natural desires, but there are no neutral ones: every one amounts to reaching for something we want that is part of God's world. Either we will reach for God's gifts to his glory and to our joy or, like the Israelites in the wilderness, we will grasp in greedy rebellion against God.

WHEN DO YOU GRUMBLE?

The Israelites' grumbling was attended with demanding, hoarding, threatening to turn back to Egypt, accusing God of ill intent toward them, ingratitude for his provision, and refusal of the terms of God's blessing. It was an all-out temper tantrum, really.

It would be all too easy to repose in your self-assured dignity and think, "Well, there's no way I would throw a fit and accuse God like that." But keep in mind that their demands probably seemed as reasonable in their own eyes as yours seem to you. It's only when we hear their complaints from God's perspective that we can discern the true sinfulness of their grumbling. So for you to relate, you'll have to take a close-up look at your life, maybe where you'd never think to look, perhaps scrutinizing desires so familiar that you never thought to question them before.

David Powlison defines grumbling simply as "dissatisfaction with what *is*."[8] Paul Tripp says, "Grumbling is the background drone of a discontented heart."[9] In other words, whatever my present situation holds is not what I want, so I grumble and grasp.

Here are three key questions you can ask to probe for natural desires that may have become grumbling lusts in your life: When are you angry? When are you anxious? When do you escape?[10] Each of these has a range of expressions, from the subtle to the more obvious. We'll focus on the subtle.

When are you angry? In its obvious forms anger is loud, hateful, and violent. But it can also be irritable, frustrated, judgmental, pushy, moody, grouchy, cranky, defensive, blunt, harsh, or impatient.

Anger makes a judgment: *this is wrong, unfair, unjust.*[11] Sometimes our assessments are correct and we have good cause for righteous anger. But even then, knowing something is wrong is only half the matter; the other half is in knowing how to make it right without increasing the wrong by unrighteous anger. Even the first half, though, is nothing to be taken for granted—anyone who is angry thinks he sees clearly what is wrong. But sin fogs the lenses through which we see the world, leading to wrong judgments about what's really wrong.

Perceived entitlements can lead to such misguided anger. An entitlement is what you believe is yours *by rights*. So a husband may believe he is entitled to sex from his wife while she believes she is entitled to his affection. If one doesn't give what is owed, the other feels righteous in condemning the failure. Or a single man or woman feels entitled to a spouse and holds God in contempt for withholding. The Israelites seemed to feel entitled to food in the wilderness, as if God had to answer to them. Grumbling insists, "I have a right to what I want, so I have a right to complain when I don't get it." The Israelites had the nerve to sit in the seat of judgment and put God to the test! (see Ex. 17:2, 7).

When are you anxious? At the extreme, anxiety can be paralyzing. But on any average day it can also be brooding, preoccupied, overly cautious, hypersensitive, perfectionistic, and worrisome, with sweating, pacing, and nail biting. Anxiety often kicks in when life feels a bit out of control or a touch too risky. Granted, a little bit of the right kind of anxiety is good for protecting your kids in a crowded place. And you want your surgeon to have enough anxiety to double-wash and double-check yet not so much anxiety that his scalpel-wielding hands tremble.

Anxiety replays the conversation you just had, calculating whether you left the right impression. It worries what people think. And it forecasts the next conversation, drilling you on all possible scenarios to ensure you don't make a fool of yourself. Anxiety frets that there's never quite enough money, attention, time, affection, leisure, or success. It assumes that the worst case is the most likely. It has a way of lingering at the back of the mind, filtering every thought.

Anxiety is a shade of fear, which is the flipside of desire.[12] You want something, and you're afraid you won't get it. Or you have something you're afraid to lose. Either way, you're on edge, agitated, discontent—fertile soil for grumbling.

When do you want to escape? Escape becomes more enticing as life becomes more difficult. Near the extreme end of the escape spectrum are addictions of all kinds: drugs, alcohol, food, sex. Near the subtle end of the spectrum are constant checking of e-mail, sports scores, or social media Web sites; aimlessly watching television or surfing the Web; unnecessary snacking; consuming hobbies; or workaholism. Even religion can be distorted and used as an escape from reality: "God is sovereign, so there's no point to dealing with _____." Fill in the blank: pain, disappointment, the past, loss. Boredom is a form of grumbling.[13] It is being discontent with what is happening now and wanting to escape into something more interesting.

Certainly there's nothing wrong with wanting to use anesthesia to escape the pain of a root canal or moving quickly through a dark alley to escape a threatening environment. Some escapes are necessary for a balanced life: a refreshing nap, a family vacation, a relaxing night out for dinner and a movie, a day away for prayer. In fact, it was for the sake of rest that God provided the Sabbath day for the Israelites. Yet these healthy escapes aren't designed to take you out of reality but to plug you back into it.

If you find yourself regularly escaping, what are you running from? What is difficult, uncomfortable, or painful that you want to avoid? Patterns of sinful escape are clues to our grumbling lusts, because they reveal where we are so dissatisfied with what *is* that we check out of reality time and again.

One stay-at-home mom found her escape in junk food. That was one thing she could control when she felt trapped in her home in the chaos of a messy house, overwhelmed by energetic and needy children. When an extended-family conflict broke out in a series of phone calls and letters, putting her into a state of almost constant anxiety, she ran to food. She knew it was sinful, but she felt entitled to some relief for all she'd suffered.

The Israelites' grumbling also had traces of all three: anxiety, escape, and finally anger. Surely they were anxious when they realized food was scarce and they had no control over their provisions. When the manna finally came later, they attempted to seize control by hoarding. Then the escape: fantasizing how plentiful the food was in Egypt, apparently forgetting how it was accompanied with slavery, and wishing God had simply killed them there while they had plenty to eat. And finally, it came out in anger and accusation: "You brought us out here to kill us, didn't you!" (see Ex. 16:3).

Can you relate to an Israelite in the wilderness, lying awake at night dreading the coming of morning—the moment of truth when you'd look outside to see whether fresh manna had fallen? How long would you feel relief in the morning to find manna before relief gave way to anxiety to get it while you could, driving you to gather quickly and obsessively? Would you have been the one making contingency plans to protect against ever being empty-handed, gathering extra manna just to make sure? Would you be angry that you had only manna to eat every day? Or would you justify your anger: "If I hadn't taken action and complained, there wouldn't *be* any manna!"

We are usually blind to our grumbling since it seems so reasonable and familiar. You'll need to pray that the Holy Spirit will search your heart and help you see what you haven't seen. You might also ask someone close to hold up a mirror to your blind spots: what you can't see may be obvious to others. When you do see something new, don't move past it too quickly. Don't just say: "Oh, well yeah, I complain about *that*, but that's because . . . " Think about what your grumbling says before God. Think about how it affects those around you. Then ask, is there any connection between this area of subtle grumbling and that obvious problem area of my life? The distance between them may not be as far as you think. For Lisa, disorderly eating expressed her grumbling heart's demand for attention.

TEMPTATION: GOD'S WAY OR MINE?

Temptation tests our desires and reveals when they are natural and when they are inordinate. As James 1:14 says, "Each person is tempted when he is lured and enticed by his *own* desire." The desire is already in the heart before the temptation arises and presents an opportunity for it to be expressed in thought, word, or deed. Sometimes, you are tempted to grumble under conditions of deprivation—when there doesn't seem to be enough of what you want. Other times, you are tempted to greed under conditions of abundance—when you have plenty to satisfy any natural desire, yet you're never quite satisfied.[14] A grumbling heart under deprivation becomes a greedy heart under abundance. Sinful desire can never be satisfied.

The Israelites grumbled in the deprivation of the wilderness, exposing their unbelief in God to provide and revealing a sinful desire to have life on their own terms. The grumbling also exposed their false belief that God wasn't good after all and had perhaps even intended to kill them with hunger. Later, the abundance of manna exposed their greed as they hoarded.

Jesus also faced temptation under conditions of deprivation in the wilderness (Matt. 4:1–11). He was hungry and thirsty after fasting forty days. At his point of greatest weakness, Satan tempted him: "If you are the Son of God, command these stones to become loaves of bread" (v. 3). He could have satisfied his hunger and proven with a miracle that he is God's Son. But Jesus knew that to do so would be to oppose the Father's will for him. Instead, Jesus depended on the Father and resisted temptation saying, "Man shall not live by bread alone, but by every word that comes from the mouth of God," the very words God had spoken through Moses to drive home the lesson about manna (v. 4; Deut. 8:3).

Jesus was tempted to greed when Satan offered the glory of all the kingdoms of the world in trade for his worship (Matt. 4:8–9). But Jesus humbled himself and was content to endure the cross, the Father's plan to exalt his Son as king. Jesus did not grasp for what he already knew was his (Phil. 2:6–11).

In the wilderness Jesus' war with Satan shows the reality of the spiritual warfare involved every time we face temptation. Yet with such subtle sins as we have seen in this chapter, we are often tempted to just let temptation happen, as if it were no big deal. The sinfulness of a desire may seem so subtle; we are content to let it linger and permit temptation to come and go as it pleases, luring and enticing us back into sin. Puritan theologian John Owen calls this not merely being tempted, but entering into temptation:

> When we suffer [allow, permit] a temptation to enter into us, then we
> "enter into temptation." While it knocks at the door we are at liberty;

but when any temptation comes in and parleys [discusses (especially with an enemy)] with the heart, reasons with the mind, entices and allures the affections, be it a long or a short time, do it thus insensibly and imperceptibly, or do the soul take notice of it, we "enter into temptation."[15]

Owen paints a vivid picture: when we harbor sinful desires and open the door to temptation, we are letting in the enemy for a conversation. We listen, consider the offer, and allow ourselves to feel drawn in. We may even give him a guest key to let himself come and go as he pleases at times we may not even be aware and alert. How foolish! If we want to be free, we can't let sin and temptation have free reign in our hearts, no matter how subtle their presence. Instead of welcoming the enemy for a conversation, we should fight him at the door. Owen also warns that if we adopt a lazy attitude about the subtle forms of sin then we shouldn't expect any great victories over the more perplexing ones.[16]

For Lisa, growing up in an emotional wilderness, barren of affection, a natural desire for love had become an inordinate desire for attention of any kind. And when temptation whispered that she could lure attention with a thinner body, her desire conceived and gave birth to sin, and so began Lisa's march toward death. She gave free reign to sin in her life instead of fighting temptation at the door.

However subtle a sinful desire may seem, Christians are called to *war* against sin. A sinful desire is never satisfied; it must be put to death by the same Spirit who empowered Jesus in the wilderness (Rom. 8:13). But war against sin consists not only of putting sin to death; we must also find our satisfaction in Christ, for he is our life. Like the Israelites, hungry in the wilderness, our souls are born hungry. We must cultivate an appetite for Christ, who alone is meant to satisfy our souls (see Ps. 107:9). John's Gospel presents Jesus as the bread of life who alone gives eternal life.

JESUS IS THE BREAD OF LIFE

Thousands had seen and heard that Jesus healed the sick, so they followed him one day to see more miracles.[17] As the day wore on, the crowd became hungry, but there wasn't enough food to feed them all and not enough money to buy it. Jesus multiplied the five loaves and two fish from a boy's lunch and fed the crowd with many baskets full to spare. Jesus' intention in this miracle was to show that he is the source of eternal life, but when the crowd followed him on to the next place, their intention was simply to get more free food. They knew the prophet Moses had provided bread in the wilderness, so if Jesus was a prophet, they reasoned, then he should be able to provide at least as much as Moses.

Knowing that they had missed the point of his miracle, Jesus said, "Do not labor for the food that perishes, but for the food that endures to eternal life. . . . It was not Moses who gave you the bread from heaven, but my Father gives you the true bread from heaven. . . . I am the bread of life; whoever comes to me shall not hunger" (John 6:27, 32, 35). He knew that they didn't want *him* so much as they wanted more bread. Or at best, maybe they wanted to be thrilled with more miracles. Either way, they didn't want eternal life from Jesus.

Many come to Jesus with wrong motives. Some come to him for mere "bread," expecting an endless meeting of everyday desires. They come to have their old appetites satisfied, not to get new ones. They don't actually believe that Jesus offers what is most satisfying. For them, bread, water, comfort, control, achievement, affirmation, pleasure—immediate and tangible, though fading quickly—seem to satisfy. These are the same ones, who, in the end, turn away from Jesus, cynical and self-righteous, saying: "*I* tried, *he* failed." Yet they never had an appetite for him at all but only absorption in themselves.

Others claim to be satisfied in Jesus, but for them, he is simply another escape from reality, for they are unwilling to face the pain of their true need, their true brokenness. Instead, they add him to their lives like a coat of varnish, concealing their true condition. Theirs is not faith, but formality.

Those who chased Jesus for more bread failed the test of manna, just as their forefathers in the wilderness did thousands of years earlier. They still failed to see that Jesus himself is the bread of eternal life; so many of them turned away from him, baffled and unbelieving (John 6:60, 66). We are often just like them, wanting Jesus only because we think he will satisfy some other desire we bring to him or that he will make us look like we lead satisfying lives, rather than wanting *him* to be our satisfaction.

Yet we cannot simply *will* ourselves to be satisfied in Jesus. Just as it is impossible to put sin to death except by the Spirit, so it is impossible to see Jesus as the bread of life except by the Spirit (Rom. 8:13; cf. 2 Cor. 3:18).

FEEDING ON THE BREAD OF LIFE

What might it have looked like if the Israelites in the wilderness had been satisfied in God? Surely they would still have asked for bread (there's nothing wrong with admitting hunger), but they would have done so in faith. Not stoically, muffling their fears with platitudes about God's sovereignty, but in genuine and desperate dependence upon the only one who could provide, knowing that he is good and that's *why* they could trust him, recalling how he'd proven his power to redeem already.

When the Spirit opened Lisa's eyes, she finally saw how her desires for love, affection, and attention had ruled her life and had even driven her destructive eating habits. She saw that even her cries to God for deliverance had been more selfish demands for temporal satisfaction, for life on her own terms. She found her heart's deepest satisfaction in Jesus, whose love for her is unending and free. After years of restlessness and desperation for a husband to love her, she was content in Christ.

Then God, in his kindness, brought a husband to Lisa. Now her marriage is both a source of great joy and a new testing ground for her heart. Will she continue to find her satisfaction in Jesus when her husband can finally give her the attention she'd always craved? Is Jesus still a greater reward to her than the husband of her dreams? There are days when her heart's old demands for affection threaten to spoil her marriage and derail her devotion to Christ. She is not out of the wilderness just yet. But when she finds her daily fulfillment in Jesus, then the joys of marriage become all the sweeter in her gratitude for this generous gift from him.

SCRIPTURE READING

- Exodus 16–17:7
- Matthew 4:1–11
- John 6:1–15, 22–71
- James 1:12–18

RECOMMENDED RESOURCES

Owen, John. *Overcoming Sin and Temptation*. Edited by Kelly M. Kapic and Justin Taylor. Wheaton, IL: Crossway, 2006. This is challenging but rewarding read. In true Puritan form, Owen takes the subtlety of sin and temptation very seriously.

Piper, John. "Be Killing Sin or Sin Will Be Killing You." Sermon, March 7, 2010. http://www.marshillchurch.org/media/special/be-killing-sin-or-sin-will-be-killing-you. Piper expounds Romans 8:13 and the command to put sin to death by the Spirit.

Powlison, David. "I Am Motivated When I Feel Desire." In *Seeing with New Eyes: Counseling and the Human Condition Through the Lens of Scripture*, 145–62. Phillipsburg, NJ: P&R, 2003.

_____. "X-ray Questions." In *Seeing with New Eyes*, 129–43. These x-ray questions are very helpful for identifying the subtle desires of the heart that exert such influence on our lives.

FOR REFLECTION AND DISCUSSION

1) What do you want badly? Resist the urge to generalize—comfort, control. Instead, be as specific as the Israelites' desire: "I want to be sure I'll have bread to eat for every meal, every day."
2) What do you feel deprived of?
3) What have you grumbled about? What does it reveal about your heart toward God?
4) Who around you bears the brunt of your grumbling, like the Israelites put upon Moses and Aaron?
5) Though the people grumbled against Moses, their anger was ultimately against God. What has your grumbling against another person revealed about your heart toward God?
6) How have you questioned God's motives toward you when you haven't received a blessing you expected? How about when you faced a trial that you weren't expecting?
7) To what temptations have you given a "guest key" to come and go as they please?

6

THE GOLDEN CALF: VOLUNTEERING FOR SLAVERY

Philip grew up in a home where the ethics were to be a good, upstanding, moral, American citizen. He gained the status of "favorite son" by demonstrating he could conform to the norms. He had self-discipline. He could play the part.

Whatever privileged status Philip enjoyed within the four walls of his home was lost when he stepped out into the world of junior high. Philip was small for his age, and he never heard the end of it, so when his peers were out socializing or playing sports, he would often stay home and pass the time bouncing a ball against a wall, alone.

One day at home, Philip found his father's porn stash. Being transported into another world where he was welcomed and treated to secret delights was exhilarating. In the real world, he had been rejected; but in this fantasy world, he was finally accepted.[1]

By the time his peers finally began inviting him out on weekends, he was already too immersed in his own world to join theirs; he couldn't wait to get home for his five hours of fantasy every Friday and Saturday night.

EGYPTIAN FANTASIES

As early as the crisis at the Red Sea, the Israelites were already attempting to escape the hardship of the wilderness in their fantasies of Egypt. Egypt had moved from their nightmares into their daydreams. There they could be left alone to their predictable labor—none of this unpredictable wandering in a wilderness. There they could drink the waters of the Nile—none of this bitter swill from occasional oases (Ex. 15:22–24). There they could sit around a buffet of meat and bread, feasting to their heart's content—none of this dependence on God's provision for just enough each day (see 16:3–4).

In the last chapter, we saw how subtle sin can be. We usually make idols out of good things, even meat and bread, not the obviously bad things like fornication. As Tim Keller says, "The greater the good, the more likely we are to expect that it can satisfy our deepest needs and hopes."[2]

In this chapter we turn to look at the deep corruption of idolatry; the affections we cultivate for that which is evil, thinking it good; the stark black-versus-white of the truth and the lie; our utter self-absorption and blindness to idolatry's great cost to God and others; and the slavery we sign up for, thinking we'll find freedom. Finally, we'll look at repentance, turning from idols to the living God.

THE TRUTH COULDN'T HAVE BEEN MORE CLEAR

After nearly fifty days of traveling through the wilderness, the Israelites arrived at Mount Sinai (Ex. 19:1–2). The next morning, Moses would go up to the mountain where God would establish his covenant with his people. By this time, they'd already seen pillars of cloud and fire, parting waters, bitter water made sweet, manna and quail in abundance every day, water from a rock, a battle fought and won against an invading army, and even God's wise concern for the harmony of their social order when Jethro helped Moses conduct a "re-org" (13:21–22; 14; 15:22–25; 16:13–18; 17:1–7, 8–16; 18). Not to mention deliverance from ruthless slavery.

Throughout the journey, God continually and intentionally blessed and intervened on behalf the people. And amidst the Israelite's wanderings, they heard the constant refrain: "I am the LORD who brought you out of the land of Egypt." God meant to emblazon this truth on their minds at the most momentous events. At the burning bush: "I promise I will bring you up out of the affliction of Egypt" (Ex. 3:17). When Pharaoh took away straw for bricks: "I am the LORD, and I will bring you out from under the burdens of the Egyptians, and I will deliver you from slavery to them" (Ex. 6:6). On the day they left Egypt: "Remember this day in which you came out from Egypt . . . for by a strong hand the LORD brought you out" (Ex. 13:3).

Now, at Mount Sinai, amidst a majestic show of thunder, lightning, smoke, and fire, God spoke the first words of the famous Decalogue: "I am the LORD your God, who brought you up out of the land of Egypt. . . . You shall have no other gods before me" (Ex. 20:2–3). The truth of God's presence could not have been clearer. In Egypt the Israelites had responded immediately in faith to Moses' message that their deliverance was at hand (Ex. 4:31). So now, too, they responded boldly to God's covenant with them: "All that the LORD has spoken we will do, and we will be obedient" (Ex. 24:3, 7).

At that, Moses prepared the elders for his departure—he would re-ascend the mountain for the next installment of God's word. He left them with instructions during his absence and told them to await his return. Then he went up into the cloud covering the mountain to meet with God for forty days (Ex. 24:1–18).

PHILIP'S SECRET LIFE

When Philip arrived at college, the traditional morality restraints were gone. Here, partying was the norm. Outwardly his behavior changed for the worse, but inwardly he merely carried forward the same ethic: conform and be accepted. The sex, drugs, alcohol, and ever-gripping fantasies of pornography allowed him to fit right in.

Then he found a new use for porn. He had come to college with great ambition and found it much harder than he expected. It had been easy to soar in his local high school, but now he was in a much bigger pond, and he felt small again. His determination to succeed and impress professors and peers often drove him into isolation and many late nights of tense and frustrated studies. Alone and online, porn became a drug, a steroid that cleared his head and helped him push through his studies.

Somewhere along the way, some Christians on campus befriended him. They accepted him genuinely and invited him to belong. More importantly, they told him of Jesus, and Philip became a Christian.

Now there were new norms for acceptance, or so Philip thought. He straightened up, reverting to many of the old moral restraints he'd grown up with. The Christian friends were amazed at such a great testimony of life change. Impressed with his seemingly quick progress in the faith, they made him a Christian small-group leader. Meanwhile, his secret porn fetish grew darker and deeper. Before becoming a Christian, he had devoured the shelves of adult video stores near the campus; now he slipped away late at night to video stores in other towns.

And then some new light broke into his darkness when he met a Christian girl who would later become his wife. She wanted to remain pure throughout their engagement, to save themselves for each other in marriage, and she made him promise they would. He promised. Then he went home to his feast of pornography and masturbation.

He reasoned to himself, "It's not like I'm breaking my promise, right? I'm just releasing the sexual tension that builds when I'm with her; *she's* the one who *really* turns me on. In fact, I'm probably doing us a favor. This *helps* us keep our promise. I'm less likely to touch her if my head's clear." Philip didn't think it was important that his fiancée know any of this.

THE GOLDEN CALF

After promising to wait and obey, the Israelites waited day after day at the base of the mountain for Moses to return. Days turned into weeks. They grew impatient. They began to doubt whether he'd *ever* return. Their hope cooled into disappointment and then crumbled in cynicism. Convinced Moses—and God himself—had abandoned them, they decided to take matters into their own hands:

> When the people saw that Moses delayed to come down from the mountain, the people gathered themselves together to Aaron and said to him, "Up, make us gods who shall go before us. As for this Moses, the man who brought us up out of the land of Egypt, we do not know what has become of him." (Ex. 32:1)

"This Moses?"[3] Their contempt was palpable as they coerced Aaron into making an idol, something they could see and feel, something to embody their hope of redemption while God and Moses were absent. Something, *anything*—now!

Aaron obliged. Here was Moses' own brother and co-bearer of God's message of deliverance caving in to the people's demands. He collected their gold jewelry, melted it down, fashioned a golden calf, and presented it to the people. They worshiped it, proclaiming: "These are your gods, O Israel, who brought you up out of the land of Egypt!" (Ex. 32:2–4).

Really? After so many miraculous and clear reminders—"I am the LORD who brought you out of the land of Egypt"—had they forgotten? Could they really have mistaken this cow for their deliverer? Maybe they meant for the cow to represent Yahweh, their true deliverer, but they'd already promised not to make any graven images of him. Either way, this was no mere forgetfulness or mistake. They chose to believe a lie. "They exchanged the glory of God for the image of an ox that eats grass" (Ps. 106:20).

WHAT IS AN IDOL?

The exchange of truth for a lie is the essence of idolatry, and idolatry, in turn, underlies all sin.[4] Paul had the golden calf incident in mind when he penned the New Testament's definitive passage on idolatry: "They exchanged the truth about God for a lie and worshiped and served the creature rather than the Creator."[5]

To modern readers, the language of idolatry may seem primitive and irrelevant to immediate concerns such as addiction. But, in fact, it is entirely relevant. According to Tim Keller, in his book *Counterfeit Gods*, "The biblical concept of idolatry is an extremely sophisticated idea, integrating intellectual, psychological, social, cultural, and spiritual categories."[6] In other words, understanding idolatry helps us understand a great deal about what goes wrong with people. Keller offers several ways of defining idolatry. An idol is:

- Anything more important to you than God.
- Anything that absorbs your heart and imagination more than God.
- Anything you seek to give you what only God can give.
- Whatever you look at and say, in your heart of hearts, "If I have that, then I'll feel my life has meaning, then I'll know I have value, then I'll feel significant and secure."
- Anything [that] becomes more fundamental than God to your happiness, meaning in life, and identity.[7]

Keller elaborates on a range of potential idols that affect and infect both individuals and whole cultures: love, sex, money, power, success, and religion.[8]

In his novel *Till We Have Faces*, C. S. Lewis tells the story of two princess sisters: Orual, the older, unattractive one, and Psyche, the kid half-sister, whose grace, beauty, and innocence captured every heart, including Orual's. Orual's life seems nearly barren of meaning and significance, except that she had been Psyche's primary caretaker (Psyche's mother had died in childbirth, and their father, the king, was a mad man). Orual sees herself as both mother and father to Psyche.

When Psyche eventually marries a husband in a far-off land, Orual is threatened.[9] She still believes that she alone holds Psyche's best interests at heart. Orual risks a journey to find Psyche and threatens to kill Psyche, and then herself, if Psyche will not choose Orual over her husband. To prove she means business, Orual stabs herself with a knife. Her love for Psyche had turned grotesque; Psyche's love and loyalty had become her idols. Maybe you can relate to Orual's jealousy, perhaps over a spouse, a child, or a friend—wanting that person's loyalty, affection, or respect more than anything.

For Philip, *being accepted by people* was more important than anything; it was an idol.[10] His morals were blown about like a weather vane. Whatever lifestyle granted him the best chance at acceptance among his party buddies, his Christian friends, or his fiancée, that was the lifestyle—at least externally—that he lived. Even his use of pornography in solitude began when he felt somehow "accepted" by porn while peers rejected him.

Philip's controlling need for acceptance is what Keller calls a "deep idol," an idol that resides deep within the motivational drive of the human heart and seeks expression through more concrete and visible "surface idols."[11] Pornography was one of the many surface idols that gave expression to Philip's much deeper idolatry of the heart.[12] The most familiar addictions are all surface idols: drugs, alcohol, sex, food, shopping, video games, gambling.

Remember Lisa from chapter 5, who wanted attention so much that she starved herself to get it? And Christine from chapter 3, who fled to the streets to indulge her drug lifestyle and seek the affection of a man? They shared a deep idol in common with Philip: they craved the love, acceptance, and attention of people in their lives. The variety of surface idols that expressed this single deep idol is surprisingly broad: pornography, food, cutting, drugs, prostitution, theft, social striving, weight loss, and religion.

An idol always lives in the heart before it is made visible by the hands.

"What the heart loves, the will chooses, and the mind justifies."[13] We may not sculpt statues or fashion golden calves, but our hearts are nonetheless "idol factories."[14] As Ed Welch says, "Drugs and sex are the modern golden calves erected by addicts to find meaning, power, or pleasure apart from God."[15]

RELIGION AND THE GOLDEN CALF

For the Israelites, the golden calf was a surface idol: immediate, concrete, and visible. But it appeared when the deep idol of their hearts demanded fulfillment. The Israelites' only access to God's presence—*ever*—had come through Moses. And up to this point in the story, he had probably never been gone more than a day.[16] So it seems the Israelites panicked, because with Moses missing, they had lost all contact with God.[17]

Christians too often take for granted their access to God's presence by the Holy Spirit, made possible by Jesus. Even as Christians, we sometimes doubt God's presence when we don't feel him. Imagine being those Israelites, facing the fear that after generations of slavery, the God who had clearly shown up and delivered them was now out of reach because Moses had disappeared. Can you not relate to their urge to try to do something about it?

There are several views about what the golden calf actually was. Did it represent some Egyptian pagan deity, or the God of Israel himself, visually represented in a culturally understandable way? Most likely, it was a pedestal they built to elevate Yahweh above them and thus ensure his continued presence in Moses' absence.[18]

It doesn't really matter whether the golden calf was an image of a pagan god or a pedestal for the true God. Either way, their rebellion was rank. They had already heard God's words—the Ten Commandments—about how he should be worshiped, and they had agreed to obey (Ex. 24:3). If the calf stood for some pagan god, then they broke the first commandment; if it represented the true God, then they broke the second.[19] Any way you look at it, they replaced God with an idol.

In a way, it's even more scandalous to think that they tried to worship the true God of Israel with a pagan image, "imitating orthodoxy through idolatry," making sacrifices before this idol that would otherwise have been appropriate for Yahweh.[20]

I knew a guy once who loved to read big theology books, and the bigger the book, the better to hide his secret sin. He justified himself by having better theology than others and wouldn't let anyone speak into his life if they didn't have the same level of theological sophistication. In the process, he traded an orthodox knowledge *of* God for relationship *with* God. He was able to appear spiritual to others according to his Christian orthodoxy while maintaining the lie of living in unrepentant sin.[21]

MORE EGYPTIAN THAN ISRAELITE

In the speech that ended with his execution, the disciple Stephen, famous for being the first Christian martyr, said of the Israelites, "Our fathers refused to obey [Moses], but thrust him aside, and *in their hearts they turned to Egypt. . . .* And they made a calf" (Acts 7:39–41). Despite all of God's wooing, deliverance, provision, and care for them, their hearts still longed for what they had left behind in Egypt. So, once again, even if the calf *was* an attempt at securing God's presence, the deep allegiance of their hearts was to Egypt and its ways.

We have already seen hints of this turning back to Egypt in the Israelites' longing looks over the shoulder for security, food, and water that began almost the day they left Egypt. But what they truly wanted was much more than food; *they wanted to go home.*

Sociologists studying what has been called the "slave mentality" have noted such paradoxes in the minds of slaves who have been freed. Seemingly counter to common sense, slaves with this mentality come to love their masters. Not only do they love their masters, but they also come to love what their masters love.[22]

History tells us the Egyptians were very proud of their land. It was part of their very identity. They even called themselves the "people of the black lands," referring to the fertility of the land around the Nile; foreigners were "people of the red land," the desert.[23] It would seem that after spending four hundred years in Egypt, the Israelites had in many ways become more Egyptian than Israelite. Rather than being mere sojourners in Egypt, they'd made their home there. And now they longed to return to their homeland.

God said he would deliver his people from the land of slavery and lead them to the land he promised Abraham. But in their Egyptian minds, God had taken them out of their homeland—the core of their identity—and banished them to the "red lands" of the wilderness.[24]

The Israelites loved Egypt and its ways. They wanted to go home. They were foolish in their idolatry, to be sure, but no more than you or I. Idolatry isn't just about bad behavior; it's about what you *love*.

PHILIP'S LOVE-HATE RELATIONSHIP WITH PORN

For many years, Philip didn't hate his dependence on pornography. He loved it. It was always there, it met his needs, and it accepted him. Even when he finally married, he had every intention of secretly bringing his obsession with him into the marriage. Even the week leading up to his wedding—and on the *very day*—he feasted. Occasionally, he fed his wife half-truths about his so-called struggles. But his main struggle was how to say it just right so that she didn't suspect anything more. Eventually, though, through some teaching at his church, he came to see pornography as sinful, so he decided to stop.

Of course, it wasn't so simple. He found that he could not stop, and then he panicked. He lambasted himself: "Why can't you do this?! You're self-disciplined! Just stop it!" But the idol which had offered acceptance, pleasure, and relief for so many years demanded his loyalty, devotion, service, and trust. It would not release him. Philip was enslaved.

DECEPTION AND VOLUNTARY SLAVERY

Sin deceives (see Heb. 3:13). It whispers lies: "The idol takes care of you; God doesn't. The idol gives you what you want, what you crave; it relieves your pain; it liberates you. Fight for your idol. Serve and defend it." To believe those lies is to declare your allegiance to the Enemy.

Here is the paradox of our slavery to sin. In one sense, we've been captured. In another sense, we want to give ourselves to our captors. It's voluntary slavery.[25] It doesn't begin as slavery, of course. In the beginning, we may make a clear-headed choice to indulge some sinful desire or to numb some pain, like Philip when he first found his father's porn stash. We feel like we control the power of the idol precisely because we choose it. The lie begins to take root. Later, some pain or temptation meets us again, and we run to the idol once again. The lie is strengthened each time, and a process of spiritual blindness sets it. Paul Tripp warns of the deceptive nature of this spiritual blindness, which affects every one of us:

> The difference between physical and spiritual blindness is that the former is blatantly obvious while the latter often goes unnoticed. A fundamental part of being spiritually blind is that you are blind to your blindness.[26]

Once we are blind, we are enslaved, because we can no longer see our way to freedom. And because we are blind to our blindness, we may think that our continued devotion to the lie *is* our exercise of freedom.

Idolaters are not only the victims of this deceit but also its perpetrators. Again, the slave who loves his master loves his master's ways, and the way of idols is deceit. To deceive is to mislead, to speak in such a way as to avoid the truth.[27] This happens by telling a lie, something factually untrue, or by telling a truth with the intention to mislead. This is what Philip did with his wife when he told her he had "struggles." It was true, but it was also deceiving because by it, he meant to keep her from knowing the whole truth.

Self-deception is when you are both the deceived and the deceiver.[28] It happens when you have both been deceived and are also unaware of the deception. Philip was self-deceived when he told himself that his porn habit actually helped his relationship with his fiancée by keeping him from making sexual advances on her. The payoff for this self-deception is that Philip could continue his porn use with less guilt and possibly even with a hint of nobility. Psychologist Diane Langberg, in her talk entitled "Self-Deception: A Supporting Column of Addiction," says that addicts are "addicted to the narcotic of deceit."[29]

GOD EXPOSES IDOLS

As Moses spoke with God on the mountain and the people built the golden calf below, God saw everything. He told Moses:

> Go down, for your people, whom you brought up out of the land of Egypt, have corrupted themselves. . . . I have seen this people, and behold, it is a stiff-necked people. Now therefore let me alone, that my wrath may burn hot against them and I may consume them, in order that I may make a great nation of you. (Ex. 32:7, 9–10).

Exposing the foolishness of their idolatry with mocking imagery, God says that they are "stiff-necked" and that they have "turned aside quickly out of the way that I commanded them" (vv. 8–9). Both phrases are allusions to the cow they worshiped. "We become what we worship," says G. K. Beale, and the Israelites who worshiped a cow had become "rebellious cows running wild and needing to be regathered."[30]

God also mockingly exposed Aaron's self-deception. When Moses descended to rebuke the people, he spoke first to his brother Aaron and said in essence: "What did they do to you that made you build a golden calf!" (v. 21). We know the truth: Aaron had told the people to pool their gold and he fashioned the calf with it (vv. 2–4). But Aaron answered Moses, "They gave [the gold] to me, and I threw it into the fire, and out came this calf" (v. 24). Shifting blame, Aaron made the *people* responsible for the gold collection, and the *calf* responsible for jumping out of the fire! But Aaron is the only one deceived here, for the story ends with the decisive words, "The LORD sent a plague on the people, because they made the calf, *the one that Aaron made*" (v. 35).

God's wrath was so hot that he had been ready to wipe out the Israelites and start over with Moses; he could still have fulfilled his promise to Abraham to bless the earth through his offspring, through Moses' line instead.[31] When he told Moses the people had corrupted themselves, the Hebrew word for *corrupt* is the same as in Genesis 6:12 where mankind's rebellion had reached such a height that God flooded everyone but Noah and his family. The connection was not lost on Moses. He understood that the people's rebellion had already reached flood levels and that the God who'd wiped everyone out once before had just cause to do it again.

INTERCESSION AND PROPITIATION

Moses faced a dilemma. He knew the people deserved God's wrath for their idolatry. And he knew that God would have been not only perfectly just to wipe them out but also faithful to his promise to Abraham if he started over with Moses. And surely, Moses was weary of the Israelites' incessant grumbling and accusation by that time. How easy it would have been for him to let them perish.

Instead, Moses was patient with the people. God had been working on

Moses' heart through the wilderness as well, and here Moses imaged not only God's anger against the sin but also his mercy. Moses interceded for the people, asking God to spare them for his (God's) name's sake. Moses neither minimized the people's sin nor accused God of being unjust in his jealous anger. God honored Moses' plea and relented (Ex. 32:11–14).

Moses' intercession prefigures Christ's intercession for us:

> My little children, I am writing these things to you so that you may not sin. But if anyone does sin, we have an advocate with the Father, Jesus Christ the righteous. He is the propitiation for our sins, and not for ours only but also for the sins of the whole world. (1 John 2:1–2)

A key similarity between the intercessions of Moses and Jesus is that, in both cases, God's glory and holy character are upheld while the sin of the people is exposed and condemned for the corruption and rebellion it truly is. A key difference between the intercessions of Moses and Jesus, however, is that while Moses would have been spared God's wrath as the Israelites were destroyed, Jesus takes God's wrath upon himself so his people are preserved. This is what is meant by *propitiation*.

REPENTANCE

If it were not for this intercession on our behalf, we would not even have the opportunity to repent. Think about it: the intercessory conversation between Moses and God was up on the mountain, far from the people who were still sinning. They weren't even there for the conversation. It happened for them, on their behalf, before they even knew they needed it. And "while we were still sinners, Christ died for us" (Rom. 5:8).

God's generous gift of forgiveness makes it possible to repent and in the culmination of that repentance, to experience greater joy. We saw in chapter 3 that receiving God's forgiveness requires accepting his condemnation of our sin and repenting of it. Now we'll pick up the rest of that process: the details of repentance. Here are six stages our repentance should include, along with some discussion of its counterfeits. Along the way, we'll see that our repentance almost always includes both a vertical dimension (our relationship to God) and a horizontal dimension (our relationship to people we've sinned against).[32]

1) *Conviction.* You have to be convinced by the Holy Spirit working through God's Word that you are guilty of sin. If you move too quickly past this point, you will spin in the cul-de-sac of self-deception because you will end up telling yourself and others that you are repenting of something that you aren't even convinced is wrong. Why do we do this? Often we do this because we love *looking* repentant more than we actually want to love God or others. We somehow know that repentance is expected and we want to show that we can meet the expectation.

Perhaps the most common counterfeit for conviction is worldly sorrow, a preoccupation with remorse for all the wrong reasons, such as the fear of consequences, falling short of one's own idealized self-image,[33] or looking bad in the eyes of others. As David Powlison says, "Remorse before the wrong eyes [one's own eyes or the eyes of others] never leads to change . . . it leads to counterfeits."[34] Our sin is always ultimately before God's eyes, and that's where conviction must start. God must be at the center of our attention; we should be concerned first and foremost about what our sin looks like in his eyes. That's what the Bible means when it says, "Godly sorrow brings repentance that leads to salvation and leaves no regret, but worldly sorrow brings death" (2 Cor. 7:10 NIV).

If we do not allow conviction to lead us to godly sorrow over our sin, then our pain-filled cries to God will degenerate into mere begging that he take away bad feelings instead of pleas for him to show his grace and mercy and change our hearts.

For Philip, conviction came only after he became desperate enough to seek the help of a discerning pastor. He'd already been in a twelve-step group for some time, and he did make some modest gains in restraining his behavior, but his marriage was still falling apart. As Philip went to meet the pastor, he still found his identity in his addiction (a perspective his twelve-step group seemed to support). It was a burden that he—and more importantly, his wife—would just have to bear; and it was stressing their marriage. Philip expected the pastor to understand this and comfort him under the weight of this burden.

But as they talked, the pastor detected Philip's blindness and worldly sorrow and instead confronted him with the reality that his habitual sin was voluntary slavery, a distortion of worship, a love of evil, and a collusion with the enemy to attack his wife and destroy their marriage. This was bigger than sexual desire, bigger than his self-misery over his many failures, and even bigger than his marriage; it was about God's glory and Philip's distorted worship. In that light, true conviction and godly grief finally swept over Philip; he had exchanged the glory of God for a lie.

2) *Confession.* You must agree with God about your sin and name it as he names it, specifically. We don't sin in general; we sin in specifics.[35] So we must confess as specifically as we sin. True confession consists in humbly telling the whole truth about our sin: *I was wrong, and God, you are right.* Counterfeits of confession, therefore, inevitably consist in pride and resistance to speaking the truth (see James 3:14).

You may, as Philip had done with his wife, confess *part* of your sin, enough to sound like a genuine confession, but you leave out significant details, leading another to believe half-truths. Half-truth telling is a form of deception.[36] Or suppose someone confronts you on your sin. You, in response, do not deny the sin outright; but you explain it, make a defense for it, or minimize it. Aaron did something like this when Moses confronted him about building the golden calf: "They gave me the gold; I just threw it into the fire, and out jumped this calf!" We must admit that our own hands have built the idols of our hearts. We have fashioned them with each indulgence of sin, with each lie we've believed and told, and with each look over the shoulder at Egypt.

Other counterfeits of confession show up in the ways we seek forgiveness from others. David Powlison describes several ways we mouth cheap, dishonest, or blame-shifting words in the name of confession and seeking the forgiveness of others. We say things like, "I'm sorry it bothered you so much"; or "I'm sorry if it hurt you, I didn't mean to"; or "Forgive me for reacting when you sinned against me."[37] These too are deceptions, sneaky ways of concealing what actually lives in the heart, which if put to words might sound like, "How about if I continue thinking and believing exactly the way I always have and you just deal with it. Oh, and I'll try to act better too, so you'll quit bugging me about it."

Counterfeit confessions pretend to reconcile, but in truth, they conceal a heart digging in its heels, unwilling to flee its idols. Even by my pointing out the bankruptcy of counterfeit confession, you may be tempted to merely tuck this away as a tip for your next confession: *Okay, remember never to say, "I'm sorry it bothered you." Say it right. Don't say it wrong.* But beware of your heart's desire to hide behind right-sounding words. God sees through the facade of those who "honor [him] with their lips, while their hearts are far from [him]" (Isa. 29:13). Confession is not about mouthing words but about telling the truth from a changing heart.

When Philip finally confessed the whole truth to his wife—no more half-truths—she was devastated. She didn't know if she could ever trust him again and didn't know whether she could remain in the marriage. His worst nightmares seemed to be coming true.

3) *Repentance.* To repent is to turn. The Israelites' sin and idolatry consisted in turning their hearts toward Egypt. Repentance consists in a heart turning back to God and away from Egypt (see 1 Thess. 1:9; 1 John 5:21). It's a total change of mind, a replacement of the false god that rules your life.[38] Because idolatry is essentially about what you *love*, repentance requires changing whom you love.[39] Repentance turns your whole heart—your whole person—to God in love, trust, and obedience instead of to idols. It trades hates and loves, hating the sin you once loved and loving the God you've hated by your sin. It trades the lie of idolatry for worship in spirit and truth.

We may promise to change; we may beg for another chance; we may even sustain a track record of improved behavior for a season, but we'll never know lasting change until we rip out the sin that's rooted in the deep idols of our hearts. In fact, it's not even enough to rip out the roots; something new must also be planted.

To recall the maxim of Puritan Thomas Chalmers: "The only way to dispossess [the heart] of an old affection, is by the expulsive power of a new one" (see Gal. 5:16–17).[40] Deep idols must be pushed out by deeper worship. This is nothing short of a miracle and is only possible by the work of the Holy Spirit in the heart of a Christian (Rom. 8:13).

Philip could not have made it through his wife's devastation over his confession had he not already begun to turn from the deep idols in his heart. The pastor had not only confronted Philip but had also patiently talked through Philip's life and helped him discover how he'd given himself to the deep idol of being accepted and had served that idol every time he deceived his wife about his porn addiction. Because Philip was finally willing to turn away from that idol, he could endure the pain of his wife's hurtful words and her initial threats of divorce while continuing to tell the truth and to hope in God to save their marriage.

4) *Restitution.* God's grace is free, but our sin takes its toll on others. Restitution is about giving back what you've stolen from others by your sin. Zacchaeus, the shady tax collector, repented and made restitution by giving half of what he owned to the poor, and by promising to restore fourfold to anyone whom he'd defrauded (Luke 19:1–10). He wasn't buying God's grace here; he was responding to it. Genuine repentance is eager to make things right with the people we've sinned against.

5) *Reconciliation.* Sin separates. It puts hostility between God and people, and it drives wedges in human relationships. God's forgiveness of sin makes peace and reconciliation possible: first with him and then with others (Rom. 5:11; 2 Cor. 5:18–19; Eph. 2:13–18; 4:3; James 3:18). Genuine repentance commits to the hard work of rebuilding relationships broken by sin. Reconciliation takes time, especially when trust has been shattered and wounds are deep. For Philip and his wife, it was a process that took place over years. It began when Philip's wife, through the help of some Christian friends, saw that because God in Christ had forgiven her in the midst of her own sin, she had the strength by the Holy Spirit to forgive Philip in the midst of his.

And by God's grace, Philip continued to walk in repentance. Because he now was assured of God's acceptance, he could live without his wife's. This freed him to pursue genuine reconciliation with her instead of manipulating her into accepting him on false pretenses. At the same time, if he ever stumbled or allowed himself to enter into temptation, he now grieved true godly grief; so when he sought his wife's forgiveness with an honest confession, it was with a humble acknowledgment of the terrible cost of his sin to her and to God.[41] As his heart changed toward God and his wife, he walked with increasing purity; her trust in him grew, and God mended their marriage.

6) *Rejoicing.* Like a thread running through each stage of this process or a light that begins to dawn early and grows to full brightness in the end, rejoicing is essential to repentance. As Tim Keller says, "Repentance without rejoicing will lead to despair."[42] Repentance is the step-by-step walking out of our redemption, the bit-by-bit turning of our hearts from the corruption of idolatry to the sweetness and rest in treasuring God above all.

Every so often, while driving the car, shopping, or fixing things around the house, the thought would cross Philip's mind, *I'm free! I don't feel anxious right now. There's no secret I'm hiding from my wife. What a relief. Thank you, Father, for freeing me.* His wife too, would have these thoughts of gratitude, and sometimes on their date nights over dinner they'd share their gratitude with each other. They delighted in the gift of intimacy and honesty in their marriage.

One of the clearest biblical examples of true repentance can be found in Psalm 51, King David's cry of repentance after being confronted by the prophet Nathan in his adultery with Bathsheba (2 Sam. 12:1–15). David is brutally honest about his own sinfulness: "For I *know* my transgressions, and my sin is ever before me" (Ps. 51:3). He knows that even though his sin brought great damage to many other people around him to whom he must make restitution, God is the most offended party: "Against you, you only, have I sinned" (v. 4). It is God with whom he must deal first and foremost; so this is where he focuses his attention, not on the consequences of his sin, not on finding someone to blame, not on extenuating circumstances, and not preoccupied with getting other people to think well of him again.

While David acknowledges God's holiness and righteous wrath, he also appeals to God's abundant mercy and steadfast love (Ps. 51:1, 4). He knows forgiveness and cleansing comes only by God's grace: God doesn't want sacrifices; he wants a broken spirit and a contrite heart (vv. 2, 16–17). Finally, David finds joy at end of his repentance: "Let the bones you have broken rejoice" (v. 8).

From the story of Philip and his wife, you might think the issue of pornography was the only sin between them—far from it. Once Philip's eyes opened to reality of sin and the joy of repentance, he saw that there were other areas of his life and in his marriage where repentance was required. His wife, too, learned that she was not merely a victim of Philip's sin; as hard as it was to face, even as badly as she'd been hurt by him, she also had her sin against him. Repentance, then, was not limited to a single issue in their marriage; it became a way of life. As Martin Luther famously said, "All of life is repentance."[43]

SCRIPTURE READING

- Exodus 32
- Psalm 51
- Romans 1:18–32

REDEMPTION

RECOMMENDED RESOURCES

Ferguson, Sinclair B. "Conviction of Sin." In *The Christian Life: A Doctrinal Introduction*, 38–46. 1981. Reprint, Edinburgh: Banner of Truth, 2009.

———. "True Repentance." In *The Christian Life: A Doctrinal Introduction*, 70–79. Reprint, Edinburgh: Banner of Truth, 2009.

Keller, Timothy. "All of Life Is Repentance." http://download.redeemer.com/pdf/learn/resources/All_of_Life_Is_Repentance-Keller.pdf.

———. *Counterfeit Gods: The Empty Promises of Money, Sex, and Power, and the Only Hope That Matters.* New York: Dutton, 2009. An excerpt of Keller's introduction can be found at http://thegospelcoalition.org/resources/a/counterfeit_gods.

———. "The Grand Demythologizer: The Gospel and Idolatry." Gospel Coalition 2009 National Conference. http://www.thegospelcoalition.org/resources/a/The-Grand-Demythologizer-The-Gospel-and-Idolatry.

———. "Smashing False Idols." Evangelists Conference 2007. http://www.evangelists-conference.org.uk/2007.php. This is a three-part lecture series that includes "Gospel Realization," "Gospel Communication," and "Gospel Incarnation" (http://thegospelcoalition.org/resources/author-index/a/Tim_Keller/scripture/jonah).

Powlison, David. "Idols of the Heart and 'Vanity Fair.'" *Journal of Biblical Counseling* 13 (Winter 1995): 40–41. Http://www.ccef.org/idols-heart-and-vanity-fair.

Welch, Edward T. *Addictions: A Banquet in the Grave.* Phillipsburg, NJ: P&R, 2001.

FOR REFLECTION AND DISCUSSION

1) What has God delivered you from that you continue to romanticize?

2) When struggling with a habitual sin that you hate, it can be confusing to understand—since you hate it—why you keep returning to it. It can be helpful to observe that the sin probably has some sort of payoff for you—some comfort, relief, power, reassurance, control, or something else. While you may find yourself hating the sin and broken over the side effects, your heart may be hooked by the payoff. So, in your situation, what's the payoff?

3) Which counterfeits of repentance do you find in your life?

4) Sometimes, we're stuck and do not change because we protect the very false belief that is the root of our sinful desires. What false belief are you protecting?

5) Using your responses to the previous two questions as clues to deep idols in your heart, what surface idols do you find in your life?

6) Considering your response to the previous question, what does your idolatry cost others around you?

7) With whom should your repentance continue in restitution and reconciliation? How will you approach this?

7

THE COVENANT-KEEPING GOD: OUR ONLY HOPE FOR LASTING CHANGE

Brooke was a normal kid, though she did make the occasional trip to the principal's office due to hyperactivity. But at the age of eleven, her life began a steep downhill spiral. She began getting in trouble at school for more serious offenses, and outside of school she started shoplifting. Her parents and teacher pressured her to reform, but this only accelerated her rebellion.

That summer, she began to sexually abuse members of her family. Given what she knew about sex at the time, she regarded such activity as taboo but relatively harmless play. It didn't last long, but she continued to spiral out of control in other ways.

She began sneaking out of the house to see friends. She broke into cars. She engaged in a sexual relationship with an adult man. Eventually, she ran away from home altogether, returning only when caught by the police after stealing a car. She was sent to a therapeutic boarding school.

There, Brooke met several men and women who had suffered sexual abuse as children. She was shocked to see how this had wrecked their lives, and she dreaded the consequences of her own actions as the full weight of what she had done came over her.

Others there cited various events that prompted their crimes: a violent boy who had an abusive father, a promiscuous girl who'd been raped, and many self-loathers who were unloved by their parents. But Brooke hadn't had a troubled life. She couldn't think of anything that might have influenced her bad behavior. So she concluded, "I am not like these people. They have reasons for their crimes, but I am simply evil. The evil that lurks in me is only waiting for the chance to abuse, corrupt, and destroy someone else. There are no reasons for it, and no boarding school therapy can stop it." Her secret crippled her with shame.

Brooke left boarding school feeling defiled and tainted and capable of tainting others. To protect herself and others from the filth within, she became obsessed with the cleanliness of her body and her environment and obsessively pursued impeccably moral behavior. She obsessed over germs, fearing that she would become dirty, and adopted cleaning rituals that gave her a sense of safety and control.

By the age of sixteen, Brooke was clinging to hope. She wanted personal change but every effort seemed to leave her worse off: she would bloody her hands from excessive cleaning, she was isolated from family and peers, and she lived every day with dread, yet still felt every bit as defiled and likely to defile another.

DISILLUSIONED

In the last chapter we saw how the Israelites' hearts turned toward Egypt in the making of the golden calf, the culmination of many smaller glances over the shoulder. The test of their faith in Moses' absence at the base of the mountain revealed their hearts' deeper affections. Despite God's relentless demonstration of faithfulness, they placed their hope in an idol. Worse yet, they committed their most rebellious act of treason only days after vowing faithfulness to God's covenant (Ex. 24:7).

But this wasn't the first time they'd lost faith. When Moses and Aaron first arrived in Egypt to announce that God had come to deliver the Israelites from slavery, they believed; shortly after, when Pharaoh retaliated by taking away the straw for their brick making, they lost faith. When God told them to paint blood on their doorposts, they believed and obeyed and were passed over; shortly after, when facing the Red Sea with the Egyptian army at their heels, they lost faith. But then God parted the waters, and on the far side, after seeing their enemy finally defeated, they sang, danced, and worshiped in faith; shortly after, they walked into a wilderness barren of food and water, and they lost faith. On the one hand, the Israelites' sin with the golden calf was their worst yet; on the other, it was only their most recent loss of faith.

Maybe you've found yourself in a similar situation. You've sinned, repented, and promised to obey. And then you do it again. You wonder, *Will I ever change?* The desperate heart that longs to be free from the bondage to sin needs some hope to hang onto. It needs some reassurance for the times when progress is painfully slow—or even moves backward. But with hope comes risk, because the higher the heart is lifted, the farther it can fall. The key is *where* do you place your hope? Too often, we set ourselves up for disappointment by hoping in all the wrong things.

Some hope to avoid indulging their sinful desires by simply busying themselves. Their diversions often include legitimate pursuits, such as working a job, spending time with friends, serving the community, or participating in church programs.

Others are not satisfied with turning a blind eye to their latent sinful desires. They hope to get to the bottom of things. They are more introspective, probing the self with reflective questions, and even subjecting themselves to the scrutiny of others, seeking to plumb the depths of their hearts and flush out all their idols. Certainly, as we saw in the last chapter, we should be asking what drives us, what we live for, what have we loved more than God—self-examination is crucial to repentance. But our mental powers are only so strong. Our insight goes only so deep.

What a heavy burden to carry if you think that the hope of change rises or falls on your ability to hunt down your idols. And how futile, for as Tim Keller says, "There's a certain sense in which we spend our entire lives thinking we've reached the bottom of our hearts and finding it is a false bottom."[1]

Some put their hope in Christian "accountability," thinking that as long as others are keeping an eye on them, they won't stray too far. Of course, it is essential to walk in the light of Christian community, confessing our sins to one another (see James 5:16; 1 John 1:7). But a wayward heart is never truly restrained by the accountability of others. If all that keeps you from sinning are watchful eyes, you won't last long. If you want to sin, you will.

Others scrap accountability altogether and just wait for the tide of sin's consequences to crash in on them and force change. Remember Christine from chapter 3? She thought, "When I hit rock bottom, I'll finally have the motivation I need to get my life back together." But Christine found that any time she thought she'd hit rock bottom, she could always sink a little deeper. The fact is that there is no rock bottom, but only a free fall into the bottomless pit of sin. The only way up is to reach out in faith to take God's rescuing hand.

Some anticipate the change that a new season of life will bring, believing that something inherent in that season will restrain their sinful desires. So a single man thinks he'll stop using pornography when he's married because he would never want to hurt his wife. Or a single woman thinks that when she's married, she'll stop flirting. The variations on this theme are nearly endless: *When I become a parent . . . When I find the right man . . . When I am in ministry . . . When I make more money . . . When I finish school . . . When I grow up . . .*

Some hope to prove themselves against insecurities that linger long after abuse by achieving success in sports, academics, a career, or even in ministry. Some hope that "true love" in a romantic relationship or being taken under the wing of a nurturing mentor will soothe the ache of their deep longing for acceptance and salve the wounds of rejection inflicted by neglecters and betrayers and finally fortify their self-esteem.

But there is no solid foundation among these false hopes. Each gives way as we grow tired, depressed, or lonely, or as others—mere humans—fail us. What is common among these false hopes is that they have nothing to do with who God is, or what change he has promised to work in us. Every one of them is an effort to trust in something or someone else. So it's not so hard to identify with the fickle faith of the Israelites. The question we now face is, what hope ensures change?

GOD, REVEALED

Most of the Israelites had a near miss with death by wrath that day. If Moses had not interceded for them, they would have all died. Commentators point out something noteworthy about Moses' character in his intercession. Moses had himself been on a journey of faith. The last time he'd spoken with God on this mountain was at the burning bush, and at the time he certainly wasn't a model of faith. God called him there to return to Egypt with the message of deliverance.

Moses responded with fear and unbelief. He said, "Who am I that I should go?" (Ex. 3:11). God reassured him, "I will be with you" (v. 12). Still, Moses resisted, asking how he could possibly prove to the Israelites that God had sent him. How could he speak to them at all as a man "slow of speech and tongue?" (v. 13; 4:10). God replied firmly and patiently, declaring his name, his character, and showing his might: "I AM WHO I AM. . . . Say to this people of Israel, 'I AM has sent me to you.' . . . 'The LORD, the God of your fathers, the God of Abraham, the God of Isaac, and the God of Jacob" (Ex. 3:14–15).

Then the Lord performed miracles right before Moses' eyes, turning his staff into a snake, and then making his hand leprous and suddenly healing it (Ex. 4:2–7). He reassured Moses once again, "I will be your mouth and teach you what you shall speak" (v. 12). But Moses, still unconvinced, pleaded: "Oh, my LORD, please send someone else" (v. 13). After contending for several rounds with Moses' unbelief, God finally became angry with him (v. 14). Yet even then, rather than consuming Moses in wrath, God sent Moses' brother Aaron, the better speaker, to go with him.

In Moses' intercession for the Israelites, he, in effect, appealed to the same qualities in God—his mercy and patience—that God had shown him in his own stubbornness. Moses had changed. He now believed God. He believed God's promises. He knew God's character, and with the resulting confidence, he made his appeal.

But Moses pressed even further. After God relented from destroying the Israelites and then again from abandoning them in the wilderness,[2] Moses made this audacious request: "Please show me your glory." Amazingly, God said yes. But he took measures to protect Moses from such a grand revelation of holiness, "for man shall not see me and live" (Ex. 33:20). God hid Moses in the cleft of a rock and allowed Moses to see only his back (vv. 21–23). No one else was permitted to come near (Ex. 34:3).

There, Moses witnessed the grandest display of God's glory yet, not so much in what he saw but in what he heard:

> The LORD passed before him and proclaimed, "The LORD, the LORD, a God merciful and gracious, slow to anger, and abounding in steadfast love and faithfulness, keeping steadfast love for thousands, forgiving iniquity and transgression and sin, but who will by no means clear the guilty, visiting the iniquity of the fathers on the children and the children's children, to the third and the fourth generation." (Ex. 34:6–7)

These words, God's revelation of himself, have echoed through the praises of his people ever since, and they always will. This is who God *is*.[3]

The Lord is compassionate. The Hebrew word for *merciful* that God applied to himself here "describes a deep love rooted in some natural bond, usually that of a superior being (God) for an inferior being (a human),"[4] or "a deep and tender feeling of compassion, such as is aroused by the sight of weakness or suffering in those that are dear to us or need our help."[5] Yahweh is bonded to Israel like a Father to his children, so says Psalm 103:13 where the same word appears: "As a father shows *compassion* to his children, so the LORD shows *compassion* to those who fear him." It was no doubt this compassion that stirred deeply in God when he heard the cries of the slaves in Egypt and promised to deliver them, the same compassion that moved him to provide a substitute for them in the Passover; for because he is compassionate, he is also forgiving.[6]

The Lord is gracious. The Hebrew word for *gracious* here "depicts a heartfelt response by someone who has something to give to one who has a need . . . but is undeserving."[7] It is a picture of a strong person helping a weak one. We get a sense of God's gracious strength at the burning bush when he reassured the weak, fearful, and undeserving Moses: "I will be *with* you. I will speak *for* you." Elsewhere in Scripture, we see that, because God is gracious, he will not turn away from the repentant (2 Chron. 30:9), nor will he forsake his people, however rebellious they are (Neh. 9:17, 31).

The Lord is slow to anger. He is patient, even when our sin warrants his righteous anger.[8] The expression in the original language includes a word for "long" and a word for "nose." "In Hebrew, the nose is associated with anger, apparently because when a person is angry, his or her face and nose may involuntarily redden and appear to 'burn.'"[9] God's face does not redden quickly; he looks kindly upon his wayward children, allowing plenty of time for their repentance.[10] So when he does finally show his anger, it is not impulsive or unjust; it chastens the obstinate unrepentant who refuse his kindness. We have seen at the burning bush how patient God was with Moses. Only after Moses' *fifth* rebuttal did God's anger burn (Ex. 4:14; cf. 3:10–4:13); and even then, he responded graciously, bringing to Moses a helper, his brother Aaron.

The Lord abounds in steadfast love. The Hebrew word *hesed* describes the "consistent, ever-faithful, relentless, constantly pursuing, lavish, extravagant, unrestrained, one-way love of God."[11] One of the most significant words in the Bible, *hesed*, summarizes the entire history of God's covenantal relationship with Israel.[12] It is God's "undeserved, selective affection by which he binds himself to his people."[13] Celebrating the Lord's victory for them at the Red Sea, the Israelites sang, "You have led in your *steadfast love* the people whom you have redeemed; you have guided them by your strength to your holy abode" (Ex. 15:13).

This abounding love will never be exhausted, because it is founded on God's infinitely gracious character (v. 13). So the psalmist rejoices, saying in essence, "Your steadfast love, O Lord, better than life, extends to the heavens and endures forever. My lips will sing aloud of your steadfast love in the morning, and I will trust it forever" (see Pss. 36:5; 52:8; 59:16; 63:3; 136:1).[14]

The Lord is faithful. His word is dependable, trustworthy, and credible. By it, his people can come to know him, for his character never changes and his Word abides. So the psalmist prays: "Lead me in your truth and teach me. . . . All the paths of the LORD are steadfast love and faithfulness, for those who keep his covenant and his testimonies" (Ps. 25:5, 10).

We saw God's faithfulness even when his people lost faith under the worsening conditions of Egypt (Ex. 5:15–21). He reminded them again of who he is and what he has promised: "I have remembered my covenant. . . . And I will bring you out. . . . I will take you to be my people" (Ex. 6:5–7). The law he delivered from Mount Sinai was filled with wisdom and justice that, if followed faithfully, would bring healing and harmony to the people once beleaguered by the harsh law of Egypt.[15]

The Lord forgives. While he is slow to anger, the Lord is quick to forgive those who have turned away from him, broken their promises of faithfulness, and fallen short of his glory by their sin. As we saw in chapter 3 on the Passover, God forgives—at great cost to himself—and makes friends out of enemies.

The Lord is just. While the Lord is full of compassion and grace, slow to anger and quick to forgive, he does not allow unrepentant sinners to go unpunished; he does not "clear the guilty" (Ex. 34:7; Num. 14:18; Nah. 1:3). There always comes a day of reckoning. For some of the Israelites, perhaps those guiltiest of golden calf worship, that reckoning came with a sword and a plague, and thousands died.[16]

But God's just wrath came also to the Israelite's rescue when he executed judgment on the gods of Egypt and punished the oppressive and unrepentant Pharaoh.[17]

In summary, God's character, which he'd already proven by his redemptive works, he now proclaimed in words.[18] It was a promise to his people; not only had he been merciful, gracious, slow to anger, just, and abounding in steadfast love, but he would always be. After such a grand revelation of God's glory, what more could Moses do? "[He] quickly bowed his head toward the earth and worshiped" (Ex. 34:8).

BROOKE'S CONFUSION

In her early twenties Brooke became a Christian. She knew that by Jesus' death, she was forgiven of her sins. To her, that meant she'd been saved from hell, but she still needed to remember all she had done; she needed to know her place, not to forget who she really was. Other Christians spoke of joy in Christ, but this, she reasoned, was not for her, not while others were still suffering because of her sin. Though as a Christian she longed for close fellowship with God and his people, she resolved that she would not become a fraud by pretending to be someone she was not. Her sense of identity was still in the worst she'd ever done, so in shame, she kept her distance.

COVENANT RENEWAL—AGAIN AND AGAIN

At the burning bush, God not only remembered his covenant with Abraham, Isaac, and Jacob, but he also promised to act upon it to deliver his people (Ex. 2:24; 3:14–22). Words became actions. And now, after revealing his abounding steadfast love, he would prove it once again. At the Israelites' most ill-deserving moment, in the aftermath of their rebellion, God demonstrated the unfathomable depths of his mercy and grace and renewed once again the covenant his people had broken (Ex. 34:10–28). Implicit in that renewal was yet another call for God's people to be faithful to that covenant.

Yet their faithfulness was once again short-lived. In fact, this generation of Israelites never entered the Promised Land (the rest of their story can be found in Leviticus and Numbers). Through the remainder of their wilderness travels, despite the occasional high point of faith, on the whole they continued in their unbelief, and in the process, their hearts hardened toward their steadfast-loving God (Heb. 3:16–19).

By the time they finally came to the brink of the Promised Land, they would not go in for lack of faith that he would preserve them in battle against the land's hostile inhabitants.[19] This God, who had already proven his might to defeat their worst enemy in Egypt, the Israelites would not trust in battle against their next enemy. So embittered in unbelief were the Israelites after their two years in the wilderness that they threatened to oust Moses and elect a new leader to take them back to Egypt! (Num. 14:4). As a consequence, God refused to take that generation into the Promised Land after all; he made them wander in the wilderness until every last one of them dropped dead in the sand, except for a faithful few (v. 33). Their children, a generation later, he would finally bring into the land.

But every generation after had its own issues. The generation after the exodus still clung to their parents' idols from Egypt (Josh. 24:14). And they didn't dispossess the godless people of the land as God had commanded; instead, they settled in with them, intermarried and served their gods (Judg. 1:27–2:3; 2:11–15; 3:5–6).

Later generations, true to their family heritage, grumbled about God's leadership of the nation through prophets and judges. They demanded to have their own king like other nations around, and in so doing, rejected God's authority (1 Samuel 8). The Lord gave them what they wanted, and the reluctant Saul—who had to be dragged out of hiding—became their first king (1 Sam. 10:17–27).

After Saul failed, the nation enjoyed its brief glory days under kings David and Solomon, only to be followed by a long line of troubled king-ships. The history of Israel's kings, found in 1 and 2 Kings and 1 and 2 Chronicles, reads like a broken record: several bad kings, then a half-decent king, followed by several more bad kings—each one representing the heart of the nation, stumbling in and out of covenant faithfulness from one gen-eration to the next.

There was never a generation that managed to wipe the slate clean and get back on track. Over hundreds of years, they declined spiritually, further and further. Yet, because of God's compassion, because he is slow to anger, he waited patiently for them to change. He persistently called them through the prophets to repentance and faithfulness to the covenant. But they only mocked the prophets until, at last, "there was no remedy," and God judged the Israelites by dispossessing *them* of the land and sending them back into captivity (2 Chron. 36:15–21).

BROOKE'S FEAR OF FALLING

As a Christian, Brooke still lived every day feeling condemnation over past sin and paralyzed with anxiety over what she might do again. In her nightmares she found herself disposing of bodies she'd only just realized she'd murdered. Harming someone else was a mere breath away, and she wouldn't even notice until it was too late. Brooke feared that if she did not remain hyper-vigilant, constantly scouring her conscience, her sin would creep up on her, and she'd taint her victim at any moment.

Before becoming a Christian, Brooke had long honored a feeling, like a voice in her head that warned her (she thought) when she was about to do something bad. It was her conscience, she reasoned, and in her rebellious years, she must have suppressed it; but now, she would obey it without question as her fail-safe against wrongdoing. Now that she was a Christian, she assumed that this feeling was the Holy Spirit. She knew, after all, that he indwells believers and convicts them of sin. So she continued to honor this voice above all others.

A NEW COVENANT PROMISED

Even while the Israelites languished in their deserved Babylonian captivity, God remained steadfast to his covenant; he continued to pursue his people, calling them back to himself through the prophets. Ezekiel, one of those prophets, was perhaps the most scathing in his rebuke of the Israelites' unfaithfulness and the most hope-giving in his promise of renewal.

According to Ezekiel, Israel was a whore, a spiritual adulteress, who had time and time again run after other lovers (Ezek. 23:4–7, 11–18). He compared the Israelites to their ancestors, inflamed with lust for Egypt and its gods (vv. 8, 19–21). Once again they had corrupted themselves, like their forefathers who had built the golden calf, and the whole human race before the flood (v. 11; Gen. 6:11; Ex. 32:7).[20] Israel's history had proven that despite countless blessings, despite God's patience and steadfast pursuit for many generations, mankind could not remain faithful to God.

But God, once again, responded according to his steadfast love. He would renew the covenant yet again. Yet this time would be different, because the faithful God of mercy, grace, and abounding steadfast love would, in this new covenant, impart the seeds of his own character into the hearts of his people. He would remove their stubborn, unbelieving, hardened hearts of stone and replace them with hearts of flesh, tender and faithfully responsive to him. He would put his own spirit within them, and write his law on their hearts.

> I will sprinkle clean water on you, and you shall be clean from all your uncleannesses, and from all your idols I will cleanse you. And I will give you a new heart, and a new spirit I will put within you. And I will remove the heart of stone from your flesh and give you a heart of flesh. And I will put my Spirit within you, and cause you to walk in my statutes and be careful to obey my rules. You shall dwell in the land that I gave to your fathers, and you shall be my people, and I will be your God. (Ezek. 36:25–28)[21]

Sometime later, the Israelites returned to their homeland with this promise ringing in their hearts. They rebuilt their temple and resettled their land, hoping to see a complete renewal of their nation inside and out.[22] Yet that renewal was never quite complete; something was missing. The Old Testament ends with this deep longing for God's best promises to be fulfilled.

Then, many years later, in the small, insignificant town of Nazareth, an angel appeared to a teenage virgin named Mary and announced that she would give birth to one called Jesus, the Son of God born into human history—the fulfillment of every promise ever made to Israel. Mary knew the significance of this. She knew those promises by heart and how they were founded upon the unchanging character of God's steadfast love. So she sang:

> My soul magnifies the Lord,
>   and my spirit rejoices in God my Savior . . .
> his mercy is for those who fear him
>   from generation to generation. (Luke 1:46–47, 50)

Her song echoed many she'd sung since childhood, including this one:

REDEMPTION

The steadfast love of the LORD is from everlasting to everlasting on those
    who fear him,
        and his righteousness to children's children,
to those who keep his covenant. (Ps. 103:17–18)

Jesus would be the new and better Moses, the Redeemer of his people
and the Mediator of the promised new covenant (Matt. 26:28; Hebrews
8). He himself is the glorious revelation of God's abounding steadfast love,
full of grace and truth, and from him we have received grace upon grace
(John 1:14–18; cf. 14:9; Col. 1:15; Heb. 1:3).

The following passage in Titus presents Jesus as the very appearance
of God's lovingkindness, reminding us of God's steadfast love revealed to
Moses on the mountain. He appears to none other than we who are foolish
and wayward, reminding us of the adulterous Israelites in their deserved
captivity; he renews us and washes us by the Holy Spirit, just as God promised through Ezekiel to cleanse his people from uncleanness and idolatry
through the sprinkling of clean water:[23]

> For we ourselves were once foolish, disobedient, led astray, slaves to
> various passions and pleasures, passing our days in malice and envy,
> hated by others and hating one another. But when the goodness and
> loving kindness of God our Savior appeared, he saved us, not because
> of works done by us in righteousness, but according to his own mercy,
> by the washing of regeneration and renewal of the Holy Spirit, whom
> he poured out on us richly through Jesus Christ our Savior, so that being
> justified by his grace we might become heirs according to the hope of
> eternal life. (Titus 3:3–7)

We are not saved by our mere resolve to good behavior, as Brooke
had thought, but by the mercy of God, by his grace to renew us (see Eph.
2:4–8). Jesus not only forgives our sin, but he also cleanses us and gives
us new hearts by the Holy Spirit. This is *regeneration*—the new birth of
the Christian (see John 3:1–14).[24] "New birth happens," says John Piper,
"because Jesus came into the world as the kindness and love of God and
died for sins and rose again."[25] The new heart finally makes faithfulness to
God's covenant—the *new* covenant—possible.

The old heart was like stone—hard and unchanging—like the "stiff
necks" of the Israelites in the wilderness (Ex. 32:9). But the new heart is a

heart of flesh: tender and responsive in faith to God. The old heart loved sin, like the Israelites longing to return to Egypt; but the new heart longs for God alone. The old heart was alive to sin and dead to God; but the new heart is dead to sin and alive to God (Rom. 6:11). While the temptation and pull of sin is still ever present, the desires of the new heart are to please God; the Holy Spirit opposes the desires of the flesh and stirs up the believers' desires for God and for fruits of righteousness (Gal. 5:16–26). The new heart has been freed from captivity to sin and obeys God freely as an enjoyable act of worship (Rom. 6:17).

Sincere Christians may be puzzled at this point, wondering why they still fight against sinful desires if they have new hearts. We still fight against indwelling sin because though we are genuinely new, we are not yet totally new.[26] We still have some of the same tendencies of the Israelites in the wilderness, one minute determined to obey and the next minute falling into sin again. The difference is that through Christ's death and resurrection, there has been a decisive break with sin and entrance into a new life in the Spirit (Rom. 6:4). So in Romans, Paul can say, on the one hand, that we have already died to sin (v. 2; cf. vv. 1–14) and, on the other, that we must continually put sin to death by the Holy Spirit (Rom. 8:13).[27]

God changes us from the inside out, first, by giving us new hearts (regeneration) with new desires, and then he continues that work in us as we walk in faith by the Holy Spirit, changing us progressively to be more like Jesus (sanctification) (see Gal. 5:16; Col. 3:9–10). We won't be perfect in this life, yet our new birth—what God alone does for us—guarantees our final perfection. We who are new *will* be perfect in the end (1 John 3:2–3).[28]

So our hope of walking faithfully is not based on our own ability to keep promises to obey, but on God's unchanging character.[29] We can hope to walk faithfully because he constantly pursues us with steadfast love and changes us, beginning with a new heart.

BROOKE'S ADVOCATE

Brooke's "feeling," that dreaded affliction of conscience, was not the Holy Spirit at all; it was her enemy, the Accuser, seeking to enslave her under condemnation (Rev. 12:10). Yes, the Holy Spirit convicts of sin (John 16:8), but for Brooke, his loving pursuit had been drowned out by her fear of sin (see 1 John 4:18). She was not merely a passive victim in this—she *chose* to believe lies. In her desperate search for hope, she had, with the enemy's urging, entrusted herself to her own powers of introspection and behavior management. And, like all sin, this led her steadily toward death (Rom. 6:23; cf. 2 Cor. 7:10).

Brooke finally found hope, not in her ability to anticipate and avoid her every sinful inclination but in God's steadfast love to make her new heart live to him by the Spirit. As she came to walk in this freedom in Christ, this life in the Spirit, she was assured of Christ's cleansing and freed from condemnation (see 1 John 1:9). She came to see Jesus no longer as a judge who, from a distance, scrutinizes her every move, but as her Advocate[30] who comes near to bear God's wrath for her sin and rescue her from despair (1 John 2:1–2).[31]

MORBID INTROSPECTION

It is worth lingering here for a moment. We have seen in the last two chapters how subtle our sinful desires can be (chapter 5) and how deep the roots can go (chapter 6). We have seen that true repentance must be specific, a particular exchange of affections, from a love for sin to a love for God. In chapters 1 and 2 we saw how significantly our sufferings can influence us and put us in situations where we must call out to God for specific help in particular times of need. There are idols from which we must turn away— both on the surface of our behaviors and in the depths of our hearts—and hurts about which we must cry out. But in order to do either, we must know something about ourselves.

David Powlison warns of two equal and parallel dangers that we can fall into in the pursuit of such self-knowledge: *idol hunting*, the danger of being caught in the vortex of self-analysis, probing for the heart's lusts, peeling an onion whose layers are infinite; and *hurt hunting*, the endless obsession with one's sorrows, sufferings, and disappointments.[32] "The Bible," he says, "is about self-knowledge; it is about knowing yourself; but it locates that process of self-knowledge in a much wider and deeper context," namely the redemptive love of God.[33] Analysis alone never changes anything, and excessive self-analysis only leads to a paralysis of a faith, as if, until I understand myself, I can't truly pray, repent, change, or love. Self-analysis is not an end unto itself; it is meant to be a "doorway of grace" through which I come to know, love, need, trust, cry out to, and depend upon my God, and there, to obey, repent, and find purpose and joy.[34]

Our hope of lasting change is not to be found in idol hunting or hurt hunting, but in the steadfast love of God. Brooke's expertise in idol hunting had left her only addicted and hopeless in an endless cycle of self-analysis. Idols promise life but lead to death; they promise sight but lead to blindness. For Brooke, idolatrous self-knowledge had in fact blinded her to the promise of God's steadfast love. And despite all her self-knowledge, she did not know her new self in Christ. In fact, she is a new creation, free to live a new life in the Spirit with full assurance of God's love.

FAITH: THE NEW HEARTBEAT

This new life in the Spirit begins with a new heart and necessarily continues in faith, life-changing belief in the gospel of Jesus Christ, in his death and resurrection. As John Piper says, "My new birth does not take place without me believing. In believing we are acting out the new birth, we are breathing in the new life."[35] In other words, regeneration causes faith, which results in change, for regeneration is inseparable from faith and repentance.[36]

When you become entangled in habitual sins and addictions, "just stop it" just won't do. You may be able to exert your willpower for a short time, resisting urges to indulge your sinful desires. But trials and temptations always return to find you in a moment of weakness, often in the very moment of weakness where you have fallen to temptation hundreds or thousands of times before. To stand firm in that moment takes more than the chanting of Bible verses, more than willpower, more than disgust at the filthiness of the sin. For the Christian, these moments are tests of faith. Do you *really* believe God? Do you *really* trust him?

Unfortunately the word *faith* has become so commonplace as to be nearly emptied of any real meaning. In our day, politicians speak of "faith traditions," generally blurring all religions and turning faith into a political category. Perhaps more confusing is the use of the word *faith* as a substitute for actual faith, as if faith in faith itself were really something. Any number of popular songs and movies come to mind, such as the song that plays with the closing credits of *The Prince of Egypt*: "There can be miracles when you believe"—in general, apparently. It's no wonder, with such hollow notions of faith, that we should at times wonder, why isn't faith working? We need biblical faith—"living personal trust in Christ."[37] This faith, according to Sinclair Ferguson, consists in knowledge, assent, and trust in Christ.[38]

First is *knowledge*, not merely an intellectual knowledge but a deep *personal* knowledge, the kind that "brings us into immediate contact with God himself."[39] A friend of mine, reflecting on his past grief over the loss of his father, admitted that he'd clung to the idea that God is a father to the fatherless as a mere platitude for comfort instead of actually embracing his heavenly Father. Biblical faith centers on knowing a person, Jesus, not on platitudes.

Second is *assent*. While faith centers on intimate fellowship with God, it also includes believing certain truths about him. For example, the apostle Paul tells us that giving mental assent to the historical fact of Jesus' resurrection is so crucial that our faith is *futile* without it (1 Cor. 15:17). There is no such thing as faith in faith itself, only faith in one who actually rose from death and imparts resurrection life to his followers.

Third is *trust in Christ*, the heart of faith. Trusting in Jesus requires that you surrender every competing hope. For the Israelites, it was the call to abandon the worship of any other god and entrust their lives to the one true God (see Ex. 20:3). For the disciples Peter, James, and John, it meant surrendering their livelihoods as fishermen the moment after pulling in their most profitable catch ever and following Jesus (Luke 5:11). For each of us, it means trusting his promise of forgiveness and *not* working to try to pay off our own debt. It means trusting his cleansing and *not* hiding in shame (1 John 1:9). It means clinging to God's steadfast love, his grace upon grace to us in Jesus Christ, as our only hope, the only true remedy against idolatry.[40]

For Brooke, there are still times when she feels weak and discouraged, times when she sins, times when some long-overlooked pattern of sin stands out and demands attention. That familiar feeling is right there, like a voice over her shoulder, and if she gives ear to it, she is quickly overwhelmed by condemnation. Before, she would have assumed that her faith was failing, and she would have resorted to obsessive self-monitoring and introspection to kick it in gear. But now she is learning that "true faith takes its character and quality from [God] and not from itself."[41] This frees her to trust God to forgive her sin and to stop trying to do penance to pay him back and to cleanse her unrighteousness, to stop isolating herself for fear that she might contaminate someone, and to change her heart and to stop fearing that she will forever be on the brink of abusing another. Her new obedience flows from this genuine faith rooted in God's love.

God didn't "barely save" Brooke, technically sparing her from hell in the end but practically leaving her hopeless in the meantime. He has crowned her with his steadfast love (Ps. 103:4) and freed her to live a new life.

SCRIPTURE READING

- Exodus 34
- Psalm 136
- Ezekiel 36:22–27
- Ephesians 2:4–10
- 1 John 2:1–2; 3:1–3

RECOMMENDED RESOURCES

Ferguson, Sinclair B. *The Christian Life: A Doctrinal Introduction.* 1981. Reprint, Edinburgh: Banner of Truth, 2009. 47–69.

Piper, John. *Finally Alive.* Ross-Shire, UK: Christian Focus, 2009.

Powlison, David. "In the Last Analysis: Look Out for Introspection." 2007 Leadership Conference. Sovereign Grace Ministries. http://www.sovereigngracestore.com/ProductInfo.aspx?productid=A2250-03-51.

FOR REFLECTION AND DISCUSSION

1) When are you tempted to feel hopeless about change?
2) What false hopes for change have you relied upon: morbid introspection? Mere accountability? Expecting to hit rock bottom? Changing life seasons (e.g., "When I am married . . . ")? Others?
3) When you face your most desperate need for mercy and forgiveness because of your sin, how do you feel about approaching God? (See Heb. 4:16).

8

IS GOD YOUR PROMISED LAND?

God's presence is everything.

I grew up in a Christian home and walked with God from an early age. I have many fond memories growing up enjoying time with him on walks, bike rides, exploring the woods, wading in the river, singing in church services, playing the drums in a worship team, and studying my Bible and learning to teach it.

As an adult, I have sometimes known seasons of great discouragement and anxiety. For reasons I don't yet understand, I don't cry often (even at times I might like to), but lately, I have shed tears when I've strongly sensed God's presence and reassurance of his love and faithfulness to me. These experiences have been so powerful they've lifted me out of my distress and refueled my hope.

There are also experiences of absence, times when God does not feel near. It is perhaps more alarming to feel such absence when you have formerly known the bliss of drawing near, as is the case for one woman I know. For the past few years she has faced one trial after another, starting with marital strife, then an unexpected and complicated pregnancy, and then another debilitating pregnancy. Then, within weeks of the second birth, a severe physical injury inhibited her from taking care of her babies. Finally, when her body and spirit could hardly bear it, her husband admitted to years of secret porn use.

Those first few years of trial, she remained hopeful. She had the kind of story most pastors are glad to tell onstage as an inspiring testimony about God's sustaining goodness amidst suffering. But with this final blow—betrayal by her husband—she was disillusioned. The only way she could make sense of it all was to conclude that God must have abandoned her—and this left her feeling the worst pain yet.

God's presence sends us into the heights of joy—and sensing his absence is unbearable.

GOD'S PRESENCE IN EXODUS

The whole of God's story can be understood in terms of his presence. His original intimacy with creation is severed by sin, and he restores that intimacy through a plan of redemption.[1] As we might expect, then, Exodus—being the Bible's pattern for redemption—is unified by this same theme, God's presence with his people (cf. John 1).[2]

In the opening chapters of Exodus, God seems to be absent while Pharaoh's presence dominates and oppresses God's people (Ex. 1:1–7, 8–22).[3] When is it that they are finally saved? It is when God comes down to deliver them (Ex. 3:8)—when he makes his presence known. In other words, he saved them by becoming present.

After the Israelites left Egypt, God's presence remained with them in the pillars of cloud and fire that led them to Mount Sinai. Again at Sinai, where he ratified his covenant with Israel, he was present amidst thunder, smoke, and lighting.

From the mountain God revealed that his whole purpose in delivering them from Egypt had to do with his presence: "They shall know that I am the LORD their God, who brought them out of the land of Egypt *that I might dwell among them*. I am the LORD their God."[4]

Both the means and the end of Israel's redemption—everything about their purpose, identity, future, and freedom—could be understood in terms of God's presence.[5]

Throughout the remainder of the Israelites' journey from the mountain to the Promised Land, he would continue to make his presence known among them through the tabernacle. This "portable Sinai,"[6] would be the centerpiece of their lives, even occupying the physical center of their camp (Num. 2:1–34). It would be a visible sign of God's continuing favor as he dwelled among them, reassuring them by his nearness. In a sense, the tabernacle was as much the Israelites' destination as the Promised Land.

On the mountain, most of the words God spoke to Moses were instructions for building the tabernacle. And right in the middle of what would otherwise have been thirteen straight chapters about the tabernacle (Exodus

25–31; 35–40) comes the unwelcome intrusion of the golden calf (Exodus 32–34).[7] This is no accident, for it shows what the golden calf was: an alternative to God's presence.[8] Yet the calf was not the ordered beauty of a tabernacle designed by God himself, but a corrupt work of their own hands (cf. Rom. 1:25).

Their plan backfired. Not only did they fail to achieve the result they'd hoped for, but they also found out that God cannot be present among unrepentant sinners without judgment. Shouldn't they have known this? After all, what had happened to Egypt—the epicenter of sin—when God arrived? It was thrown into chaos and consumed by the plagues of God's judgment. In the final plague, the death of the firstborn, the firstborn died when God *passed through* the land of Egypt (Ex. 12:12).

God's first response to the Israelites' sin with the golden calf was to have Moses stand back while he consumed the people in his wrath (Ex. 32:10). Because of Moses' intercession and appeal to God's mercy, God spared them; yet this was not the end of the consequences. When it was time for Moses to set out from Sinai and lead the people toward the Promised Land, God said, "Go up to a land flowing with milk and honey; but I will not go up among you, lest I consume you on the way, for you are a stiff-necked people" (Ex. 33:3).

God had delivered his people so that he might dwell among them, but now, from the look of things, the entire mission was at risk.[9] It would seem that the only way God could keep from consuming them was to *not* be present among them,[10] because sinners cannot survive the presence of a holy God (Ex. 19:16–25; 24:2; 33:20).[11] The gravity of this "disastrous" consequence fell so heavily upon the people that they threw off their jewelry and mourned (33:4). This was no mere setback. It was the end of the road.[12] There really was no point in going on.

GODLESS HEAVENS

This moment in Exodus should stop you dead in your tracks. We are all forced to wrestle with the question, What am I striving for? The cold facts are that we tend to set our sights on godless promised lands, destinations that promise every good thing but God himself.

No doubt, you have some situation in your life that demands attention:

that enslaving addiction, fear, or wound, an unfulfilled longing to have children, or a marriage in crisis. You long for freedom. You know what it is to wander in the wilderness, and you are desperate to arrive at "home."

Heaven, prefigured by the Promised Land, is the true home of every Christian. But what do you imagine awaits your arrival there? John Piper asks:

> Would you be satisfied to go to heaven—have everybody there in your family that you want there, have all the health and restoration of your prime, and everything you disliked about yourself fixed, have every recreation you've ever dreamed available to you, and have infinite resources of money to spend—would you be satisfied . . . if God weren't there?[13]

If you were completely free from the urge to look at porn and were totally fulfilled emotionally, spiritually, relationally, and sexually, would you be satisfied without Jesus?

If you were finally assured that your friends, your spouse, and your pastor had your best interests at heart, loved you, and would never hurt you, would you be satisfied without Jesus?

Most Americans who have any concept of God never conceive that he is the central treasure and goal of life. In fact, 82 percent of them believe that the maxim "God helps those who help themselves" is a verse from the Bible.[14] He is there at most to help us get where we are going and to tell us how we should behave along the way. Some have called it *moralistic therapeutic deism*, described by the following beliefs that characterize most of the so-called Christianity in America today:

1) A god exists who created and orders the world and watches over human life on earth.
2) God wants people to be good, nice, and fair to each other, as taught in the Bible and by most world religions.
3) The central goal of life is to be happy and to feel good about oneself.
4) God does not need to be particularly involved in one's life except when God is needed to resolve a problem.
5) Good people go to heaven when they die.[15]

Such ambivalence stands in sharp contrast to the grief-stricken Israelites in the wilderness throwing off their jewelry and mourning at the thought that

God would not remain with them at the center of their lives because of their sin. Yet even the most Christian of Christians—those who know better (including myself, I'm afraid)—still tend to use God as a means to achieve their chosen ends of personal transformation. As Mark Galli warns:

> If you're a Christian mainly because you want to be changed, that's a problem. If you've given your life to God mostly because you are tired of yourself and want to be a different person—well, that may suggest you're merely using God to fix you. That's not faith. That's not love of God. That's love of self.[16]

Once, when I was a member of a small group—part of a week-long, twelve-hour-a-day training for leaders—my group confronted me *hard*. They felt like I'd been aloof, placing myself above them in self-righteousness. In my view, of course, they were wrong. But there seemed to be something in their warning that was worth chewing on. So I kept chewing—for a year.

Near the end of that year, I sat in a lecture taught by Winston Smith, and he said something like, "You are not the standard for others," and it hit me: that's what I'd been doing, seeing myself as the standard for others, looking down upon them from my supposed great height.[17] Furthermore, I had been using God to pursue personal transformation that I sometimes used as a self-justification to place myself further above others (in my private thoughts, at least). I had never realized any of this. With Winston's help and God's providential timing, this was forced to the forefront of my mind, and I was on my knees in conviction.

Here, near the end of a book that you probably picked up because you were seeking transformation and freedom, it may be hard to swallow the idea that such goals could be hollow. But here's the catch: they are only hollow when they are not filled with God. To put it differently, they are best enjoyed as gifts wrapped in the much larger and all-satisfying gift of being in God's presence, which is to say, the gift of God himself.

You see, we don't just get peace *from* God; God *is* our peace—he gives us himself (Rom. 15:33; 2 Cor. 13:11; Eph. 2:14; Phil. 4:9; 1 Thess. 5:23; 2 Thess. 3:16; Heb. 13:20).[18] We don't just get joy from God; he is our joy—he gives us himself. He is our hope, and he gives us himself (Rom. 15:13); our love, and he gives us himself (2 Cor. 13:11; 1 John 4:8, 10, 16).

Where do we find our freedom? "Where the Spirit of the Lord is, *there* is freedom" (2 Cor. 3:17). It is in the presence of God, beholding his glory in the face of Jesus Christ. That is where we are changed (2 Cor. 3:18; 4:6).

So it isn't that we should stop wanting freedom from addiction, healing for the wounds of our past, or repair for our broken relationships today. It is that these blessings all come to us in God's presence and lead us further into his presence. He is the greatest gift he gives.

GOD WITH MOSES

The blessing of God's presence—the very lifeblood of human existence—*this* is what was at stake for the Israelites when God said, "I will not go [with] you" (Ex. 33:3). Moses, however, continued to enjoy God's presence. He pitched a tent outside the camp and called it the "tent of meeting," a sort of alternate tabernacle.[19] There, God would meet with Moses and they would speak face-to-face like friends (Ex. 33:7, 9, 11).[20] Because of the golden calf incident, plans for the real tabernacle had been suspended, and because God would no longer dwell *among* the people, the tent had to be pitched outside the camp, *away* from them.

His presence, descending upon the tent in a pillar of cloud, was such an awesome spectacle that even from a distance, the people rose up, stood beside their tents, and gazed in wonder and worship (Ex. 33:8). But they had to stand back. They were permitted to seek the Lord's counsel only through Moses, who would encounter God on their behalf (v. 7).

In one of these encounters Moses pleaded for God to remain with the Israelites (vv. 12–13). God's response was to say (in effect): "I will remain with you, Moses, but I will not go with the people" (v. 14).[21] But Moses persisted in his plea for the people:

> [Moses] said to [God], "If your presence will not go with me, do not bring us up from here. For how shall it be known that I have found favor in your sight, I and your people? Is it not in your going with us, so that we are distinct, I and your people, from every other people on the face of the earth?" (vv. 15–16)

Moses was essentially saying: "What's the point of our going into the Promised Land if you aren't there? This whole exodus has been about restoring your people to your presence. That's what makes us who we are as a people. If you aren't with us, we have nothing. We have no other identity, no other purpose." He knew that the fate of the people hung on God's response. There was no plan B.

At last, God was satisfied with Moses' plea and he made a promise: "This very thing that you have spoken I will do, for you have found favor in my sight, and I know you by name" (v. 17). Why did God relent and agree to go with the people? Did it have *anything* to do with them? No. God remained with the people because of Moses, his friend and (crucial for the Israelites) the people's mediator.[22] Without the favorable mediation of Moses, they would have lost everything.

After God renewed his promise to remain with the Israelites and revealed his character ("The LORD, the LORD, merciful and gracious, abounding in steadfast love and faithfulness," Ex. 34:1–28), the building of the tabernacle resumed (Exodus 35–40). Not surprising, the people responded generously when Moses called for the collection of gold, silver, bronze, and other fine materials required for the building of God's tabernacle (Ex. 35:5–9, 20–29). What other response but grateful generosity would befit their having received the greatest gift imaginable? Six times in Exodus 35, we hear of the people's hearts being stirred or their spirits being moved. The giving, gathering, and construction of the tabernacle was a great celebration by a people who knew what a precious gift they'd been given in God's presence (vv. 5, 21, 22, 26, 29). After the sorrowful aftermath of the golden calf, this was a joyous time of restoration. And the people set their hearts and hands to it with great eagerness.

GOD WITH US

What no one yet expected is that the intimate promise of *God with us* held an even greater, more personal fulfillment in the ages to come. His protection and grace would come embodied in another person whom he would favor and know by name, Immanuel, *God with us*.[23] Jesus was born Immanuel, God with us, in human form (Matt. 1:22–23). The eternal Son of God—the Word who was with God at creation—was now with us. He took on flesh to dwell among us (John 1:1, 14).[24] Jesus embodies all the mercy, grace, peace, joy, and steadfast love that abounds from God's character and anchors his promises. "Jesus fulfills the purpose for which the tabernacle was built."[25]

Jesus is also our mediator, making it possible for us to know God's presence, like Moses mediating God's presence to the Israelites (1 Tim. 2:5). Yet, far surpassing Moses, the covenant promises Jesus binds to those who trust him are greater than those made to the Israelites in the wilderness (Heb. 3:1–6; 8:6). He makes peace between us and God, and gives us access to God's presence. Now, we may confidently draw near to the throne of grace any time we need his grace and mercy (Rom. 5:2; Eph. 2:18; 3:12; Heb. 4:16).[26] Hear this: "Let us then with confidence draw near to the throne of grace, that we may receive mercy and find grace to help in time of need" (Heb. 4:16).

What is the throne of grace but the very presence of God? This passage recalls the Most Holy Place in the tabernacle where only one person once per year ever "drew near." The high priest approached only after elaborate preparations, including cleansing sacrifices and the donning of specially designed garments (Lev. 16:2–34; cf. Exodus 28). He then prepared coals to burn incense, producing smoke that would cover the mercy seat. Why? *So that he wouldn't die* (Lev. 16:12–13).

What compares with the breathtaking experience of drawing near to such an exceptionally dangerous blessing as God's presence?[27] Imagine you're at the Grand Canyon, gazing into its vast grandeur, feeling swallowed up by its immensity. Now imagine walking right up to the edge to get a closer look and leaning over a sheer cliff that falls away over a mile deep. Do you feel safe to draw so near? For your foot to slip in that moment would mean the end.[28]

This is perhaps similar to the exhilarating terror that the high priest would have felt in the Most Holy Place. He survived only when he followed the very precise instructions he'd been given (which some failed to do, and died; Lev. 16:1; cf. 10:1–2). Hebrews says that because Jesus is our great high priest, our mediator, we can draw near with confidence and experience the greatness of God. It is as if we stand at the edge of the Grand Canyon with full assurance that Jesus holds us fast, that we might take in the breathtaking view without fear of falling.

As if that were not enough blessing—far more than the Israelites ever knew—God has done even more to make his presence known to his children. He has sent his Holy Spirit to dwell within those who are in Christ. We have become the tabernacle where God dwells by his Spirit (1 Cor. 3:16–17; cf. Rom. 8:10). He could not be nearer, and he will never be farther away, for he will never forsake us, and nothing can separate us from his love (Rom. 8:38–39; Heb. 13:5).

Going even further, we also await the hope of the new creation when God will dwell with us directly—no temple, no tabernacle and no walls. There will be just the boundless presence of God, the ultimate eternal blessing:

> And I heard a loud voice from the throne saying, "Behold, *the dwelling place of God is with man. He will dwell with them*, and they will be his people, and God himself will be with them as their God. He will wipe away every tear from their eyes, and death shall be no more, neither shall there be mourning, nor crying, nor pain anymore, for the former things have passed away." (Rev. 21:3–4)

So significant and satisfying is this finale in God's story that Graeme Goldsworthy says:

> This one verse [Rev. 21:3] could be said to sum up and to contain the entire message of the Bible. The whole of the history of the covenant and of redemption lies behind this glorious affirmation. Every aspect of the hope of Israel . . . is woven into this one simple and yet profound statement: the *dwelling of God is with men*.[29]

ENCOUNTERING GOD

We have seen how God's story—past, present, and future—is all about making his presence known. He has worked his mighty deeds time and again to deliver his people and make it possible for them to be restored to his presence. In Christ, he has forever made his home with humankind. But how do we engage with this truth in *our* lives? Sure, he has shown up in history—and the new creation holds an even greater future—but how does he show up in our struggles today? And how do we experience his presence when he does?

The Psalms invite us to just such a personal, present encounter with the living God of history.[30] Listen to David's encounter with God in Psalm

16: "In your presence there is fullness of joy; at your right hand are pleasures forevermore" (v. 11). What are the vast joys and pleasures he finds there? In this psalm he enjoys protection and refuge; savoring all good things; delighting in an inheritance from God; finding counsel, wisdom, and guidance; and assurance of his final destination in God's presence (vv. 1–2, 5–8, 10–11).

Or consider the anticipation of the worshiper in Psalm 84, making his pilgrimage to the temple, the place of God's presence:[31] "My soul longs, yes, faints for the courts of the LORD; my heart and flesh sing for joy to the living God" (v. 2). He remembers how good it is to be in God's presence, where he bursts out in song from the depths of his whole being. That memory and his anticipation of his next encounter sustain him in his long journey through arid lands; yet even before he reaches his destination, he finds the Lord strengthening him and quenching his thirst, as if the Lord comes out to meet him on his way home (vv. 5–7). Finally, in God's presence—where even one day is better than a thousand anywhere else—he finds blessing, and favor, and honor (vv. 4, 10–12).

In Psalm 131 David has calmed and quieted his soul in God's presence; there he rests, free of the noise and nag of high-minded preoccupations that stir anxiety. "Like a weaned child with its mother; like a weaned child is my soul within me" (v. 2). He is satisfied just to be near the all-satisfying God, asking for nothing more than what is naturally enjoyed in his presence, for in God lies all his hope, his peace, his wisdom, and fullness of joy (v. 3).[32]

So not only is the entire message of the Bible summarized by the truth that the dwelling place of God is with man, but the apex of our daily hope and happiness is delivered in the same promise—*God is with us.*[33]

WHAT ABOUT WHEN GOD DOESN'T FEEL NEAR?

So "the Lord is near," period (Phil. 4:5 NIV). This truth stands firm to ground a Christian's hope and confidence every minute of every day. It is true because God has made it true in Christ through the Holy Spirit, not because we perfected some spiritual disciplines. He promises that he will not leave us, and he has secured that promise in Christ and sealed it by the Holy Spirit. That's how we know he is near, no matter what.

Yet the fact is that Christians don't always experience the euphoria of peace and joy associated with being in God's presence. Why is that? The short answer is that we may not know. There just seem to be days that we sense God's absence rather than his presence, and we can't always put our finger on some suffering or some sin that might be the cause.

These times of apparent absence put our faith to the test. His presence is far more than the feeling of his presence; he is unchanging even if our feelings wax and wane. Will we believe what we know to be true, even when we don't feel it? For the Christian, God remains faithfully present, always. Even when we think our grip is slipping, he never lets go of his child's hand.

Faith—believing God is near—is what binds our hearts to him. And faith is most true to its nature when it continues in hope having nothing tangible to hold onto but the promise of a person who has already proven *I am near* (see Heb. 11:1).

Sensing God's Absence amidst Suffering

There are, however, times when our trust in God's presence is shaken by intense or prolonged suffering, as we saw in the opening story of the woman who had come to believe that after years of devastating trials, God had abandoned her to suffer alone.

When we suffer, God's presence holds the promise of *refuge*, a sanctuary, that place of peace amidst chaotic surroundings.[34] He is a very present help in our time of trouble, and he promises to be our strong tower where we can hide when dreaded enemies encroach or the earth beneath our feet seems to give way (Pss. 46:1–3; 61:3; Prov. 18:10). In those moments—and sometimes through year after year of such moments—our faith is tested. Will we believe that God is near and run to him for refuge? Or will the test of faith expose our latent unbelief as we grow anxious and run to some false refuge, as if God were not really our strong tower. In the words of David Powlison:

> When someone feels tempted to pack it in because they don't want the long hard fight, they are basically saying, "There is somewhere else where I'm going to find a better refuge and a better rest. Let me just go to the Caymans, let me just watch TV . . . " and somehow that is going to stand for rest for your souls, and it never does. . . . Any person who's laboring

167

. . . in a hard situation in life is going to go somewhere for rest, and you either go to the Lord who is our refuge—[a] refuge that is full of living water—or you turn to something that beckons and never delivers.[35]

We are meant to seek refuge in a storm, and the Lord is near. Is it not precisely when we *don't* feel him that we most need to cling to this truth? (Phil. 4:5–6). For us, as for the Israelites in the wilderness, there really is no plan B. When we run to false refuge, we abandon the only sure rest for our souls.

Sensing God's Absence amidst Sin

There are also times when we sense God's absence because we are content with the presence of sin in our lives, sin we are unwilling to confess or put to death. God said that he would not go into the Promised Land with the Israelites because if he were to remain near them in their sinful state, they would die. His holiness and wrath mean death to sin and sinners.

On the cross, Jesus died bearing the wrath of God for sinners. We don't die for our sin only, because, in Christ, we died *to* sin in him (Rom. 6:1–11). This is how we have come to have peace with God (Rom. 5:1). And that is the only reason God's presence can ever be a delight to a Christian. Otherwise, it would be terrifying and life-threatening. In this sense, we have been saved *by* God, *from God*.[36]

While in Christ we have already died to sin and we now have peace with God, indwelling sin remains. That is why Jesus calls his followers to *consider* themselves dead to sin and alive in him (Rom. 6:10–11). This is obedient faith: believing that we are dead to sin in Christ and therefore no longer enslaved to it, we exercise our freedom to live in obedience to him (vv. 6:6–8). We are free to put sin to death in our lives because Jesus already put it to death on the cross.[37]

But what if we don't do this? What if we don't declare war on sin and put it to death by the Spirit but instead we make peace with it? This is effectively to declare a preference for sin's presence over God's. God is never less present in a Christian's life, even when he sins, but if a Christian chooses hardhearted unbelief, if he makes peace with sin, he will not enjoy the peace of God's presence. The Christian who is content with the presence of sin should not be surprised to feel the absence of God's peace.

Kate was depressed and had cried every day for months. She groaned that God seemed so far from her. Kate had grown up in a Christian home and had vowed to keep her virginity; she wore a promise ring. But when her boyfriend—whom she thought she would marry—broke up with her, she sank. In her resulting loneliness and desperation, she succumbed to a one-night stand with some guy at a party. All she wanted was to be with her ex-boyfriend again. She couldn't get over his absence in her life. He was her golden calf, her substitute for the presence of God. The fact is that, given the chance, she would have run back to him and away from God. But since the boyfriend wouldn't have her and because she wouldn't put her sin to death to make way for God's presence, she lost both.

In my own life, God's presence has been both a severe warning against my habitual sin and the greatest reason to put that sin to death. For a number of years in college, I hid an addiction to Internet pornography. I hid behind religiosity—the outward appearance of morality and the trappings of Christian religion.[38] I also hid behind rigorous academics and long periods of time alone late at night. But I could not hide from the presence of God.

I remember that many times in those decisive moments—to click or not to click—I felt what seemed like the Holy Spirit tapping me on the shoulder. I knew better than this. I also knew what was better than this; the peace of God's presence was better than a rush from porn. But in that moment, I didn't believe it. I shrugged him off, and my body would chill as I reached a trembling hand for the mouse.

God was never less present with me. In fact, he was there convicting me of my sin. But it wasn't a good feeling; it was terrible because I traded the peace of God to make peace with sin. When I felt guilty afterward, I would cry out to God, "Why won't you take this from me? Don't you promise a way of escape?" (see 1 Cor. 10:13). The truth is that he *had* given me a way of escape—his presence—but I ignored him. Sure, there were lots of times that it felt like I was out of control—as if porn was choosing me—but now I see that it was only because I had willingly hardened my heart in unbelief so many times before. Yet still, he was there, my way of escape.

His presence, finally, was my rescue. Not because he finally came to rescue me—he had always been there—but because I finally believed that enjoying him is better than anything else. I believed it all the way into those decisive moments, all the way down to a mouse click. By the Spirit, I declared war on my sin and came out of hiding because I could no longer stand the self-inflicted pain of forsaking the joy of God's presence.[39]

There is a curious phrase in Psalm 16: "The lines have fallen for me in pleasant places" (v. 6). What does that mean? It is the language of land allotment or, more specifically, of Promised Land allotment. When the next generation of the Israelites finally made it into the Promised Land and God drove out their enemies, each tribe was allotted its portion of the Promised Land (Joshua 13–21). Here was the land they'd longed for all their lives, the land that they'd spoken of from generation to generation throughout their entire captivity in Egypt and their journey through the wilderness. It was a new Eden, a fertile land flowing with milk and honey, ready to be cultivated and enjoyed. They were finally home.

The psalmist speaks as one already in the Promised Land, enjoying the best it has to offer. And above it all, God himself is his greatest blessing: his portion, his inheritance, and everything he has that is good (Ps. 16:2, 5–6).

The book of Exodus ends with the glory of the Lord filling the tabernacle. God himself, the greatest portion of the Israelites' future Promised Land, had already come to them in the wilderness. And he has come near to you and me by his Holy Spirit. In him, we can already begin to enjoy the very best of what our future holds. God *is* our Promised Land.

SCRIPTURE READING

- Exodus 33
- Psalms 16 and 84
- 2 Corinthians 3:12–18
- Hebrews 4:14–16

FOR REFLECTION AND DISCUSSION

1) To what refuges do you run when you are hurting? Afraid of something threatening? Anxious about an uncertain future? Bored? Tired and wanting some relief?
2) Describe a time when you can recall strongly sensing the presence of God.
3) Is there some sin that you've made peace with that robs your enjoyment of God's presence?
4) What "promised land" are you tempted to get whether God is there or not?

EPILOGUE:
THE REDEEMER'S MISSION

God doesn't redeem you and me just so we can be happier all by ourselves; he is on a mission to make his name known to the whole world. We who have been redeemed are swept up into his story and sent out on his mission.

It was God's mission that was at stake when he sent plagues upon Pharaoh and Egypt, for he said to Pharaoh: "For this purpose I have raised you up, to show you my power, so that my name may be proclaimed in all the earth" (Ex. 9:16). Terence Fretheim comments, "Hence God's purposes in these events are not focused simply on the redemption of Israel. *God's purposes span the world.* God is acting in such a public way so that God's good news can be proclaimed to everyone (see Rom. 9:17)."[1]

God had his mission in mind when he made the covenant with Israel at Mount Sinai. He reminded them of their identity as his chosen people, his treasured possession, whom he had redeemed from slavery in Egypt. Then he called them to his mission: as a nation they would be his priests, making his presence known to the whole world:

> You yourselves have seen what I did to the Egyptians, and how I bore you on eagles' wings and brought you to myself. Now therefore, if you will indeed obey my voice and keep my covenant, you shall be my treasured possession among all peoples, for all the earth is mine; and you shall be to me a kingdom of priests and a holy nation. (Ex. 19:4–6)[2]

Everything about the life of Israel was to be an imitation of God: their attitudes, actions, relationships, commerce, possessions, sexuality—everything. The Ten Commandments and the rest of the laws given by God through Moses were expressions of God's good character and wisdom. By keeping them, the people would proclaim his name and display his greatness to a watching world:

> Keep them and do them [God's commands], for that will be your wisdom and your understanding in the sight of the peoples, who, when they hear all these statutes, will say, "Surely this great nation is a wise and under-standing people." For what great nation is there that has a god so near to it as the LORD our God is to us, whenever we call upon him? And what great nation is there, that has statutes and rules so righteous as all this law that I set before you today? (Deut. 4:6–8)

If your story of redemption stops at your healing or your freedom, then you do not yet have God's vision for redemption. If you are content to keep God's presence all to yourself, then you haven't been truly changed. He wants to do something in you, yes; but beyond that, he wants to do something through you.[3] He wants to make his name known.

"Let the redeemed of the LORD say so, whom he has redeemed from trouble" (Ps. 107:2). How will you proclaim the name of your Redeemer? Here are a few ways God calls us onto his mission.

First, *living holy lives that reflect his grace.* The New Testament picks up on the idea that God's redeemed people are his priests, making his name known in the world:

> But you are a chosen race, a royal priesthood, a holy nation, a people for his own possession, that you may proclaim the excellencies of him who called you out of darkness into his marvelous light. . . . Keep your conduct among the Gentiles honorable, so that when they speak against you as evildoers, they may see your good deeds and glorify God on the day of visitation. (1 Pet. 2:9, 12)

What in this passage motivates us to live holy lives? He has called us out of darkness and into his marvelous light. That is God's grace to us, not because of anything we've done but because he has called us his people and redeemed us. How could we not live by that grace for all to see and know who he is?

Second, *forgiving those who sin against us, especially within the body of Christ.* As Jesus wrapped up his ministry on earth and commissioned his disciples to make his name known, he told them this: "A new commandment I give to you, that you love one another: just as I have loved you, you also are to love one another. By this all people will know that you are my disciples, if you have love for one another" (John 13:34–35).

As we saw in chapter 3, Jesus shows his love for us in that while we were yet sinners, he died for us (Rom. 5:8). He loved us that much—while we were still his enemies. If we are to love others as he has loved us, then we must forgive those who sin against us. This expression of his love working through us out toward others shows that we belong to him; and by showing how great his love is, we make him known to the world.

Third, *approaching those we've sinned against in humble repentance.* Everything about us (in our flesh, that is) resists admitting when we're wrong, truly wrong, and in need of God's forgiveness and the forgiveness of others. It is pride that keeps us from it, pride that suppresses the knowledge of God and the Holy Spirit's conviction of our sin. But when we go to others in sorrow for our sin against them—for godly reasons, not selfish reasons—we, in a sense, step out of the way and let God be seen as the righteous one who loves to work "righteousness and justice for all who are oppressed" (Ps. 103:6). He loves those we've sinned against so much that he softens *our* hearts and makes us willing to repent and make things right with them. This is yet one more way that his love and goodness are made known to others.

Fourth, *incarnating the love of Christ to others.* To redeem you, Jesus descended deep into your darkness with his light. He left the comfort of heaven to reach you. How far will you stretch out of your comfort zone to reach those who don't yet know him? Everyone around you has been touched by evil; they are hurting and enslaved. If you've been redeemed by Jesus, you bear a message of hope that is unmatched by any therapy, medication, or support group the world has to offer. The only question is, how will you—the redeemed of the Lord—say so?

APPENDIX:
RELIGIOUS ADDICTION

Religious addiction is one of the most pernicious addictions of all. David Powlison makes the surprising claim that religion and addiction have much in common, and to make the point he offers this definition: *To addict is to bind, devote, or attach yourself as a servant, disciple or adherent of something.*[1] Both religion and addiction have to do with what you "wrap your life around" and to whom or what you surrender as your master. Religion in the good sense implies genuine devotion to God and love of neighbor (see James 1:26–27). But the practice of religion can be so distorted and counterfeited that it becomes religious addiction, which Powlison calls "religiosity."[2]

Religiosity is about the show, the "impression management," and the trappings of religion, but not its faith and certainly not its God. Like any other addiction, religiosity serves as an escape from reality. Are you devastated by the loss of a loved one? "God is sovereign," blurts the stoic religious addict, like a knee reflex, and by this he means, "Don't feel it; don't think about it; just detach yourself from it. Since God is sovereign, why should you bother?"

The religious addict escapes the reality of his own sin too. If he doesn't deny his sin altogether, he finds some way to justify himself, often by noticing how he's not as bad as the next guy. He's not like *those* heathen. He also justifies himself by the doing of and associating with religious stuff: serving, reading, teaching, praying, and church-going, along with adopting the lingo, aesthetic tastes, and moral lifestyle typical of other religious people. These are his "sacrifices" to gain his god's favor and retain his righteous standing. But he is as deceived and rebellious as the Israelites imitating orthodoxy through idolatry.[3] He is as much trapped in a fantasy world as Philip was in pornography.

According to Powlison, religious addictions are harder to break than addictions to cocaine or heroin because they are the hardest to see, and this blindness seems to be strongly reinforced by the authorities of church culture, certain Bible passages, personal experience, and even God himself.

In his *Religious Affections*, Jonathan Edwards lists many traits that are "no certain sign" of true faith, including:

- intense affections
- fluency, fervency, or abundance of religious speech
- spontaneous spiritual experiences
- a tendency for the words of Scripture to come to mind at just the right time
- showing love
- conviction and confession followed by comfort and joy
- great confidence as to the genuineness of the affections experienced.[4]

Edwards goes on and on, tearing away just about every sign you ever thought would be sure-fire evidence of genuine faith. His point isn't that any of these signs are bad. In fact, he's saying that when true faith is present, these signs will be also. The problem is that they can be counterfeited, and they often are. And because all idolatry is essentially deceptive, those who counterfeit them often don't realize it; they themselves, the religious addicts, are deceived.

BIBLIOGRAPHY

Allender, Dan B., and Tremper Longman III. *The Cry of the Soul: How Our Emotions Reveal Our Deepest Questions about God*. Colorado Springs: NavPress, 1994.

Bauer, W., F. W. Danker, W. F. Arndt, and F. W. Gingrich. *A Greek-English Lexicon of the New Testament and Other Early Christian Literature*. 3rd ed. Chicago: University of Chicago Press, 2000.

Beale, G. K. *We Become What We Worship: A Biblical Theology of Idolatry*. Downers Grove, IL: InterVarsity, 2008.

Cheong, Robert Kenneth. "Towards an Explicitly Theocentric Model of Forgiveness Based on God's Two-Fold Commandment to Love." PhD diss., Southern Baptist Theological Seminary, 2005.

Driscoll, Mark, and Gerry Breshears. *Death by Love: Letters from the Cross*. Wheaton, IL: Crossway, 2008.

Dumbrell, William J. *The Search for Order: Biblical Eschatology in Focus*. Eugene, OR: Wipf and Stock, 1994.

Elwell, Walter E. *Evangelical Dictionary of Theology*. 2nd ed. Grand Rapids, MI: Baker Academic, 1984.

Enns, Peter. *Exodus*. NIV Application Commentary. Grand Rapids, MI: Zondervan, 2000.

Ferguson, Sinclair B. *The Christian Life: A Doctrinal Introduction*. 1981. Reprint, Edinburgh: Banner of Truth, 2009.

Fretheim, Terence E. *Exodus*. Interpretation: A Bible Commentary for Teaching and Preaching. Louisville, KY: Westminster, 1991.

Goldsworthy, Graeme. *According to Plan: The Unfolding Revelation of God in the Bible*. Downers Grove, IL: InterVarsity 1991.

_____. *The Goldsworthy Trilogy*. Waynesboro, GA: Paternoster, 2000. Reprint, 2006.

Keller, Timothy. *Counterfeit Gods: The Empty Promises of Money, Sex, and Power, and the Only Hope That Matters*. New York: Dutton, 2009.

Lane, William L. *Hebrews 1–8*. World Biblical Commentary. Dallas: Word, 1991.

Lister, John Ryan. "'The Lord Your God Is in Your Midst': The Presence of God and the Means and End of Redemption." PhD diss., Southern Baptist Theological Seminary, 2010.

Longman, Tremper, III. and Daniel G. Reid. *God Is a Warrior*. Studies in Old Testament Biblical Theology. Grand Rapids, MI: Zondervan, 1995.

Mackay, John L. *Exodus*. A Mentor Commentary. Ross-Shire, UK: Mentor, 2001.

Morgan, Christopher W., and Robert A. Peterson. *Suffering and the Goodness of God*. Wheaton, IL: Crossway, 2008

Murray, John. *Redemption Accomplished and Applied*. Grand Rapids, MI: Eerdmans, 1955.

Owen, John. *Overcoming Sin and Temptation*. Edited by Kelly M. Kapic and Justin Taylor. Wheaton, IL: Crossway, 2006.

Piper, John. *Finally Alive*. Ross-Shire, UK: Christian Focus, 2009.

Plantinga, Cornelius. *Not the Way It's Supposed to Be: A Breviary of Sin*. Grand Rapids, MI: Eerdmans, 1995.

Powlison, David. *Seeing with New Eyes: Counseling and the Human Condition Through the Lens of Scripture*. Phillipsburg, NJ: P&R, 2003.

_____. *Speaking the Truth in Love*. Greensboro, NC: New Growth Press, 2005.

Sailhamer, John H. *The Pentateuch as Narrative*. Grand Rapids, MI: Zondervan, 1992.

Sarna, Nahum M. *Exploring Exodus: The Origins of Biblical Israel*. New York: Schocken, 1986.

Stuart, Douglas K. *Exodus*. New American Commentary 2. Nashville, TN: Broadman, 2006.

Ten Elshof, Gregg A. *I Told Me So: Self-Deception and the Christian Life*. Grand Rapids, MI: Eerdmans, 2009.

Tripp, Paul David. *Instruments in the Redeemer's Hands: People in Need of Change Helping People in Need of Change*. Phillipsburg, NJ: P&R, 2002.

Volf, Miroslav. *Free of Charge: Giving and Forgiving in a Culture Stripped of Grace*. Grand Rapids, MI: Zondervan, 2005.

Welch, Edward T. *Addictions: A Banquet in the Grave, Finding Hope in the Power of the Gospel*. Phillipsburg, NJ P&R, 2001.

_____. *Blame It on the Brain: Distinguishing Chemical Imbalances, Brain Disorders, and Disobedience*. Phillipsburg, NJ: P&R, 1998.

_____. *When People Are Big and God Is Small: Overcoming Peer Pressure, Codependency, and the Fear of Man*. Phillipsburg, NJ: P&R, 1997.

Wenham, Gordon J. *The Book of Leviticus*. New International Commentary of the Old Testament. Grand Rapids, MI: Eerdmans, 1979.

Wright, Christopher J. H. *Knowing Jesus through the Old Testament*. Downers Grove, IL: InterVarsity, 1992.

_____. *The Mission of God: Unlocking the Bible's Grand Narrative*. Downers Grove, IL: InterVarsity, 2006.

Wright, N. T. *Evil and the Justice of God*. Downers Grove, IL: InterVarsity, 2006.

NOTES

PREFACE

1. "Redemption Groups" and "Redemption Group" are trademarks and may only be used under a licensing agreement. The Redemption Group Network helps churches develop and license Redemption Groups. See www.redemptiongroups.com for more information.

2. Diane Langberg, *Power Dynamics*, www.dianelangberg.com.

INTRODUCTION

1. The story as it's told here is an adaptation of Joseph's story. The actual account can be found in Genesis 37 and 39.

2. Paul David Tripp, *Instruments in the Redeemer's Hands: People in Need of Change Helping People in Need of Change* (Phillipsburg, NJ: P&R, 2002), 41.

3. Ibid., emphasis original.

4. G. Abel, J. Becker, et al., "Self-Reported Sex Crimes on Nonincarcerated Paraphiliacs," *Journal of Interpersonal Violence* 2 (1987): 3–25. See http://www.darkness2light.org/KnowAbout/statistics_2.asp (accessed November 6, 2009).

5. Centers for Disease Control and Prevention, "Adverse Childhood Experiences Study," http://www.cdc.gov/nccdphp/ace/prevalence.htm (accessed January 1, 2010).

6. Ibid.

7. David Powlison, "Broken through Child Abuse," Hope for Broken Relationships, CCEF Annual Conference 2006, http://ccef.org/broken-through-child-abuse (accessed December 14, 2009).

8. Ibid.

9. Jessica Ravitz, "Rape Victims Offer Advice to Today's College Women," CNN.com, December 15, 2009, http://www.cnn.com/2009/LIVING/12/15/sexual.assaults.college.campuses/index.html (accessed January 1, 2010).

10. John F. Bettler, "Counseling and the Problem of the Past," *Journal of Biblical Counseling* 7 (Winter 1994): 10; emphasis original.

11. Powlison, "Broken through Child Abuse."

12. Ibid.

13. "Statistics on Pornography, Sexual Addiction and Online Perpetrators," SafeFamilies.org, http://www.safefamilies.org/sfStats.php (accessed January 1, 2010).

14. Focus on the Family poll, October 1, 2003, cited in ibid.

15. Jerry Ropelato, "Internet Pornography Statistics," *Top Ten Reviews*, http://internet-filter-review.toptenreviews.com/internet-pornography-statistics.html (accessed August 9, 2010).

16. "Alcoholism Facts," http://www.learn-about-alcoholism.com/alcoholism-facts.html (accessed December 11, 2009).

17. U.S. Department of Justice, Office of Justice Programs, Bureau of Justice Statistics, "Drug and Crime Facts: Drug Use," http://www.ojp.usdoj.gov/bjs/dcf/du.htm (accessed December 11, 2009).

18. "Addiction Types," http://www.myaddiction.com/addiction_categories.html (accessed November 6, 2009). This list is cited for illustrative purposes, not as a recommended resource for gaining a biblical understanding of addiction.

19. "Treatment Programs for Drug or Alcohol Addiction," Shick Shadel Hospital, http://schickshadel.com/programs/treatment_programs_overview.php (accessed November 6, 2009).

By calling into question Shick Shadel's philosophy, I don't intend to discount the legitimate physiological components of addiction; rather, to comment that a strictly physiological and nonmoral view is short-sighted from a biblical perspective, where everything happens before the face of God and the (spiritual) heart is even more fundamental to human functioning than the brain. See Edward T. Welch, *Blame It on the Brain: Distinguishing Chemical Imbalances, Brain Disorders, and Disobedience* (Phillipsburg, NJ: P&R, 1998).

20. Ibid. The Shick Shadel Web site cites the *American Heritage Dictionary of the English Language*, 3rd ed., for its definition of addiction.

21. Patrick Carnes, *Out of the Shadows*, 3rd ed. (Center City, MN: Hazelden, 2001), 107–15.

22. I have also heard more positive stories from people going through Twelve Step groups.

23. *Abuse, addiction,* and *assorted troubles* are not intended to be technically precise categories. They arise more from pastoral counseling experience and reflect the frequency of occurrence of these issues among members in the counseling office—many have experienced abuse of some kind, many have experienced addiction of some kind, and then there are many other troubles of all kinds. So when I run Redemption Groups and write this book for use in those groups, these are the three audiences I have in mind.

24. "Alcoholism Facts," http://www.learn-about-alcoholism.com/alcoholism-facts.html (accessed December 11, 2009).

25. Mental Health America, "Factsheet: Eating Disorders," http://www.mentalhealth america.net/go/eating-disorders (accessed January 1, 2010).

26. National Eating Disorders Association, "General Information," http://www.nation-aleatingdisorders.org/information-resources/general-information.php#facts-statistics (accessed January 1, 2010).

27. Mental Health America, "Factsheet: Anxiety Disorders: What You Need to Know," http://www.mentalhealthamerica.net/go/information/get-info/anxiety-disorders/anxiety-disorders/anxiety-disorders-what-you-need-to-know (accessed January 1, 2010).

28. S.A.F.E. Alternatives, "FAQ," http://www.selfinjury.com/resources_faq.html (accessed January 1, 2010).

29. American Psychological Association, "Suicidal Thoughts among College Students More Common Than Expected," press release, August 17, 2008, http://www.apa.org/news/press/releases/2008/08/suicidal-thoughts.aspx (accessed January 1, 2010).

30. American Psychiatric Association, "Let's Talk Facts about Depression," http://healthy minds.org/Document-Library/Brochure-Library/Lets-Talk-Facts-Depression.aspx (accessed November 6, 2009).

31. Ibid.

32. Patrick F. Fagan and Robert E. Rector, "The Effects of Divorce on America," The Heritage Foundation, http://www.heritage.org/research/family/BG1373.cfm (accessed November 6, 2009).

33. Laurie Moison, "Infidelity: From Media to Cubicle, Many American Marriages Affected by Affairs," Divorce360.com, http://www.divorce360.com/divorce-articles/news/trends/adultery-in-the-mainstream.aspx.aspx?artid=300 (accessed November 6, 2009).

34. Special thanks to Bill Clem, who has taught me what it means to see my story within God's story, and whose idea it was to emphasize this concept early in our Redemption Group curriculum. He also drafted the original corresponding curriculum module that guided me in writing portions of this introduction.

35. Sexaholics Anonymous, "Why Stop Lusting," http://www.sa.org/whystopbroch.php (accessed November 6, 2009), 2.

36. Eric L. Johnson, *Foundations for Soul Care: A Christian Psychology Proposal* (Downers Grove, IL: InterVarsity, 2007), 11.

37. William J. Dumbrell, *The Search for Order: Biblical Eschatology in Focus* (Eugene, OR: Wipf and Stock, 2001), 9; emphasis added.

38. For a more comprehensive yet concise and readable survey of God's story see Vaughan Roberts, *God's Big Picture: Tracing the Story-Line of the Bible* (Downers Grove, IL: InterVarsity, 2003).

39. The one exception, of course, is Jesus Christ himself, the eternal Son of God who added to himself humanity.

40. By the way, we hit turbulence as I completed this sentence! I survived.

41. To explore the implications of *coram Deo* against the modern trend toward the "bio-psychologizing" of human life (explaining human beings purely in terms of biology) see David Powlison, "Biological Psychiatry," in *Seeing with New Eyes: Counseling and the Human Condition through the Lens of Scripture* (Phillipsburg, NJ: P&R, 2003), 239–51.

42. Thanks to Tim Keller for the idea that worship is about *what you live for*, from his plenary sessions at The Evangelist Conference 2007: Smashing False Idols, http://www.evangelists-conference.org.uk/2007.php (accessed July 2008).

43. See Cornelius Plantinga, *Not the Way It's Supposed to Be: A Breviary of Sin* (Grand Rapids, MI: Eerdmans, 1995), 10; Francis Brown, Samuel Rolles Driver, and Charles Augustus Briggs, *Enhanced Brown-Driver-Briggs Hebrew and English Lexicon*, electronic ed. (Oak Harbor, WA: Logos Research Systems, 2000), 1022.

44. Plantinga, *Not the Way*, 10.

45. Ibid.

46. Actually, just as God's story does not begin in Genesis, neither does the Serpent's. The serpent that was Satan was an angel created by God who later rebelled against God and was thrown down from heaven (Rev. 9:1, 12:9; Luke 10:18).

47. By "agnostic" here, I'm referring to any idea, mainly scientific ones, that either implicitly or explicitly do not depend on the knowledge of God.

48. The term "worship disorder" comes from Edward T. Welch, *Addictions: A Banquet in the Grave* (Phillipsburg, NJ, P&R, 2001).

49. Plantinga, *Not the Way*, 14. Plantinga defines evil as "any spoiling of shalom, whether physically (e.g., by disease), morally, spiritually, or otherwise." He defines sin as any moral and spiritual evil "for which some person (or group of persons) is to blame. In short, sin is culpable shalom-breaking."

50. Shalom is also spoiled by impersonal evils such as diseases, birth defects, or natural disasters. Plantinga, *Not the Way*, 14.

51. David Powlison warns against the bad habit of fragmenting the problem of evil, of overemphasizing either sin (evil I do), or suffering (evil that comes at me). Either fails to see the world as God sees it, and, as a consequence, we fail to comprehend our situations and ourselves. "Counseling through the Lens of Scripture," CCEF.org, http://ccef.org/counseling-through-lens-scripture (accessed January 1, 2010).

52. The "Gospel Gaps" in Timothy S. Lane and Paul David Tripp, *How People Change* (Greensboro, NC: New Growth Press, 2006) explore some of those solutions we tend toward (pp. 8–12).

53. It can also be partially due to simple unbelief and hardness of heart.

54. Really, the whole Bible tells God's story, which is the context of the good news of the gospel. Also, there is another story you have to know to grasp the significance of Jesus as your redemption—your own.

55. For a survey of biblical passages that show that the exodus is the prototype of redemption see Ex. 15:1–18; Deut. 7:8; 15:15; 2 Sam. 7:23; 1 Chron. 17:21; Isa. 51:10; and Mic. 6:4.

56. Christopher J. H. Wright, *The Mission of God: Unlocking the Bible's Grand Narrative* (Downers Grove, IL: InterVarsity, 2006), 265.

57. Christopher J. H. Wright, *Knowing Jesus through the Old Testament* (Downers Grove, IL: InterVarsity, 1992), 29.

58. Mark Driscoll and Gerry Breshears, *Death by Love: Letters from the Cross* (Wheaton, IL: Crossway, 2008), 61.

59. http://www.merriam-webster.com/dictionary/slave.

60. The idea of "voluntary slavery" comes from Welch, *Addictions*.

61. John Murray, *Redemption Accomplished and Applied* (Grand Rapids, MI: Eerdmans, 1985), 46–47.

62. Dumbrell, *The Search for Order*, 9.

63. Terrance E. Fretheim, *Exodus*, Interpretation: A Bible Commentary for Teaching and Preaching. (Louisville, KY: Westminster, 1991), 13–14. See also, Dumbrell, *The Search for Order*, 42; Noel Due, *Created for Worship: From Genesis to Revelation to You* (Ross-Shire, UK: Mentor, 2005), 73.

64. Meredith G. Kline, *God, Heaven, and Har Magedon: A Covenantal Tale of the Cosmos and Telos* (Eugene, OR: Wipf and Stock, 2006), 22.

65. In the firstfruits metaphor, because Christ, the firstfruits (of the harvest), rises first, the rest of the harvest (us) is sure to follow.

66. Anthony Hoekema, "The Reformed Perspective," in *Five Views on Sanctification*, ed. Stanley Gundry (Grand Rapids, MI: Zondervan, 1987), 76–77.

67. Graeme Goldsworthy, *According to Plan* (Downers Grove, IL: InterVarsity, 1991), 137.

68. G. K. Beale, *We Become What We Worship: A Biblical Theology of Idolatry* (Downers Grove, IL: InterVarsity, 2008), 76–78.

69. Thomas Chalmers, *The Expulsive Power of a New Affection*, http://www.monergism.com/Chalmers%2C%20Thomas%20-%20The%20Expulsive%20Power%20of%20a%20New%20Af.pdf (accessed January 17, 2010).

70. Thanks to James Noriega for this line.

CHAPTER 1: WHEN YOU SUFFER, GOD IS NEAR

1. "Haiti Earthquake of 2010," *New York Times*, http://www.nytimes.com/info/haiti-earthquake-2010/ (accessed January 17, 2010); "Haiti quake death toll may hit 200,000-minister," Reuters, http://www.alertnet.org/thenews/newsdesk/N15143632.htm (accessed January 18, 2010).

2. John L. Mackay, *Exodus: A Mentor Commentary* (Ross-Shire, UK: Mentor, 2001), 34.

3. "Pharaoh" is the title for the king of Egypt, not the name of a particular man. In Egyptian, it simply means "The Great House." Originally it referred to the royal palace, but eventually became synonymous with the ruler, like saying, "The White House," to refer to the administration of the president of the United States. Nahum M. Sarna, *Exploring Exodus: The Origins of Biblical Israel* (New York: Schocken, 1986), 18.

4. By "innocent" here, I mean that they were not suffering because of anything they did wrong. We'll see later in the story, though, even under their slavery, they were not innocent in the absolute sense of sinlessness.

5. Sarna, *Exploring Exodus*, 21.

6. Adolf Erman, *Life in Ancient Egypt* (New York: Dover, 1971), 433.

7. Peter Enns, *Exodus*, NIV Application Commentary (Grand Rapids, MI: Zondervan, 2000), 50–51.

8. John Feinberg helpfully distinguishes the *religious* problem of evil—an emotional problem—from the *philosophical* problem of evil—an intellectual problem. Feinberg himself tells of how he had written his doctoral dissertation and published a book on the problem of evil—he had the intellectual answers—and then tragedy struck his own family and none of those answers made any difference in how he felt. That is the so-called religious problem of evil. "A Journey in Suffering," in *Suffering and the Goodness of God*, ed. Christopher W. Morgan and Robert A. Peterson (Wheaton, IL: Crossway, 2008), 219.

9. Douglas K. Stuart, *Exodus.* New American Commentary 2 (Nashville, TN: Broadman, 2006), 103, 305–6.

10. "The idea seems to be that God took personal knowledge of, noticed, or regarded them. In other passages the verb *know* is similar in meaning to 'save' or 'show pity.'" Richard E. Averbeck, "Exodus 2:25," NET.

11. William Edgar, "Suffering and Oppression," in *Suffering and the Goodness of God*, 174.

12. Ibid., 175.

13. In his sermon "God So Loved the World, Part 2," May 10, 2009, John Piper shows how God's special covenant love for his people surpasses his more general love for all people, http://www.desiringgod.org/ResourceLibrary/Sermons/BySeries/86/3883_God_So_Loved_the_World_Part_2/ (accessed December 24, 2009).

14. David Powlison, "What If Your Father Didn't Love You?" in *Seeing with New Eyes: Counseling and the Human Condition Through the Lens of Scripture* (Phillipsburg, NJ: P&R, 2003), 171–81. Powlison empathizes with the plight of those whose fathers sinned against them, while challenging the popular solution of re-parenting. At the end, he offers in nine points, "a simple summary of the way to grow in the knowledge of God your Father even if your father sinned against you."

15. See Matt. 1:23 ("God with us"); Luke 10:22; John 10:30; 14:5–11; 15:9; 16:27; Rom. 5:5; 8:14; Eph 2:18; 1 John 1:2–3).

16. W. Bauer, F. W. Danker, W. F. Arndt, and F. W. Gingrich, *Greek-English Lexicon of the New Testament and Other Early Christian Literature*, 3d ed. (Chicago: University of Chicago Press. 2001), s.v. "ἀββα."

17. Michael R. Emlet, "When It Won't Go Away: A Biblical Response to Chronic Pain," *Journal of Biblical Counseling* 23 (Winter 2005): 25.

18. Tim Keller makes the point that while Jesus suffered great physical agony, there have been Christian martyrs who've suffered physical torments as bad or worse, even while maintaining greater composure than Jesus. But what made Jesus' suffering and death "qualitatively different from any other death" is that he not only faced physical agony but also—infinitely worse—separation from the Father, a loss beyond our comprehension. Keller says, "On the cross [Jesus] went beyond even the worst human suffering and experienced cosmic rejection and pain that exceeds ours as infinitely as his knowledge and power exceeds ours" (*The Reason for God: Belief in an Age of Skepticism* [New York: Dutton, 2008], 30).

CHAPTER 2: BRICKS WITHOUT STRAW

1. "Satan's first device to draw the soul into sin is, to present the bait [temptation]—and hide the hook" (Thomas Brooks, *Precious Remedies Against Satan's Devices* [1652; repr. Carlisle: Banner of Truth, 2000], 29–34).

2. Nahum M. Sarna, *Exploring Exodus: The Origins of Biblical Israel* (New York: Schocken, 1986), 22.

3. Ibid., 23.

4. Ibid.

5. Ibid. This comes from an ancient inscription.

6. James B. Pritchard, ed. *Ancient Near Eastern Texts Relating to the Old Testament* (repr. 1969; Princeton: Princeton University Press; New York: Dover, 1955), 433.

7. Thanks to James Noriega for this provocative question.

8. Richard E. Averbeck, "Exodus 5:22," NET.

9. See D. A. Carson, *Scandalous: The Cross and Resurrection of Jesus* (Wheaton, IL: Crossway, 2010), 32–37.

10. Jesus did learn obedience by what he suffered (Heb. 5:8)—and so can we—but that doesn't mean we should always infer that the purpose of our suffering is to teach us a lesson. We may never know the purpose, nor do we always need to know. Job, for example, suffered for entirely mysterious reasons, as far he ever knew. See Walter C. Kaiser Jr., "Eight Kinds of Suffering in the Old Testament," in *Suffering and the Goodness of God*, ed. Christopher W. Morgan and Robert A. Peterson (Wheaton, IL: Crossway, 2008), 65–78.

11. Cf. Acts 13:35. In Psalm 16:10, *Sheol* seems to mean "the grave." See W. A. Van Gemeren, "Sheol," *Evangelical Dictionary of Theology*, 2nd ed., ed. Walter A. Elwell (Grand Rapids, MI: Baker, 2001).

CHAPTER 3: THE PASSOVER

1. Douglas K. Stuart, *Exodus*, New American Commentary 2 (Nashville, TN: Broadman, 2006), 131–32. Stuart notes that Osiris was also identified as the god of the Nile, along with some other gods who were associated with the river's flood cycle.

2. John H. Sailhamer, *The Pentateuch as Narrative* (Grand Rapids, MI: Zondervan, 1992), 255.

3. See Ex. 7:22; 8:15, 19, 32; 9:7, 12, 34–35; 10:1, 20, 27; 11:10. By the sixth plague (9:12), we are clearly told not only that Pharaoh hardened his own heart but also that God hardened Pharaoh's heart. This hearkens back to what God had told Moses: on the one hand, Pharaoh would refuse to let the people go (i.e., it was his own will to resist; 3:19), and on the other hand, ultimately God would harden Pharaoh's heart (4:21). The question is often raised as to the fairness of this: How can God judge Pharaoh if God is the one who hardens Pharaoh's heart? It may help to see the heart-hardening process in its full context here. Pharaoh never acted against his own will; rather, his responses to the plagues showed that he consistently willed to resist God. In fact, in each new plague Pharaoh had an opportunity to change his mind; instead, he chose to harden further. The heart-hardening process shows both that God is ultimately sovereign over Egypt—even over the heart of its king—and that God did not violate Pharaoh's will in bringing about the occasions for his sinful heart to be further exposed and increasingly hardened. See also Peter Enns, *Exodus*, NIV Application Commentary (Grand Rapids, MI: Zondervan, 2000), 130–31; Stuart, *Exodus*, 146–150; Nahum M. Sarna, *Exploring Exodus: The Origins of Biblical Israel* (New York: Schocken, 1986), 63–65.

4. Sailhamer, *The Pentateuch as Narrative*, 257.

5. Thanks to Bill Clem for pointing out these assumptions we often bring to this story.

6. It's significant, though, that Exodus itself first presents the story as God's saving innocents from suffering; it's only later that the depth of their idolatry is revealed. God has compassion toward his suffering children, even while they also sin.

7. Steve Jeffery, Michael Ovey, Andrew Sach, *Pierced for Our Transgressions: Rediscovering the Glory of Penal Substitution* (Wheaton, IL: Crossway, 2007), 38; G. K. Beale, *We Become What We Worship: A Biblical Theology of Idolatry* (Downers Grove, IL: InterVarsity, 2008), 126.

8. David Powlison says that our sin compounds our suffering, resulting in an overall worse effect. "Second Big Arrow: Transaction Leads to Action," in Lecture 10, *Dynamics of Biblical Change*, Christian Counseling and Educational Foundation, Glenside, PA (2005).

9. I'm thankful to Bill Clem for this vivid illustration.

10. This is the theme of *ransom*—the price paid for freedom—that we first saw in the Introduction.

11. Enns, *Exodus*, 254–55.

12. Sarna, *Exploring Exodus*, 93–94.

13. Timothy Keller, *Counterfeit Gods: The Empty Promises of Money, Sex, and Power, and the Only Hope That Matters* (New York: Dutton, 2009), 9.

14. John L. Mackay, *Exodus*, Mentor Commentary (Ross-Shire, UK: Mentor, 2001), 206–7; Enns, *Exodus*, 247n7.

15. It is by grace through faith that we are saved; yet true faith always expresses itself in obedience. If we merely *hear* God's word but do not *do* it, we deceive ourselves and our faith is dead (James 1:22; 2:17).

16. The word *propitiation* in this passage refers to the "satisfaction or appeasement of God's wrath, turning it to favor." Thomas R. Schreiner, "Romans 3:25," in *ESV Study Bible*, ed. Wayne Grudem, et al. (Wheaton, IL: Crossway, 2008), 2163.

17. Miroslav Volf, *Free of Charge: Giving and Forgiving in a Culture Stripped of Grace* (Grand Rapids, MI: Zondervan, 2005), 130.

18. Ibid., 153.

19. See chapter 6 for a more comprehensive treatment of repentance.

20. To make such changes apart from faith in God would be mere moralism and self-righteousness (Phil. 3:4–9), and to claim to have faith but not work it out in actual obedience would be self-deception (James 1:22).

21. Tim Keller says, "Repentance without rejoicing will lead to despair" (*Counterfeit Gods*, 172).

22. Ibid., 149.

23. Ibid.

24. David Powlison, "First Big Arrow," in Lecture 10, *Dynamics of Biblical Change*.

25. Volf, *Free of Charge*, 154.

26. *Penance* is "an act of self-abasement, mortification, or devotion performed to show sorrow or repentance for sin," *Merriam-Webster's Collegiate Dictionary*, 11th ed. But we can't satisfy God by doing such works of penance. He does not delight in sacrifice but only in the broken and contrite heart that looks to him in faith for forgiveness (Ps. 51:1–2, 16–17).

27. Cf. Volf, *Free of Charge*, 152, 154.

28. Robert Kenneth Cheong, "Towards an Explicitly Theocentric Model of Forgiveness Based on God's Two-Fold Commandment to Love," PhD diss., Southern Baptist Theological Seminary (2005), 121; emphasis added. I owe much of my understanding of forgiveness to my friend Robert Cheong, whose dissertation, personal guidance, and wisdom gained from years practicing his model on the front lines of pastoral ministry have been invaluable to me. Because Robert's dissertation is unpublished, I have tried to footnote other published materials that tend to reflect similar views (as clearly as I can tell), namely, Volf's *Free of Charge*.

29. How can we ever view another person as an enemy, especially a friend or family member, without harboring ongoing bitterness? David Powlison distinguishes between objective and subjective senses of the word *enemy*. He claims that the Bible primarily uses the term objectively to refer to one who acts destructively and wrongs you. That person becomes an enemy with respect to the particular wrongdoing, not necessarily as a global assessment that the person is *your* enemy (subjectively) in every sense. To regard someone as an enemy in this objective sense is merely to make an honest assessment that he or she is treating you like an enemy. "Review of Last Lecture," in Lecture 11, *Dynamics of Biblical Change*.

30. "Gospel love" is love as expressed by God's love for us at the cross. This is how we are also to love others.

31. Cheong, "Towards an Explicitly Theocentric Model of Forgiveness."

32. Ibid., 24.

33. Leo Tolstoy, *The Complete Works*, in Russian, vol. 53 (Moscow: Terra, 1992), 197. Also related is the biblical idea of meekness, which John Piper says is "the power to absorb adversity and criticism without lashing back" ("Blessed Are the Meek," sermon, February 9, 1986, http://www.desiringgod.org/ResourceLibrary/Sermons/ByDate/1986/529_Blessed_Are_the_Meek [accessed February 26, 2010]). See Num. 12:1–3.

34. Volf, *Free of Charge*, 168.

35. Phil McGraw, "Dr. Phil's Ultimate Weight Loss Solution," *O, The Oprah Magazine*, October 15, 2003, http://www.oprah.com/omagazine/Dr-Phil-The-Ultimate-Weight-Loss-Solution/8 (accessed January 22, 2010).

36. Cheong, "Towards an Explicitly Theocentric Model of Forgiveness," 34–35.

37. What we'll find is that while our forgiveness should be similar to God's, there are some things about who God is that makes his forgiveness special, ultimate, and final in ways that ours could never be, so our forgiveness will not always be exactly like his.

38. Volf, *Free of Charge*, 145–51, 200.

39. There may be times, as we'll see below, that our desire for reconciliation may be thwarted by the other person's unrepentance, especially when being near that person would be dangerous.

40. Volf, *Free of Charge*, 203.

CHAPTER 4: CROSSING THE RED SEA

1. Dan B. Allender and Tremper Longman, *The Cry of the Soul: How Our Emotions Reveal Our Deepest Questions about God* (Colorado Springs, CO: NavPress, 1994), 195.

2. June P. Tangney and Ronda L. Dearing, *Shame and Guilt* (New York: Guilford, 2004), 56, 117.

3. Cornelius Plantinga, *Not the Way It's Supposed to Be: A Breviary of Sin* (Grand Rapids, MI: Eerdmans, 1995).

4. Plantinga, *Not the Way*, 10; Francis Brown, Samuel Rolles Driver, and Charles Augustus Briggs, *Enhanced Brown-Driver-Briggs Hebrew and English Lexicon*, electronic ed. (Oak Harbor, WA: Logos Research Systems, 2000), 1022.

5. Plantinga, *Not the Way*, 30. I borrow the language of "vandalism of shalom" from Plantinga.

6. About this passage Dave Mathewson observes: "Within this chiastic arrangement [Rev. 21:1–5] the removal . . . of the sea in [v. 1] . . . is paired lexically and syntactically with the removal . . . of death, sorrow, and pain [v. 4]." "New Exodus as a Background for 'The Sea Was No More'" in Revelation 21:1C," *Trinity Journal* 24 (Fall 2003): 245.

7. "The cosmic sea . . . symbolizes the continued threat the forces of chaos pose against God and creation. . . . As Creator, God controls the sea, both producing and calming its waves. . . . Thus the threat of chaos and evil which the sea symbolizes is ultimately hollow." *Dictionary of Biblical Imagery*, ed. Leland Ryken, James C. Wilhoit, Tremper Longman III (Downers Grove, IL: InterVarsity, 1998), s.v. "sea"; see also Tremper Longman III and Daniel G. Reid, *God Is a Warrior* (Grand Rapids, MI: Zondervan, 1995), 65.

8. Plantinga, *Not the Way*, 30.

9. In the following section I summarize the narrative of Ex. 13:17–14:14. I encourage you to read through that passage of Scripture before continuing here and leave your Bible open to refer back to it along the way.

10. A question is raised at this point about God hardening Pharaoh's heart and Pharaoh making his own choices. Does one override the other? The bottom line is that Pharaoh never did anything he didn't want to do and is therefore morally culpable for every choice. See Nahum M. Sarna, *Exploring Exodus: The Origins of Biblical Israel* (New York: Schocken, 1986), 65.

11. Fretheim highlights the close relationship between the Passover and Red Sea, suggesting the close linking of death and resurrection as one event in two parts. *Exodus*, Interpretation: A Bible Commentary for Teaching and Preaching (Louisville, KY: Westminster, 1991), 152. Noting a similar pattern, Longman and Reid show how the Gospel of Matthew records an earthquake both at Jesus' crucifixion (Matt. 27:51) and at his resurrection (Matt. 28:2), suggesting that these are two episodes in a single event, The Day of the Lord. *God Is a Warrior*, 133.

12. Meredith G. Kline, "The Old Testament Origins of the Gospel Genre," *Westminster Theological Journal* 38 (Fall 1975): 10.

13. Fretheim, *Exodus*, 153.

14. Ibid., 153. Fretheim says that while the creation theme is prominent throughout Exodus, "it is the sea crossing that . . . [brings] God's creational goals to a climax." Peter Enns elaborates on the re-creation theme in the Exodus in "Creation and Re-Creation: Psalm 95 and Its Interpretation in Hebrews 3:1-4:13," *Westminster Theological Journal* 55 (Fall 1993): 256. See also Longman and Reid, *God Is a Warrior*, 32, 86; William J. Dumbrell, *The Search for Order: Biblical Eschatology in Focus* (Eugene, OR: Wipf and Stock, 2001), 42; Meredith G. Kline, *God, Heaven, and Har Magedon: A Covenantal Tale of the Cosmos and Telos* (Eugene, OR: Wipf and Stock, 2006), 116.

15. Timothy Keller, "Before the Beginning," sermon, November 16, 2008, http://sermons.redeemer.com.

16. Ibid.

17. Dumbrell, *Search*, 184; For more on the relationship between the kingdom of God and the new creation, see Graeme Goldsworthy, *According to Plan: The Unfolding Revelation of God in the Bible* (Downers Grove, IL: InterVarsity, 1991), 210–16.

18. See Longman and Reid, *God Is a Warrior*, 101–2.

19. Isa. 29:18–19; 35:5–6; 42:1–3; 53:5; 61:1–2; cf. Matt. 12:15–21; Luke 4:16–21; 7:22; 1 Pet. 2:24. Our focus here is on the spiritual significance of Jesus' healing ministry and its relevance to the healing of our spiritual wounds, though Christians also have the privilege of laying hands on the sick and praying for physical healing (James 5:14).

20. Allender and Longman, *Cry of the Soul*, 196–97.

21. Here, my emphasis in on the shame that results in false beliefs and accusations by the Enemy. But shame can also tell the truth about our guilt from sin; e.g., when Adam and Eve ran and hid in their shame, their shame was the natural consequence of their guilt (Gen. 3:8). In fact, Scripture condemns those who are guilty of sin and feel no shame (Rom. 1:27).

22. Meredith G. Kline, *By Oath Consigned: A Reinterpretation of the Covenant Signs of Circumcision and Baptism* (Grand Rapids, MI: Eerdmans, 1975), 55; http://www.covopc.org/Kline/By_Oath_Consigned.html. Kline cites this example from a case in Hammurapi's [Hammurabi's] Code.

23. Ibid., 56

24. Ibid., 55. Yamm was a sea god in ancient Near Eastern religion. Also, the Egyptians believed Pharaoh was a god. John Sailhamer, *The Pentateuch as Narrative* (Grand Rapids, MI: Zondervan, 1992), 252.

25. *The American Heritage Dictionary of the English Language*, 4th ed., s.v. "despise."

26. Ibid.

27. W. Bauer, F. W. Danker, W. F. Arndt, and F. W. Gingrich, *Greek-English Lexicon of the New Testament and Other Early Christian Literature*, 3d ed. (Chicago: University of Chicago Press, 2001), s.v. "καταφρονέω."

28. "Thinking only of the evaluation of God ('the joy that was set before him') ... Jesus despised (i.e., considered valueless) the disgraceful reputation a cross would bring him in the eyes of the Greco-Roman world. His own vindication came afterward, when he 'sat at the right hand of the throne of God.' While in the public court of opinion, Jesus took the most disgraceful seat—on a cross—in God's court of reputation, Jesus was worthy of the highest honor" (David A. deSilva, "Despising Shame: A Cultural-Anthropological Investigation of the Epistle to the Hebrews," *Journal of Biblical Literature* 113 [1994]: 44).

29. Thanks to James Noriega for the original "light" metaphor, which I've adapted here.

30. "Shame creates an absorption with self that can make us feel as if we're drowning in quicksand," Allender and Longman, *Cry of the Soul*, 192.

CHAPTER 5: DEMANDING MANNA

1. In the following section, I summarize the narrative of Ex. 16:1–30. I encourage you to read through that passage of Scripture before continuing here and leave your Bible open to refer back to it along the way.

2. Douglas K. Stuart, *Exodus*, New American Commentary 2 (Nashville, TN: Broadman, 2006), 372.

3. Ibid.

4. John H. Sailhamer, *The Pentateuch as Narrative* (Grand Rapids, MI: Zondervan, 1992), 274; emphasis added.

5. In "I Am Motivated When I Feel Desire," David Powlison discusses the distinctions between what John Calvin calls *natural desires* or *affections* and *inordinate desires* (*Seeing with New Eyes: Counseling and the Human Condition Through the Lens of Scripture* [Phillipsburg, NJ: P&R, 2003], 149).

6. See Powlison, *Seeing with New Eyes*, 147–48.

7. David Powlison discusses the errors of the "love-need" psychologies and how some Christian counselors too uncritically "baptize" this secular notion, rendering the gospel as merely the preferred way to meet these supposed "in-built" and "absolutized" yearnings for love. This psychology, he says, tends to be popular only within cultures and for individuals prone to "intimacy idols" ("Idols of the Heart and 'Vanity Fair,'" *Journal of Biblical Counseling* 13 [Winter 1995], 40–41, http://www.ccef.org/idols-heart-and-vanity-fair [accessed January 28, 2010]).

8. David Powlison, "Redeeming Relationships in an Empty Marriage," CCEF Annual Conference 2006: Hope for Broken Relationships, http://ccef.org/relationships-empty-marriage (accessed December 14, 2009).

9. Paul David Tripp, "Grumbling—A Look at a 'Little' Sin," *Journal of Biblical Counseling* 18 (Winter 2000): 51.

10. I ask *when* do you escape, for example, instead of *why* because, while the *why* question is what we want to search out with the Holy Spirit's guidance, the *when* question helps us begin that search in a concrete and particular time and place (or recurring pattern of times and places). These details anchor our findings to specific pains, temptations, emotions, thoughts, and beliefs. A theme of David Powlison's teaching is that we sin and suffer in specific ways, not just in general; so our cries to God for rescue and our repentance from sin, while interpreted by an understanding of broad patterns, should be made just as specific as the sin and suffering. "Change happens in specifics," in *Seeing with New Eyes*, 132; See also Powlison, "Think Globally, Act Locally" in *Speaking the Truth in Love* (Greensboro, NC: New Growth Press, 2005), 61–72. I am also indebted to Powlison for the categories of anger, anxiety, and escape in the following analysis. He estimates that if we could understand these three basic human problems, it would account for some 95 percent of life's struggles. David Powlison, "Anxiety," in Lecture 4, *Dynamics of Biblical Change* (2005), Christian Counseling and Educational Foundation (Glenside, PA).

11. "[Anger] weighs something or someone, finds it lacking, wrong, or displeasing, and then moves into action. Anger arouses us to attack or discredit what we find displeasing. . . . It is a self-contained judicial system, reacting to perceived wrong with energy" (David Powlison, "Anger, Part 1: Understanding Anger," *Journal of Biblical Counseling* 14 [Fall 1995]: 48).

12. "A fear is simply desire turned on its head: 'I *don't want*'" (Powlison, *Seeing with New Eyes*, 145n1); emphasis original.

13. Powlison, "Redeeming Relationships in an Empty Marriage."

14. There are also desires which are always evil, and there is never a question about whether they are natural or inordinate, such as a desire to murder.

15. John Owen, *Overcoming Sin and Temptation*, ed. Kelly M. Kapic and Justin Taylor (Wheaton, IL: Crossway, 2006). Bracketed comments are from the translator's notes.

16. Ibid., 86–87. Owen calls this principle of fighting sin "sincerity and diligence in a universality of obedience."

17. The following is a summary of John 6:1–15, 25–59.

CHAPTER 6: THE GOLDEN CALF

1. While many men will likely find much in common with Philip, a male character, porn is not just a man's issue. In fact, though Philip's story is a composite of a few men's stories, it also borrows from some women's stories. I have heard some women say that the shame and fear of exposure that haunt any porn addict is for them compounded by the stereotype that porn is a male sin.

2. Timothy Keller, *Counterfeit Gods: The Empty Promises of Money, Sex, and Power, and the Only Hope That Matters* (New York: Dutton, 2009), xvii.

3. Peter Enns comments that the phrase "this Moses" both in English and in the original Hebrew conveys "a sense of derision and contempt" (*Exodus*, NIV Application Commentary [Grand Rapids: Zondervan, 2000], 569).

4. G. K. Beale, *We Become What We Worship: A Biblical Theology of Idolatry* (Downers Grove, IL: InterVarsity, 2008), 203–4.

5. Ibid., 204–8; Rom. 1:25a.

6. Keller, *Counterfeit Gods*, xix.

7. Ibid., *xix, xvii, xviii*.

8. Ibid., *vii*, 203–4. Also theological, magic/ritual, political/economic, racial/national, relational, philosophical, and cultural idols.

9. There's much more to this plot, of course: Psyche's being far away was probably Orual's least significant concern. But I won't spoil any more than this for those who haven't read this fascinating tale.

10. For a book-length treatment of what the Bible calls "fear of man," here expressed as a controlling desire for the approval of others, see Edward T. Welch, *When People Are Big and God Is Small: Overcoming Peer Pressure, Codependency, and the Fear of Man* (Phillipsburg, NJ: P&R, 1997).

11. Ibid. A similar distinction is made by Richard Keys, who says "idols come in pairs. He says there is the more visible and tangible "nearby" idol, a counterfeit of the true God's immanence, and the less tangible and more meaning-making "faraway" idol, a counterfeit of God's transcendence ("Idols of the Heart," in *No God but God: Breaking with the Idols of Our Age*, ed. Os Guinness and John Seel [Chicago: Moody, 1992], 37–38). Keller claims that Keyes's concept of a "far idol" is more of a cognitive false belief system, whereas his own concept of a "deep" idol refers to a motivational drive (Keller, *Counterfeit Gods*, 188n46).

12. Keller, *Counterfeit Gods*, 64–66. For more on understanding addiction in terms of the biblical concept of idolatry, see Edward T. Welch, *Addictions: A Banquet in the Grave* (Phillipsburg, NJ: P&R, 2001), 47–55.

13. So Anglican historian Ashley Null summarizes the anthropology of Archbishop Thomas Cranmer. He goes on, "The mind doesn't direct the will. The mind is actually captive to what the will wants, and the will itself, in turn, is captive to what the heart wants" ("Interview with Dr. Ashley Null on Thomas Cranmer: Primary Author of the Book of Common Prayer," http://www.acl.asn.au/old/null.html [accessed March 10, 2010]).

14. Ezekiel tells us that idols are more than works of the hands for outward worship; they are taken "into the heart" (Ezek. 14:3). Picking up on this theme John Calvin says, "Man's nature . . . is a perpetual factory of idols. . . . Man tries to express in his work the sort of God he has inwardly conceived . . . therefore the mind begets an idol; the hand gives it birth" (*Institutes of the Christian Religion*, ed. John T. McNeill [Westminster Press: Philadelphia, PA, 1960], 108).

15. Welch, *Addictions*, 53.

16. Douglas K. Stuart, *Exodus*, New American Commentary 2 (Nashville, TN: Broadman, 2006), 661.

17. Ibid.

18. Peter Enns notes that calves or bulls were commonly used in the ancient Near East as pedestals to elevate a god above the people, ensuring that the gods' presence was with them. He concludes: "The Israelites are not saying that this calf and *not* Yahweh brought them out of Egypt, but that Yahweh's *presence* is now associated with this piece of gold" (*Exodus*, 569–70; emphasis original); cf. Beale, *We Become What We Worship*, 84–85; Nahum M. Sarna, *Exploring Exodus: The Origins of Biblical Israel* (New York: Schocken, 1986), 215–18.

19. First commandment: "You shall have no other gods before me" (Ex. 20:3); second commandment: "You shall not make for yourself a carved image, or any likeness of anything that is in heaven above, or that is in the earth beneath, or that is in the water under the earth" (Ex. 20:4).

20. Stuart, *Exodus*, 666.

21. See also the appendix in this volume.

22. Timothy M. Pierce, "Enslaved to Slavery: An Application of a Sociological Method to the Complaint Motif," *Journal of the Evangelical Theological Society* 49 (December 2006): 646–97. A similar phenomenon called "the Stockholm Syndrome" has been documented, where a hostage develops a loyalty to the hostage-taker, http://en.wikipedia.org/wiki/Stockholm_syndrome (accessed June 26, 2009).

23. Pierce, "Enslaved to Slavery," 689.

24. Lest we underestimate the seductiveness of idolatry to the Israelites, Douglas Stuart describes nine attractions of idolatry that would have enticed them. It's not too hard to imagine yourself in their shoes. Idolatry was (1) *guaranteed*: ensuring a god's presence without having to depend on his goodwill or faithfulness. (2) *Selfish*: gods were thought to be nearly all-powerful, except for the ability to feed themselves; worshipers who "fed" the idol obligated the god to use his power on their behalf. (3) *Easy*: idolatry didn't require ethical behavior, only consistency and generosity of sacrifices to the idol. (4) *Convenient*: idol shrines were ubiquitous and could be worshiped at the worshiper's convenience anywhere and anytime. Yahweh by contrast required that they worship on his inconvenient terms. (5) *Normal*: everyone around the Israelites worshiped idols; it was simply the way of the world. Worshiping Yahweh made them as conspicuous as Noah building an ark under dry skies. (6) *Logical*: the idea of entrusting all of life to a single God was scandalous; there were too many facets of existence to be ruled by a single god. (7) *Pleasing to the senses*: idolatry involved ornate carvings and depictions of gods that could be seen, touched, and admired. Yahweh was invisible and had to be worshiped by faith, not by sight. (8) *Indulgent*: idol worship involved "pigging out" on the meat offered in sacrifices. Israelites were permitted to eat meat whenever they wanted as part of a normal diet, but the idol's invitation to gluttony was hard to resist. (9) *Erotic*: ancient pagans believed that all creation required procreation; if you wanted a flock of sheep, some gods somewhere had to have sex and give birth to this provision. So there

was temple prostitution: worshipers imagined themselves role-playing the gods giving birth to the objects of their desires (Stuart, *Exodus*, 450–54).

25. I borrow the term "voluntary slavery" from Welch, *Addictions*, 46.

26. Paul David Tripp, *Instruments in the Redeemer's Hands* (Phillipsburg, NJ: P&R, 2002), 278–79.

27. For the following discussion of deception and self-deception, see Gregg A. Ten Elshof, *I Told Me So: Self-Deception and the Christian Life* (Grand Rapids, MI: Eerdmans, 2009), 22–23.

28. Ibid., 25.

29. Diane Langberg, "Self-Deception: A Supporting Column of Addiction," CCEF Annual Conference 2008: The Addict in Us All, http://ccef.org/self-deception-supporting-column-addiction (accessed February 26, 2010).

30. Beale, *We Become What We Worship*, 78.

31. Cf. Enns, *Exodus*, 571–72.

32. These stages are taken from Driscoll and Breshears, *Death by Love*, 65–67, except for the sixth, which is from Keller, *Counterfeit Gods*, 172–73.

33. David Powlison, "First Big Arrow," in Lecture 10, Dynamics of Biblical Change (2005), Christian Counseling and Educational Foundation (Glenside, PA).

34. Ibid.

35. Specificity is a theme in David Powlison's teaching. I'm sure I've heard him use this exact phrase before, probably in his lectures for Dynamics of Biblical Change.

36. Ten Elshof, *I Told Me So*, 22–23.

37. David Powlison, "2006 Workbook," Dynamics of Biblical Change (2006).

38. Driscoll and Breshears, *Death by Love*, 66.

39. Keller, *Counterfeit Gods*, xxi, 55–56. Keller echoes Brian S. Rosner's observation that idolaters do three things with their idols: *love*, *trust*, and *obey* them (Brian S. Rosner, *Greed as Idolatry: The Origin and Meaning of a Pauline Metaphor* [Grand Rapids, MI: Eerdmans, 2007], 43–46, 149–71).

40. Thomas Chalmers, *The Expulsive Power of a New Affection*, http://www.monergism.com/Chalmers%2C%20Thomas%20-%20The%20Expulsive%20Power%20of%20a%20New%20Af.pdf (accessed January 17, 2010).

41. For John Owen's distinction between "being tempted" and "entering into temptation" see chap. 5.

42. Keller, *Counterfeit Gods*, 172.

43. Martin Luther, "Martin Luther's 95 Theses," Project Gutenberg, http://www.gutenberg.org/catalog/world/readfile?fk_files=773195&pageno=2 (accessed February 3, 2010).

CHAPTER 7: THE COVENANT-KEEPING GOD

1. Timothy Keller, *Counterfeit Gods: The Empty Promises of Money, Sex, and Power, and the Only Hope That Matters* (New York: Dutton, 2009), 176.

2. For now, I'm skipping over another round of intercession in Ex. 33:12–17. We'll revisit this in the next chapter.

3. The following points are adopted from J. Carl Laney, "God's Self-Revelation in Exodus 34:6–8," *Bibliotheca Sacra 158* (January 2001): 36–51.

4. Ibid., 43; cf. L. J. Coppes, "*raham*," in *Theological Wordbook of the Old Testament*, ed. R. Laird Harris, Gleason L. Archer, and Bruce K. Waltke (Chicago: Moody, 1980), 2:841.

5. Laney, "God's Self-Revelation," 43; cf. R. B. Girdlestone, *Synonyms of the Old Testament* (Grand Rapids, MI: Eerdmans, 1970), 108.

6. Laney, "God's Self-Revelation," 44; cf. Ps. 78:38.

7. Laney, "God's Self-Revelation," 44; cf. Edwin Yamauchi, "*ḥanan*," in Harris, et al., *Theological Wordbook of the Old Testament*, 1:302.

8. Cf. Laney, "God's Self-Revelation," 45. Laney says that the Hebrew expression ["slow to anger"] is used ten times to refer to God's patience in dealing with those whose sins arouse his wrath.

9. Ibid.

10. God's kindness leads to repentance (Rom. 2:4).

11. Mark Driscoll and Gerry Breshears, *Doctrine: What Christians Should Believe* (Wheaton, IL: Crossway, 2010), 178.

12. *Vine's Complete Expository Dictionary of Old and New Testament Words*, s.v. "Loving-Kindness."

13. Laney, "God's Self-Revelation," 47.

14. The Psalms sing of God's steadfast love 248 times.

15. For a discussion of the theology of the Mosaic law in the Pentateuch, see John H. Sailhamer, *The Pentateuch as Narrative* (Grand Rapids, MI: Zondervan, 1992), 62–65. Sailhamer argues that the Pentateuch, including its laws, intends to teach not law keeping but faith in God. By analogy to other ancient Near Eastern law codes of the same literary genre, he shows that the laws given by God through Moses were first and foremost a description of the divine wisdom and justice of the Lawgiver.

16. Ex. 32:26–28, 35. According to Enns, the death penalty exacted here is not extreme by the standards of Exodus. After all, failure to precisely follow instructions for building the tabernacle also incurred a death penalty, as well as working on the Sabbath (Ex. 31:15). It was probably only carried out on the most guilty of the Israelites, while everyone else—still guilty but less so—had to be atoned for (Ex. 32:30) (*Exodus*, NIV Application Commentary [Grand Rapids: Zondervan, 2000], 576–78).

17. David Powlison, expounding Psalm 10 to comfort the victimized, says, "The wrath of God is a central piece of the hope of God's people." So the victim can trust that God will not clear their unrepentant abusers (*Seeing with New Eyes: Counseling and the Human Condition Through the Lens of Scripture* [Phillipsburg, NJ: P&R, 2003], 101). The phrase "visiting the iniquity of the fathers on the children and the children's children to the third and the fourth generation" is commonly misunderstood to mean that the sins of parents are put upon their children, but Ezekiel 18 clarifies that this is not the case. Children may experience the ongoing consequences set in motion by their parents' sin; however, they are only accountable for their own (Laney, "God's Self-Revelation in Exodus 34:6–8," 50). Peter Enns says this particular consequence is applicable only to the present context, an echo of Ex. 20:5 (*Exodus*, 415–16, 585).

18. Laney, "God's Self-Revelation in Exodus 34:6–8," 43.

19. The original inhabitants of the Promised Land, including the Amorites, Canaanites, Hittites, Perizzites, Hivites, and Jebusites (Ex. 34:11), were idolaters on whom God's judgment for sin was now warranted. After promising the land long before to Abraham, God had allowed plenty of time for their repentance, but they would not. In the conquest of the land and the defeating of these people, we see God's justice, "who will by no means clear the guilty" (Ex. 34:7); cf. Gen. 15:16; Ex. 34:11–16; Lev. 18:24–27; Deut. 9:4–5.

20. The same word "corrupt" appears in each case.

21. This passage parallels the other primary Old Testament prophecy on the new covenant (Jer. 31:31–34).

22. See Nehemiah for the account of the returning exiles and the rebuilding of the temple in Jerusalem.

23. Cf. John Piper, *Finally Alive* (Ross-Shire, UK: Christian Focus, 2009), 94.

24. The passage in John 3, where Jesus tells Nicodemus about the necessity of the new birth, is a key passage on the new birth, which this passage in Titus echoes. I have focused attention on Titus 3, because of its strong verbal connection to Ezekiel and allusion to our texts in Exodus. John Piper in *Finally Alive*, a work on the new birth, gives sustained attention to Ezekiel 36, John 3, Ephesians 2, 1 John, 1 Peter 1, and Titus 3.

25. Piper, *Finally Alive*, 94.

26. Anthony Hoekema, "The Reformed Perspective," in *Five Views of Sanctification*, Melvin E. Dieter, et al. (Grand Rapids, MI: Zondervan, 1987), 74; see also "Already-and-not-yet" in the Introduction.

27. See Hoekema, *Five Views*, 75.

28. See Piper, *Finally Alive*, 68, 88–90.

29. David Powlison says it this way, from a lecture where he role-plays counseling a woman struggling with panic attacks: "You view being a Christian as you upholding your end of the deal as the central dynamic. But you know, in the way the Bible presents it, God upholds. That's first. And we uphold our end only in response to what he does" ("Panic Attacks: A Counseling Case Study," Christian Counseling and Educational Foundation, http://ccef.org/panic-attacks-counseling-case-study-part-1 [accessed March 3, 2010]).

30. I'm thankful to Bill Clem who planted the seeds for this chapter with his original teaching on advocacy from Moses' intercession throughout Exodus 32–34; he also suggested the current title, "Covenant Keeping God."

31. See Piper, *Finally Alive*, 141, 150.

32. David Powlison, "In the Last Analysis: Look Out for Introspection," 2007 Leadership Conference, Sovereign Grace Ministries, http://www.sovereigngracestore.com/ProductInfo.aspx?productid=A2250-03-51 (accessed February 18, 2010).

33. Ibid.

34. Cf. Keller, *Counterfeit Gods*, 176.

35. Ibid., 105.

36. Piper, *Finally Alive*, 138; Sinclair B. Ferguson, *The Christian Life: A Doctrinal Introduction* (1981; repr., Edinburgh: Banner of Truth, 2009), 61.

37. Ferguson, *Christian Life*, 63.

38. The following points are adopted from Ferguson, *Christian Life*, 63–67.

39. Ibid., 64.

40. Keller, *Counterfeit Gods*, 164.

41. Ferguson, *Christian Life*, 67.

CHAPTER 8: IS GOD YOUR PROMISED LAND?

1. Enns, *Exodus*, NIV Application Commentary (Grand Rapids: Zondervan, 2000), 561.

2. Durham, *Exodus*, Word Biblical Commentary (Waco, TX: Word, 1987), *xxi*.

3. See Enns, *Exodus*, 50–51.

4. Ex. 29:46. While we have focused our attention here and through this book on the redemption of individuals, God's story works through the redemption of individuals who become missionaries involved in the redemption of others. The larger purpose for Israel was not only to know God's presence but to make his presence known among the nations of the earth (see Ex. 19:6; Deut. 4:6–8). Likewise, God's purpose in redeeming us from sin and suffering is not merely for our own happiness but ultimately for his glory, which he wants us to reflect to the world around.

5. John Ryan Lister, "'The Lord Your God Is in Your Midst': The Presence of God and the Means and End of Redemptive History," PhD diss., Southern Baptist Theological Seminary (2010), 184–85.

6. Terence E. Fretheim, *Exodus*, Interpretation: A Bible Commentary for Teaching and Preaching (Louisville, KY: Westminster, 1991), 294.

7. These chapters form a unit; together they tell of the intrusion of the golden calf and the consequences thereof (Enns, *Exodus*, 568).

8. Nahum M. Sarna, *Exploring Exodus: The Origins of Biblical Israel* (New York: Schocken, 1986), 215–17; Enns, *Exodus*, 568.

9. Of course, it was not ultimately at risk. But we must not let our theology of God's sovereignty neutralize the sense of crisis in this moment.

10. Of course, because God is omnipresent, he is always present everywhere. At stake here is not God's omnipresence but the special, covenantal, relational way that he is present with his people, represented by the tabernacle. See Lister, "The Lord Your God Is in Your Midst," 31–33; Adam Johnson, "God's Being in Reconciliation: The Theo-Ontological Basis of the Unity and Diversity of the Doctrine of the Atonement in the Theology of Karl Barth," PhD diss., Trinity Evangelical Divinity School, n.d.

11. Lister shows that God's presence must be mediated because of the presence of sin, "The Lord Your God Is in Your Midst," 38–40. Humankind's unmediated access to the presence of God was lost in Eden with the entrance of sin but will be restored in the new creation, when the dwelling place of God is once again with man (Rev. 21:3). In the meantime, God's presence is an "exceptionally dangerous blessing" (Johnson, "God's Being in Reconciliation").

12. Enns, *Exodus*, 578.

13. John Piper, "The Echo and Insufficiency of Hell, Part 2," sermon (June 21, 1992), http://www.desiringgod.org/ResourceLibrary/Sermons/BySeries/20/801_The_Echo_and_Insufficiency_of_Hell_Part_2/ (accessed March 10, 2010). I first heard this quotation as a sample of a John Piper sermon in Shai Linne's song "My Portion," *The Solus Christus Project*. Thanks to Shai for helping me track down Piper's original sermon.

14. Michael Horton, *Christless Christianity: The Alternative Gospel of the American Church* (Grand Rapids, MI: Baker, 2008), 31. Horton traces the aphorism's true source to Benjamin Franklin, an avowed deist.

15. Christian Smith, *Soul Searching: The Religious and Spiritual Lives of American Teenagers* (New York: Oxford University Press, 2005), 162–63; cf. Horton, *Christless Christianity*, 41. Horton also explains this idea in the video interview "What Is Moralistic Therapeutic Deism?" http://there-surgence.com/what-is-moralistic-therapeutic-deism (accessed March 6, 2010).

16. Mark Galli, "Point of Crisis, Point of Grace: Why It's Crucial to Recognize How Little We're Being Transformed," *Christianity Today* (January 21, 2010), http://www.christianitytoday.com/ct/2010/januaryweb-only/13-43.0.html?start=1 (accessed March 6, 2010).

17. Winston Smith, "Go Away, I Need You," CCEF National Conference 2007: Running Scared: Fear, Worry and the God of Rest.

18. Thanks to James Noriega for introducing me to this way of thinking about the relationship between these gifts and the way God gives them to us in himself.

19. Enns, *Exodus*, 579.

20. Commentators assert that Moses' "face time" with God in the tent of meeting is a metaphor for intimacy. Moses did not actually see God's face, for no man can look upon God's face and live (Ex. 33:20); see Enns, *Exodus*, 580.

21. See Enns, *Exodus*, 581. The word "you" in Exodus 33:14 is singular, indicating that God would go with Moses alone.

22. See Enns, *Exodus*, 581.

23. See Ex. 33:17; Luke 3:22. The literal meaning of the word *Immanuel* is "with us [is] God," found in Isa. 7:14; 8:8; Matt. 1:23 (R. L. Reymond, "Immanuel," *Evangelical Dictionary of Theology*, 2nd ed., ed. Walter A. Elwell [Grand Rapids, MI: Baker, 2001]).

24. Or, more literally, "'pitched his tent' (Gk. *skēnoō*), an allusion to God's dwelling among the Israelites in the tabernacle (cf. Ex. 25:8–9; 33:7)" (Andreas J. Köstenberger, "John 1:14," in *The ESV Study Bible*, ed. Wayne Grudem, et al. (Wheaton, IL: Crossway, 2008), 2020. "In other words, Jesus came and 'tabernacled' among his people," Enns, *Exodus*, 555.

25. Enns, *Exodus*, 555.

26. According to commentator William Lane, "The throne of Grace [in Hebrews 4:16] is the place of God's presence, from which grace emanates to the people of God. The only one who was permitted to 'draw near' under the provisions of the Mosaic covenant was the high priest, who could approach the altar in the most holy place of the tabernacle once a year, on the Day of Atonement. If his ministry was acceptable, the altar of judgment became the place from which mercy was dispensed to the people (cf. Lev. 16:2–34; Heb. 9:5). In bold extension of the language of worship the writer calls the community to recognize that through his high priestly ministry Christ has achieved for them what Israel never enjoyed, namely, immediate access to God and freedom to draw near to him continually" (William L. Lane, *Hebrews 1–8*, Word Biblical Commentary [Nashville, TN: Thomas Nelson, 1991], 115).

27. Thanks to Adam Johnson for this provocative phrase, "God's Being in Reconciliation."

28. I have adapted this word picture from John Piper, "Gospel," sermon, March 10, 2010, http://www.marshillchurch.org/media/special/john-piper-gospel (accessed March 18, 2010).

29. Graeme Goldsworthy, *The Goldsworthy Trilogy* (Waynesboro, GA: Paternoster, 2006), 313; emphasis original.

30. "The Psalms . . . show that the history of redemption, the covenant and the prophetic word from God, are not merely religious ideas or statements about the past but *encounters with the living God*. The great objective facts of God's work for his people to save them can never remain merely out there. . . . They are the indispensable means by which the Spirit of God regenerates the heart, mind and soul of those whom he calls into fellowship with himself" (Graeme Goldsworthy, *According to Plan: The Unfolding Revelation of God in the Bible* [Downers Grove, IL: InterVarsity, 1991], 177). Thanks to Ryan Lister for highlighting this quotation in his dissertation.

31. The temple in Israel's later history functioned similarly to the tabernacle in the wilderness.

32. Cf. David Powlison, "Peace, Be Still: Psalm 131," in *Seeing with New Eyes: Counseling and the Human Condition Through the Lens of Scripture* (Phillipsburg, NJ: P&R, 2003), 75–89.

33. David Powlison, "Intimacy with God," *Journal of Biblical Counseling* 16 (Winter 1998): 4; emphasis original.

34. Pss. 11:1; 14:6; 16:1; 17:7; 18:30; 25:20; 34:8; 46:1; 71:1, 3, 7; 91:2, 4, 9. These are but a few highlights in the Psalms of this mega-theme that runs throughout the Scriptures.

35. David Powlison, "Ask the Counselor," http://www.youtube.com/watch?v=paG59x CDn8I (accessed March 8, 2010).

36. Cf. R. C. Sproul, *Saved from What?* (Wheaton, IL: Crossway, 2002), 121.

37. John Piper clarifies that we can only put to death sin that Jesus has already died for, cancelled, and forgiven ("Be Killing Sin or Sin Will Be Killing You," sermon, March 7, 2010, http://www.marshillchurch.org/media/special/be-killing-sin-or-sin-will-be-killing-you [accessed March 10, 2010]).

38. See Appendix in this volume.

39. "Genuine, heartfelt pain over sin flows only from genuine, heartfelt pleasure in God" (John Piper, "The Echo and Insufficiency of Hell, Part 2," sermon, June 21, 1992, http://www.

desiringgod.org/ResourceLibrary/Sermons/BySeries/20/801_The_Echo_and_Insufficiency_ of_Hell_Part_2/ [accessed March 10, 2010].

EPILOGUE

1. Terence E. Fretheim, *Exodus*, Interpretation: A Bible Commentary for Teaching and Preaching (Louisville, KY: Westminster, 1991), 125; emphasis original.

2. See Christopher J. H. Wright, *The Mission of God: Unlocking the Bible's Grand Narrative* (Downers Grove, IL: InterVarsity, 2006), 224–25.

3. Thanks to Steve Tompkins for this line.

APPENDIX

1. David Powlison, "Addicted to Religion," CCEF Annual Conference 2008: The Addict in Us All.

2. Ibid.

3. Tim Keller addresses this issue masterfully through the parable of the Prodigal Son(s). Within our framework, the younger brother who runs off would be the porn, food, or gambling addict, while the older brother, the religious addict, stays home and follows the rules (*The Prodigal God: Recovering the Heart of the Christian Faith* [New York: Dutton, 2008]).

4. Jonathan Edwards, *The Religious Affections* (Carlisle: Banner of Truth, 2004), 54–110. By "religious affections," Edwards means something like emotions that arise in the context of faith. His phrase "no certain sign" basically means that these religious expressions don't prove one way or another whether someone's faith is genuine—both a genuine believer and a counterfeit may show the same sign.

GENERAL INDEX

SCRIPTURE INDEX